The Practice of
English Fundamentals

The Practice of English Fundamentals

by the late JOSEPH M. BACHELOR
and HAROLD L. HALEY

Department of English
Miami University

FORM B

Prentice-Hall, Inc., Englewood Cliffs, New Jersey

©1949, 1945
by PRENTICE-HALL, Inc.,
Englewood Cliffs, New Jersey

All rights reserved. No part of this book
may be reproduced in any form or by any means,
without permission in writing from the publisher.

Printed in the United States of America

ISBN: 0-13-689299-X

10 9 8 7 6 5 4 3 2 1

PRENTICE-HALL INTERNATIONAL, INC., *London*
PRENTICE-HALL OF AUSTRALIA, PTY. LTD., *Sydney*
PRENTICE-HALL OF CANADA, LTD., *Toronto*
PRENTICE-HALL OF INDIA PRIVATE LIMITED, *New Delhi*
PRENTICE-HALL OF JAPAN, INC., *Tokyo*

FOREWORD

The title of this book, *The Practice of English Fundamentals*, gives an unusually accurate description of it. The emphasis is upon the *use* of English, and only the essentials of correct English are treated, but these are treated with considerable thoroughness. This book is intensive rather than comprehensive.

In the textual discussions and the illustrative sentences, debatable refinements and questionable points of usage have been ignored; the principles stated are those necessary to be observed in formal writing and speaking. Of course, a great deal of freedom, not to say laxity, is permissible in colloquial English, but this book is concerned only with that plane of English designated as formal.

The primary value of the book is in the exercises. To help the student acquire correct language habits, the exercises repeat the fundamentals of good English until they are established as thought processes. More exercises are given than some classes will need. These optional exercises may be omitted, or they may be assigned to individual students who may require additional practice. To avoid monotony in the exercises, repetition is put, wherever possible, into varied forms. However, no attempt has been made to disguise the fact that mastering good English is hard but—let it be added quickly—rewarding work.

Sometimes a problem in correct usage has been treated under two or more headings in the text. This repetition is intentional. Since the parts of speech are interrelated, discussion concerning errors in their use cannot be isolated into a sort of linguistic vacuum. The misuse of language occurs in *sentences*.

Answers to the exercises are not to be indicated by various sorts of lines nor by complicated systems of numbers and letters. The former, by being superficially easy to make and by psychologically encouraging the spirit of a game, result in progressive carelessness; the latter usually require so much effort to remember the "system" that the exercise itself receives divided attention. In this book almost all answers are to be written in columns: the writing insures concentration, care, and the formation of good language habits; the arrangement of answers in columns allows easy correction by the class or teacher.

At the back of the book are materials which should provide convenient reference for both student and teacher: synopses of verb conjugations, a list of principal parts of irregular verbs, the declensions of pronouns, and comparisons of adjectives and adverbs. Also at the back of the book, for reference and study, is a list of 450 frequently misspelled words. Finally, at the very end, is a chart for recording the scores obtained on all exercises. The student should make these entries faithfully and honestly, for this chart will be a kind of picture of his ability and, it is to be hoped, of his progress.

J. M. B.
H. L. H.

CONTENTS

	PAGE
PREFACE	v
DIAGNOSTIC TESTS	1

I. UNDERSTANDING THE SENTENCE

The Sentence	15
The Sentence Fragment or Period Fault	16
The Comma Fault	18
The Run-on or Fused Sentence	20
Exercises 1–5	21

II. GRAMMAR

Agreement of Subject and Verb	33
Exercises 6–9	39
Agreement and Reference of Pronouns	47
Exercises 10–14	51
Case	61
Exercises 15–21	67
Mood and Tense	81
Exercises 22–24	85
Problems in the Use of Certain Verbs	91
Exercises 25–32	95
Problems with Modifiers	111
Exercises 33–35	117
Dangling and Misplaced Modifiers	123
Exercises 36–39	127
Problems with Connectives	135
Exercises 40–47	141
Problems with Clauses	157
Exercises 48–49	161
Words Misused from Similarity of Sound or Meaning	165
Exercises 50–54	173

III. PUNCTUATION AND MECHANICS

	PAGE
End Punctuation	185
Strong Internal Punctuation	186
Enclosing Punctuation	188
Weak Internal Punctuation	190
Conventional Punctuation	195
Mechanics	196
Exercises 55–81	203

IV. SPELLING

Rules for Spelling	259
Exercises 82–88	263

APPENDIX

Outline of Inflections	279
450 Words Frequently Misspelled	285

ACHIEVEMENT TESTS 289

INDEX 301

Diagnostic Tests

NAME .... DATE .... SCORE ....

GENERAL TEST—UNDERSTANDING THE SENTENCE

Decide whether each group of words appearing below is a complete sentence, two or more sentences run together, or an incomplete construction. In supplying your answers, use the following abbreviations:

S—*A complete sentence*

RT—*Sentences run together*

F—*Incomplete construction or fragment*

1. Although John Brown has been characterized as an unbalanced, ruthless fanatic, he was regarded by his followers as an inspired old prophet with a vision of glory.
2. Wishing to turn on the light in the dining room, I pressed the switch on the wall, but with no result.
3. The biology instructor, walking about and peering over our shoulders, sometimes pausing to help a student who was having difficulty in adjusting a microscope.
4. Mosquitoes are prevalent in the north as well as in the tropics, even in the region of Hudson Bay they appear in dense swarms.
5. Having no desire to start an argument, I replied that he had a right to his own opinion in the matter.
6. The soldiers under fire were under constant tension every minute, every second, hence there were many cases of battle fatigue.
7. My mother, being an ardent collector of old furniture and other bric-a-brac, never misses an auction sale within fifty miles of our home.
8. Countless adventurers having flocked into Alaska, where they expected to make their fortunes as prospectors.
9. He was so startled to see us that he could not speak he just stood there with his mouth agape.
10. Then, too, there is the person who, when he is late for work, tries to invent an excuse that has never been used before.
11. Whenever Aunt May tries to relate a joke, she becomes confused and forgets the main point of the anecdote.
12. He has held a position as assistant manager of a department store, therefore he is familiar with the common problems of retail merchandising.

.... 13. The janitor, a squat, dark-complexioned man who hurled threats at the children as they raced across the green turf in front of the apartment house.

.... 14. He tossed and turned in a siege of wakefulness, when dawn came he pulled on his clothing and walked hurriedly through the village streets toward the station.

.... 15. Particularly when, just as you are returning from a party, you remember all the clever things that you might have said.

.... 16. The campaign over, the leaders of both parties predicted success at the polls on the following day.

.... 17. The forest fire was making rapid headway, nevertheless the volunteer fire fighters grimly continued their battle.

.... 18. A successful young poet who, after speaking before local clubs on a few occasions, discovered that his services as a lecturer were in constant demand.

.... 19. The early returns, which were based on incomplete reports from cities in the upstate area, showed that Senator Burt had a commanding lead over his opponent.

.... 20. Although it was nearly midnight, hundreds of people milled about in the huge concourse, the holiday rush was at its peak.

.... 21. Many people think that birds migrate to find a warmer climate, but this view is incorrect they migrate to find better feeding grounds and nesting areas.

.... 22. Essentially because a world language would promote international trade, simplify travel, and create better understanding among nations, to mention only a few of its goals.

.... 23. The daily society page is dear to the hearts of most women, it is even read by a few men.

.... 24. Perhaps the most trying experience in the life of an amateur airman is his first solo flight, made after he has undergone several weeks of training with an experienced pilot.

.... 25. That evening, while playing the rôle of Othello in a Detroit theater, he missed his cue and faltered, waiting for the prompter to give him the line.

To obtain score, multiply number of errors by 4 and subtract total from 100.

NAME .... DATE .... SCORE ....

GENERAL TEST IN GRAMMAR

Draw a circle around any word incorrectly used and write the correct word in the margin on the left. If the sentence is correct as it stands, let the space remain blank. Errors are not to be corrected by rewriting the sentences or by fundamentally changing their meaning.

.... 1. As usual, I had lain the change on the kitchen shelf.

.... 2. Most every region has its folklore and legends.

.... 3. Why don't he get a haircut now and then?

.... 4. May I demonstrate how this vacuum cleaner works?

.... 5. The captain, together with thirty members of his crew, were saved.

.... 6. Which of us would you say is the tallest, my brother or I?

.... 7. Otis Skinner was one of the most versatile actors that has ever appeared on the American stage.

.... 8. His only objection to chemistry were its laboratory requirements.

.... 9. Anyone could do the work as well as him.

.... 10. Each of the girls pay a quarter for the refreshments.

.... 11. These stories are to juvenile to suit me.

.... 12. You could of stayed at our house.

.... 13. He has not wore this suit very often.

.... 14. Most readers thought the most interesting character of the novel to be him.

.... 15. These magazines are your's, aren't they?

.... 16. Between you and me, his prospects do not seem favorable.

.... 17. In the attic there was an old-fashioned organ and a red plush stool.

.... 18. They can afford to pledge as much as us.

.... 19. Do not apply for this job except you are a hustler.

.... 20. We shall get better results if we sing altogether.

.... 21. Dust the books good before you put them back.

.... 22. They intended to have stayed in Florida until March.

.... 23. Your method of solving the problem is different than his.

.... 24. I believe there telephone must be out of order.
.... 25. We shall give the dog to whomever will provide a good home for it.
.... 26. The committee took its places around a large table.
.... 27. There have been hardly no plays in town this season.
.... 28. Everyone should have their household goods insured.
.... 29. Try to scatter the grass seed more even.
.... 30. Constant worry can soon effect one's health.
.... 31. The dog looked hopefully at the plate of cookies.
.... 32. I thought that the milk tasted sourly.
.... 33. I have known few persons more generous than he.
.... 34. She baked a chocolate cake for my father and I.
.... 35. Ten of us stamp collectors formed a club.
.... 36. We saw his sister and he at the game.
.... 37. Is that the man whom she is engaged to?
.... 38. Who do you think they have elected?
.... 39. He always seemed kind of bashful.
.... 40. Whom are you working for at the present time?
.... 41. The locust tree sheds its leaves early in the fall.
.... 42. He swung the bat like he intended to hit the ball out of the park.
.... 43. The reason for my taking down the shutters was because I intended to paint them.
.... 44. I read in *Time* where a robot had punched its owner.
.... 45. A shortage of labor and materials have seriously handicapped the building contractors.
.... 46. Due to a sprained ankle he was unable to walk far.
.... 47. Your only wasting time in trying to argue with him.
.... 48. Who do you suppose picked up my book?
.... 49. Arrest whoever is responsible for this outrage.
.... 50. Dave Sims and myself were working as cub reporters on the paper.

To obtain score, multiply number of errors by 2 and subtract total from 100.

NAME .... DATE .... SCORE ....

GENERAL TEST IN PUNCTUATION

Decide whether any changes should be made in the punctuation of the following sentences. To make changes, follow these directions. First, set down in the space at the left the word (or number) which immediately precedes the mistake. Then, if you wish to add *punctuation, insert the proper mark after the word. To take out* unnecessary *punctuation, insert the faulty mark after the word and draw a circle around the mark. If the sentence is correctly punctuated, leave the space at the left blank.*

EXAMPLE:

    house,   = comma to be added
    house (,)   = comma to be taken out

1. Salem, not Plymouth, was the scene of the witch trials in New England.
2. The sun blazed down from a cloudless sky, and the village drowsed in the heat of the summer afternoon.
3. A sign on the door announced that supper would be served at 5:45 P.M.
4. From the kitchen came the pungent, appetizing aroma of coffee.
5. He always buys the Sunday edition of the New York Times.
6. The man entering the house is my brother-in-law.
7. The word irrelevant is often misspelled.
8. Every woman, who attends the demonstration, will be given a book of recipes.
9. Gregor Mendel, a nineteenth-century Austrian biologist made important studies in the field of genetics.
10. I saw in this week's issue of *Life* an article called The World of Mirth.
11. Three Justices of the Supreme Court—Brandeis, Cardozo, and Holmes—cast the dissenting votes.
12. Under his arm was a bulging, brief case.
13. His argument I must say, is logical and persuasive.
14. On September 18, 1948, he was transferred to Atlanta, Georgia.

_____ 15. Where he went after leaving here we do not know.
_____ 16. Mark Twain's experiences on a Western trip are described in a book titled <u>Roughing It</u>.
_____ 17. Including today there are exactly thirty days until Christmas.
_____ 18. The Empire Hotel is a three-story brick structure with about forty-five rooms.
_____ 19. The small tugboat noisy and officious pulled the huge liner away from the pier.
_____ 20. The boy seized the large bundle of newspapers and tossed it into his cart.
_____ 21. The income tax laws permit deductions for the following items dependents, medical fees, charities, and business expenses.
_____ 22. "How old is this child" the conductor asked sharply.
_____ 23. No I do not wish to subscribe to any more magazines.
_____ 24. The need for a new city hall is apparent to anyone who has visited the shabby building on Court Street recently.
_____ 25. Ellen is this your handbag?
_____ 26. The hotel did not look promising nevertheless we decided to stop for the night.
_____ 27. Three of our national parks Yellowstone, Glacier, and Zion attract thousands of visitors every summer.
_____ 28. My employer who is usually a mild-mannered individual began shouting at the salesman.
_____ 29. The children applauded whole-heartedly when the animated cartoon was announced.
_____ 30. We stayed at the Piedmont Inn, Conway, North Carolina for one week.
_____ 31. Officials of the company have recently announced that an extra dividend will be declared on the common stock.
_____ 32. "My what a long day it has been" she said wearily.
_____ 33. The radio drama having ended my aunt went to the kitchen and began to prepare lunch.
_____ 34. Since I had not seen him for several years I could not recall his name.

35. You should have your winter clothes dry-cleaned in the spring then you should store them in garment bags.
36. July the fourteenth, which is a national holiday in France commemorates the fall of the Bastile.
37. That American slang is sometimes very picturesque and amusing no one will deny.
38. I think to be perfectly frank, that the plan is quite unworkable.
39. We have had orders recently from the following manufacturers the Eastman Kodak Company, Rochester; the General Electric Company, Schenectady; and the Spencer Lens Company, Buffalo.
40. Because a pilot must have good eyesight, steady nerves, and physical endurance many applicants cannot meet the rigid qualifications for flight training.
41. Wasn't it Thoreau who said On a pleasant autumn morning all men's sins are forgotten
42. He finished trimming the window and then went outside to study the effect.
43. "If you'll come back in half an hour" the mechanic said "your car will be ready."
44. Before the fireplace stood a pair of gleaming brass andirons.
45. The earliest phonograph was a strange contrivance it looked somewhat like a megaphone.
46. Pick out any card you like, George and then put it back into the deck.
47. The hat which she was wearing matched her suit.
48. That the dress was a remarkable bargain, the clerk kept insisting.
49. The Dead Sea it is a salt lake is more than a thousand feet below sea level.
50. Prominent in Lincoln's Cabinet were William H. Seward, Secretary of State Salmon P. Chase, Secretary of the Treasury and Simon Cameron, Secretary of War.

To obtain score, multiply number of errors by 2 and subtract total from 100.

NAME .... DATE .... SCORE ....

GENERAL TEST IN SPELLING

In the space at the left, write each italicized word in full.

.... 1. Plans for a new airport will be made after city officials have *confer—d* with representatives of the airlines.
.... 2. There was no sign of *rel—f* from the stifling heat.
.... 3. The actor had a long, narrow face with a *prom—n—nt* chin.
.... 4. Some *val—ble* antiques were sold at the auction.
.... 5. The *c—ling* of this room needs papering.
.... 6. A large *attend—nce* is expected for the outdoor concert.
.... 7. As a result of last year's earnings, the company finds itself in an *advantag—us* position.
.... 8. The copperhead is a *pois—n—s* snake.
.... 9. The hero finally outwits the *vill—n* and marries the beautiful heiress.
.... 10. At the last meeting of the club we argued about a certain rule of parliamentary *proc—dure*.
.... 11. Do not go to any *unne—sary* trouble.
.... 12. The Indians frequently made use of *med—cinal* herbs.
.... 13. His letter ended with the polite phrase "Yours *tr—ly*."
.... 14. These fabrics, which are guaranteed against shrinkage, come in a wide *var—ty* of colors and patterns.
.... 15. National ambitions are a serious *obst—cle* to world peace.
.... 16. Through his long service with the firm, Carlson has become an *ind—spens—ble* man.
.... 17. It is often said that *exp—r—nce* is the best teacher.
.... 18. Mrs. Rand took her *n—ce* and nephew to the circus.
.... 19. Sociologists point out that *envi—mental* influences help to explain one's personality or temperament.
.... 20. They *occasion—y* have guests for dinner.
.... 21. The last *p—formance* will start at nine o'clock.
.... 22. The tame crow was a *misch—v—us* creature.
.... 23. He was a *for—gn* correspondent for a Chicago newspaper.
.... 24. The *doct—r* will be here within an hour.
.... 25. He *l—d* the papers on his desk.

.... 26. The robbery *occur—d* sometime after midnight.
.... 27. When accused of the crime, the prisoner said that he was a victim of mistaken *iden—ty*.
.... 28. In his laboratory notebook, he made a very careful drawing of the *specim—n*.
.... 29. He has recently *appl—d* for a position at the bank.
.... 30. Barnum knew that *curi—sity* is a universal human trait.
.... 31. We do not yet know the full *signifi—nce* of atomic energy.
.... 32. She cannot read for ten minutes without *becom—ng* bored.
.... 33. He is said to be a *conscien—us* worker.
.... 34. Early diagnosis and treatment of the *d—sease* are important.
.... 35. This problem is *compar—tively* simple.
.... 36. General Marshall was *ch—sen* to serve as Secretary of State.
.... 37. The *princip—* of the high school gave a short talk.
.... 38. The cathedral at Chartres is one of the finest examples of Gothic architecture in *exist—nce* today.
.... 39. Careless *prep—ration* is often the cause of poor grades.
.... 40. The clerks at the post office were *b—s—ly* engaged in sorting over the morning mail.
.... 41. He has been named chairman of the membership *com—t—e*.
.... 42. One *—fect* of the war was a general increase in taxes.
.... 43. We were *listen—ng* to the news broadcast.
.... 44. They are *quit—ng* work at five o'clock.
.... 45. Faulty *pro—nciation* often leads to errors in spelling.
.... 46. He is a skillful *pol—tician*.
.... 47. There was a *contin—us* line of cars on Castle Street.
.... 48. He stubbornly *pers—veres* in one line of action.
.... 49. Romeo is the hero of a Shakespearean *tr—g—y*.
.... 50. It was a *pl—s—nt* Sunday afternoon in early spring.

To obtain score, multiply number of errors by 2 and subtract total from 100.

SECTION I
Understanding the Sentence

UNDERSTANDING THE SENTENCE

I. The Sentence

The sentence is the unit of thought in writing and speaking. To write and speak correctly one must have a thorough and sound knowledge of the sentence.

A sentence is a group of words which contains a subject and a predicate and which makes a grammatically and logically complete assertion, or asks a question, or gives a command. Since neither a subordinate clause nor a phrase fulfills these requirements, neither can be a sentence.

The subject of a sentence is the person about whom or the thing about which something is said. The predicate is always a finite verb which says something about the subject. A sentence may have objects, direct or indirect; it may have modifiers and connectives; but as valuable as these may be in elaborating the writer's thought, they are not grammatically essential to a sentence. "It rains," which has only a subject and predicate, is a perfectly good sentence; but "Raining the whole night through and far into the next morning" is not a sentence. This word-group has a verbal and modifiers and connectives, but it does not have a subject and predicate.

Normally the subject precedes the predicate in declarative sentences, rarely precedes the predicate in interrogative sentences, and frequently is omitted in imperative sentences. The italicized words in the following sentences are the subjects.

The little *girl* put her doll in the buggy.
Does *he* intend to return to college this fall?
You are going with me? (a less frequent form of a question)
You put down that stone. (imperative sentence with the subject expressed)
Get out of the way! (imperative sentence with the subject *you* understood)

The subject in declarative sentences sometimes follows the predicate. Do not be deceived by position. No matter what the order is, the person about whom or the thing about which something is said is the subject.

Gone was every *evidence* of the red man.
Whom are *you* looking for?
Which one do *you* want?
Slowly and anxiously passed the *hours*.
In the far corner of the pasture lot stood an old apple *tree*.
There is no *sugar* in the bowl.
Endless are the *things* one has to do on a farm.

To find the subject of any sentence, ask *who* or *what* of the predicate (finite verb).

It is true that every subordinate clause has a subject and a predicate, but a subordinate clause is not a sentence because it does not express a complete thought. "When the sun dropped over the horizon" is a subordinate clause with *sun* as the subject and *dropped* as the predicate, but it does not make a complete statement. "When the sun dropped over the horizon, a beautiful afterglow illuminated the western sky." Now we have a complete predication with *afterglow* the subject and *illuminated* the predicate of the main or independent clause.

Remember that neither length nor word order has anything to do with a group of words being a sentence. The command "Go!" is a sentence; a whole paragraph of a hundred and fifty words may be one sentence: length does not determine a sentence. The words may be in a simple and logical sequence; they may be inverted and involved: word order does not determine a sentence. To repeat: a sentence must have a subject, stated or implied, and it must make a complete statement about the subject, ask a question of the subject, or give a command to the subject.

II. THE SENTENCE FRAGMENT OR PERIOD FAULT

A sentence fragment is a related group of words which is punctuated as a sentence but which does not logically and grammatically express a complete thought. Most sentence fragments are subordinate clauses, or verbal and prepositional phrases, punctuated as complete sentences. We had best begin by understanding subordinate clauses and the various kinds of phrases.

A subordinate clause is a group of words introduced by a subordinate conjunction, having both a subject and a predicate but not expressing a complete thought when standing alone. These subordinate conjunctions introduce clauses of time, place, condition, purpose, result, cause, reason, concession, manner, comparison, and degree. Such clauses are related to and dependent upon main clauses for their meaning. The subordinate clauses are italicized in the following sentences.

Give me a call *when you are ready.*
After he had finished his work, he went to a show.
He could not see well *because there was a heavy fog.*
Although I am very busy, I hope to read this book soon.

You will note that these subordinate clauses do not make complete sense by themselves.

A phrase is a group of related words having neither subject nor predicate and used as a noun, an adjective, or an adverb. (You may disregard the fact that an infinitive is sometimes said to have a subject. Such a word is in no true sense a subject since it is in the *objective* case.)

To repeat gossip is a vicious habit. (infinitive phrase used as a noun, subject of *is*)
He wanted *to leave early in the morning*. (infinitive phrase used as a noun, object of *wanted*)
The flowers *to plant early* are the nasturtiums and the petunias. (infinitive phrase used as an adjective, modifying *flowers*)
He worked in a factory *to get experience*. (infinitive phrase used as an adverb, modifying *worked*)
Working at night is an unnatural way of living. (gerund phrase, subject of *is*)
He did not like *working at night*. (gerund phrase, object of *did like*)
Taking his coat from the hook, the boy started for the barn. (participial phrase used as an adjective, modifying *boy*)
She walked slowly *around the beautiful yard*. (prepositional phrase used as an adverb, modifying *walked*)
The apples *in the small barrel* are beginning to rot. (prepositional phrase used as an adjective, modifying *apples*)

There are two basic ways by which to correct sentence fragments: (1) incorporate the fragment into the sentence of which it is logically a part; (2) expand the fragment into a complete sentence.

WRONG: He kept on trying in the face of difficulties. Trusting he would ultimately find a solution.
CORRECTION BY INCORPORATION: He kept on trying in the face of difficulties, trusting he would ultimately find a solution.
CORRECTION BY EXPANSION: He kept on trying in the face of difficulties. He trusted that he would ultimately find a solution.

Do not punctuate subordinate clauses as complete sentences.

WRONG: He said he would not do the work in a hurry. Only when he was ready.
RIGHT: He said he would not do the work in a hurry but only when he was ready.
WRONG: I would not lend him my car. Not even if he were a good friend of mine.
RIGHT: I would not lend him my car, even if he were a good friend of mine.
WRONG: He said that he had never cast a ballot. Though he was surely old enough to vote.
RIGHT: He said that he had never cast a ballot, though he was surely old enough to vote.
RIGHT: He said that he had never cast a ballot. However, he was surely old enough to vote.
WRONG: The candidate for this office is Mr. Chapman. Who has, I am sorry to say, done some questionable things to obtain votes.
RIGHT: The candidate for this office is Mr. Chapman, who has, I am sorry to say, done some questionable things to obtain votes.
WRONG: He said that he was no longer interested in the house. That he would not buy it even at half price.
RIGHT: He said that he was no longer interested in the house, that he would not buy it even at half price.

Do not write phrases as complete sentences.

WRONG: She had a very bad habit. To repeat gossip up and down the street.
RIGHT: She had a very bad habit: to repeat gossip up and down the street.
RIGHT: She had a very bad habit; she repeated gossip up and down the street.

WRONG: I should like very much to call at your office next Monday. And to have a personal interview with you then.
RIGHT: I should like very much to call at your office next Monday and to have a personal interview with you then.
BETTER: I should like very much to call at your office next Monday in order to have a personal interview with you.
WRONG: Lots of things may undermine one's health. Eating and drinking excessively for one thing. And staying up late at night for another.
RIGHT: Lots of things may undermine one's health: eating and drinking excessively for one thing and staying up late at night for another.
WRONG: Every boy comes to that uncomfortable age sometime. Being too old to play with children and being too young to associate with grown-ups.
RIGHT: Every boy comes to that uncomfortable age sometime when he is too old to play with children and too young to associate with grown-ups.

Do not use appositives as complete sentences.

WRONG: He was a man everyone respected. A man of the highest integrity.
RIGHT: He was a man everyone respected, a man of the highest integrity.
WRONG: There was an amazing accumulation of old stuff in the attic. Namely, old clothes, trunks, discarded furniture, broken pictures, and rusty guns.
RIGHT: There was an amazing accumulation of old stuff in the attic, namely, old clothes, trunks, discarded furniture, broken pictures, and rusty guns.

Do not use ablative absolutes as complete sentences.

WRONG: There were several reasons why he did not want to be transferred to South America. The chief being that he did not speak Spanish.
RIGHT: There were several reasons why he did not want to be transferred to South America, the chief being that he did not speak Spanish.
RIGHT: Of the several reasons why he did not want to be transferred to South America, his inability to speak Spanish was the chief one.

There are several recognized uses in English in which partial sentences may be punctuated as complete sentences.

Mercy! Oh! (interjections)
How remarkable! (exclamatory statement)
"What time is it?" "Five o'clock." (answer to question)
Would she do such a thing as that? Certainly not. (rhetorical question and answer)
Now, for the next point. To digress for a moment. Finally, to summarize briefly. (transitions in a discourse)

It is true that you will find sentence fragments in good magazines and in standard books by reputable writers. These incomplete sentences are used intentionally to obtain vividness or to catch the reader's attention by the unusual or the unexpected. To teach such stylistic devices is not the purpose of this book; its purpose is rather to inculcate accepted practices of sound, correct English.

III. THE COMMA FAULT

The second of the two basic errors in writing sentences is the so-called comma fault, the use of a comma as the punctuation between two sentences.

Two points must be kept clearly in mind in correcting the comma fault: (1) the comma as the sole connection between the two sentences must be eliminated by writing the two parts as separate sentences, by inserting a co-ordinating conjunction after the comma, by substituting a semicolon for the comma, by using a semicolon before a linking adverb, by subordinating one of the sentences to the other, by reducing one of the sentences to a phrase, or by making a single sentence of the two sentences; (2) the correction should give the most logical expression of the thought.

The following sentences illustrate the various ways in which the comma fault may be corrected. The sentences will be grammatically correct, but they will vary considerably in the shades of meaning they will convey. Which correction to use will depend upon the writer's intended meaning.

WRONG: The salesman had not sold a vacuum sweeper all day, he was discouraged.
TWO SENTENCES: The salesman had not sold a vacuum sweeper all day. He was discouraged.
CO-ORDINATING CONJUNCTION: The salesman had not sold a vacuum sweeper all day, and he was discouraged.
SEMICOLON: The salesman had not sold a vacuum sweeper all day; he was discouraged.
SEMICOLON AND LINKING ADVERB: The salesman had not sold a vacuum sweeper all day; consequently, he was discouraged.
SUBORDINATION: Since he had not sold a vacuum sweeper all day, the salesman was discouraged.
PARTICIPIAL PHRASE: Not having sold a vacuum sweeper all day, the salesman was discouraged.
SINGLE SENTENCE: His not having sold a vacuum sweeper all day discouraged the salesman.

If the two sentences require separate emphasis, use a period as the correction for the comma fault.

WRONG: He was not a native American, he was a Pole.
RIGHT: He was not a native American. He was a Pole.

If the two sentences are logically related and of equal importance, use a semicolon to correct the comma fault.

WRONG: There was nothing more to do, he had exhausted all his resources.
RIGHT: There was nothing more to do; he had exhausted all his resources.

If the two sentences are co-ordinated in thought and of equal importance, insert *and*, *or*, or *but* after the comma to correct the comma fault.

WRONG: He was not a good writer, he was an excellent mathematician.
RIGHT: He was not a good writer, but he was an excellent mathematician.

If one of the sentences is of less importance than the other or is dependent upon it, use a semicolon and a linking adverb or a subordinate conjunction as the correction.

WRONG: He had had little experience, he was not offered the position.
RIGHT: He had had little experience; therefore he was not offered the position. (linking adverb)
RIGHT: Since (or As) he had had little experience, he was not offered the position. (subordinate conjunction)

If the sentences are rambling or "stringy," a simple sentence is often the best correction.

WRONG: The kitten was young and playful, it belonged to Harry.
RIGHT: The young and playful kitten belonged to Harry.

In very informal writing the comma is being used increasingly between sentences. The purpose of this book, however, is to teach correct punctuation at the formal level of writing.

IV. THE RUN-ON OR FUSED SENTENCE

The run-on sentence results from the omission of all punctuation between two sentences. Basically the mistake is the same as that in the comma fault, only the error is carried to a higher degree. Fused sentences may be eliminated by any of the methods given as corrections of the comma fault.

WRONG: He kept on playing finally he won a game.
RIGHT: He kept on playing, and finally he won a game.
RIGHT: He kept on playing; finally he won a game.
RIGHT: He kept on playing until he finally won a game.

NAME .... DATE .... SCORE ....

1. UNDERSTANDING THE SENTENCE—I

Identifying Subject and Verb

Pick out the subject and the verb in each of the following sentences and enter them in the space at the left. Enter the subject in the left column and the verb in the right. Be sure to include both parts of a compound subject or verb.

EXAMPLE:
SUBJECT   VERB
guide   rode   At the head of the column rode a lanky, sunburned guide.

SUBJECT	VERB	
bandstand	was painted / Decorated	1. In the center of the park was a bandstand, painted a gleaming white and decorated with bunting.
toil, hardships	are gone	2. Gone forever are the toil and hardships of pioneering days.
pictures, jumble	were	3. On Helen's desk were pictures of her family and a jumble of books and papers.
you	inspect	4. Inspect carefully the numerous wires leading to the instrument board.
Palace	stands	5. In the restored portion of Williamsburg stands the Palace, a replica of the building once used by the colonial governors.
Reporter	ran / telephoned	6. After jotting down a few rough notes at the scene of the train wreck, the reporter ran to a farmhouse and telephoned the story to the news room.
John	had won / gone	7. A person of exceptional ability, John had won a Rhodes scholarship and gone to Oxford for three years.
Prestige	grew	8. Following his famous "Cross of Gold" speech, Bryan's prestige as an orator steadily grew.
Rubber	came	9. Much of the natural rubber imported before the war came from the Dutch East Indies.
Italy	holds	10. Because of her many contributions to Western culture, Italy holds unusual interest for the student of art or literature.

21

SUBJECT	VERB		
Judge	*Rapped/warned*	11.	Because of the noise in the courtroom the judge rapped his gavel and warned the spectators.
Clowns	*were*	12.	In the circus there were three clowns, all of them having cherry-red noses and bizarre costumes.
Joan	*worked*	13.	During the Christmas season Joan worked as a salesgirl in the department store.
record	*can be used*	14.	A single record can now be used to play an entire symphony.
leaves	*change*	15.	In the fall the leaves of the beech tree change to a golden-yellow hue.
Normandie	*was destroyed*	16.	The *Normandie*, once a luxury liner, was almost completely destroyed by fire.
New York	*witnessed*	17.	Not since 1888 had New York witnessed such a snowstorm as this one.
juke box	*was*	18.	In a corner of the restaurant was a juke box, a garish monstrosity of chrome and onyx.
statue	*stood*	19.	At Rhodes, according to legend, stood a gigantic statue, its legs spanning the entrance to the harbor.
Books	*have influenced*	20.	Books like Plato's *Republic* and More's *Utopia* have influenced men's thinking about ideal commonwealths.

To obtain score, allow 5 points for each sentence in which the subject and the verb are correctly identified.

NAME .... DATE .... SCORE ....

2. UNDERSTANDING THE SENTENCE—II

Completing Sentence Fragments

Revise each of the passages below in which a sentence fragment occurs. You may make the correction either by joining the fragment to a complete sentence or by expanding the fragment into a complete sentence. With either procedure, make such changes in capitalization, punctuation, or phrasing as may be necessary. If the passage is made up of complete sentences, or if it contains a partial sentence which is in recognized use, write the word "Correct" in the blank space.

EXAMPLE:

We find it difficult to provide a satisfactory definition for the word *democracy*. Knowing, however, what the word means in terms of our experience.

We find it difficult to provide a satisfactory definition for the word democracy. *We know, however, what the word means in terms of our experience.*

1. In a hasty glance he took in the details of the room. Namely, the overstuffed furniture, the bulbous lamps, the faded blue rug, and the ornate chandelier.

   Such articles as the overstuffed furniture, the bulbous lamps, the faded blue rug, and the ornate chandelier.

2. Before going on the air, radio comedians often joke with the studio listeners. In order to get themselves into the right mood for the actual show.

   In order to get themselves into the right mood for the actual show, radio comedians often joke with the studio listeners before going on the air.

3. The truck came to a jolting stop. At the very moment that the old lady serenely stepped off the curb.

   At the very moment that the old lady serenely stepped off the curb, the truck came to a jolting stop.

4. Would any clear-headed individual risk his life savings in such a fly-by-night scheme as that? Absolutely not.

   Any clear headed individual absolutely would not risk his life savings in such a fly-by-night scheme as that.

5. Silversmithing is an old and distinguished American craft. The craft, incidentally, that was followed by Paul Revere of Revolutionary fame.

   The craft that was followed by Paul Revere of Revolutionary fame, ~~Silversmithing~~ [Silversmithing] is an old and distinguished American craft.

6. It is acknowledged that there are many abuses in our present jury system. To do away with juries, however, would violate the traditions of American justice.

7. To the open road every Sunday go thousands of motorists. Speeding along the wide express lanes or slowing down to a crawl on the crowded approaches to metropolitan centers.

8. The well-meaning friend at my bedside told of accidents involving broken needles left in the patient and of other medical mishaps. Such as deaths caused by a quantity of air being carelessly pumped into a blood vein.

To obtain score, allow 12½ points for each sentence which is properly revised or for each sentence which is identified as correct.

NAME .... DATE .... SCORE ....

3. UNDERSTANDING THE SENTENCE—III

Completing Sentence Fragments

Revise each of the passages below in which a sentence fragment occurs. You may make the correction either by joining the fragment to a complete sentence or by expanding the fragment into a complete sentence. With either procedure, make such changes in capitalization, punctuation, or phrasing as may be necessary. If the passage is made up of complete sentences, or if it contains a partial sentence which is in recognized use, write the word "Correct" in the blank space.

EXAMPLE:

I found my way about the streets of Boston without any difficulty. Although I had never visited a large city before.

I found my way about the streets of Boston without any difficulty, although I had never visited a large city before.

1. A tornado in Illinois plucked off a man's wig. Later depositing it on the head of another man several blocks away.

....
....

2. At sundown the road-weary motorist must choose between two types of accommodations. Either the tourist cabin with its box-like compactness or an upstairs room in one of the innumerable tourist homes along his route.

....
....
....
....

3. The years between 1920 and 1930, sometimes called the "era of normalcy," brought America the Model T, the airplane, and the mechanical refrigerator. An era of great technological changes, but of few important social advances.

....
....
....
....

4. When electricity was first introduced, alternating current was for a long time under suspicion. The main objection being that it was too dangerous for ordinary use.

　　..
　　..
　　..

5. The standard curriculum of the American colleges is patterned on the elective system. Which was first introduced at Harvard more than half a century ago.

　　..
　　..
　　..

6. In England, this writer asserts, advertising is directed chiefly toward men. In America, on the other hand, it being directed toward women.

　　..
　　..

7. Miss Willett was the society editor. A shrewd, affable woman who knew how to deal with the debutantes and the dowagers of the local "400."

　　..
　　..
　　..

8. First of all, a book review should tell what the book is about: its theme, scope, and purpose. Now for the next requirement. It should convey to the reader something of the quality or flavor of the writing.

　　..
　　..
　　..
　　..

To obtain score, allow 12½ points for each sentence which is properly revised or for each sentence which is identified as correct.

NAME .... DATE .... SCORE ....

4. UNDERSTANDING THE SENTENCE—IV

Correcting Comma Faults and Fused Sentences

By supplying the proper punctuation, eliminate every comma fault or fused (run-on) construction which appears among the sentences below. To make a correction, give the proper mark of punctuation in the space at the left, together with the word which precedes it and the word which follows it. If the sentence is correct as it stands, leave the space at the left blank.

EXAMPLES:

summer; then   I worked for my father until last summer, then I secured a job in a shoe factory.

window. It   Here is the hat you saw in the window it is just your size.

1. Annie's hair is seldom in evidence; in fact, there is some doubt as to its existence, for at work she always wears a silk stocking pulled down tightly over her ears.

moderate; it   2. The sky was clear and the wind moderate, it was truly a beautiful day for flying.

3. A section of the street had been blocked off for dancing, the music being provided by a local three-piece orchestra with its repertoire of dreamy waltzes and lively polkas.

4. My grandmother has a queer hobby she collects all sorts of old buttons.

5. He spent his early life in Montana, however, he has lived in the East for the past twenty years.

6. Murphy would often say, "Boys, I haven't had a cold for forty years, it's simply because I wear my long red flannels and take C.B.Q. pills."

7. I had written to my mother to tell her that I would not be home until late in the summer, hence she was greatly surprised to see me.

8. Frank's talk reflected a lively curiosity about his neighbors' affairs, moreover, he enjoyed listening to their conversations over the old-fashioned party-line telephone.

9. Standing near the forward ventilator on the forecastle deck, we watched the gulls which were flying in long, graceful arcs above the ship.

.... 10. Mr. Wilkins Micawber was an unfailing optimist; he was forever waiting for something to turn up.
.... 11. Ten students live in the house operated by the home economics department, each of these girls being assigned certain tasks for a specified period.
.... 12. Ready-mixed ingredients for muffins, rolls, biscuits, cake, gingerbread, and even pies can now be purchased at every grocery store; consequently, the problem of home baking has been greatly simplified.
.... 13. The general horror of snakes is hard to explain, for psychologists tell us that this fear is acquired, not instinctive.
.... 14. Why do some people always insist on taking pictures? my whole life has been blighted by wretched snapshots.
.... 15. Returning alumni will have an opportunity to see the baseball game in the afternoon, later they will be able to meet with old friends at the various class reunions.
.... 16. The practice of falconry was largely confined to aristocrats and noblemen; thus it came to be known as "the sport of kings."
.... 17. We never really asked Charlie to be caretaker of our fishing lodge; he just stepped in and casually took over the job.
.... 18. A good start may not be especially important in some of the longer running events, like the mile and the half-mile; however, it is a crucial matter in the dashes.
.... 19. On a hill above the village is an old fort that overlooks the Straits of Mackinac; it had a strategic importance in the colonial wars between the British and the French.
.... 20. Landing a giant tuna is an exciting sport, a battle that tests the skill and ingenuity of the deep-water fisherman.

To obtain score, multiply number of errors by 5 and subtract total from 100.

NAME .... DATE .... SCORE ....

5. UNDERSTANDING THE SENTENCE—V

Correcting Comma Faults and Fused Sentences

By supplying the proper punctuation, eliminate every comma fault or fused (run-on) construction which appears among the sentences below. To make a correction, give the proper mark of punctuation in the space at the left, together with the word which precedes it and the word which follows it. If the sentence is correct as it stands, leave the space at the left blank.

EXAMPLES:

sky; its   The moon was rising in the eastern sky its orange glow made the street lights seem pale and anemic.

neighborhood; consequently   Prowlers had been reported in the neighborhood, consequently we were careful to lock our doors every night.

.... 1. Dottie is pretending to model the latest style in hats; a white lamp shade trimmed with pink satin ribbon is slanted at a becoming angle over her right eye.

.... 2. A man may think that he is choosing his suit; nevertheless, it is his wife who invariably makes the final decision.

.... 3. An old dog, Bubbles was fat and ungainly; hence she quickly grew tired when she attempted to follow us on our rambles.

.... 4. There were flashes of lightning accompanied by volleys of thunder; then the storm broke in all its savage fury.

.... 5. After the fuselage, wings, and tail assembly had been put together, it was time for the tissue-paper covering to be applied.

.... 6. A runner who is kept too long in the starting position relaxes his muscles; he is not ready for a good start when the gun is fired.

.... 7. In the early hours of the morning, a sleet storm had covered the roads with a sheathing of ice; as a result, there were several minor accidents.

.... 8. The coach, a nervous little man, strode back and forth across the room, giving last-minute instructions before the start of the game.

.... 9. The slum-clearance project must be carried through, however long it may take or whatever expense is involved.

29

.... 10. In an army camp, humor serves as an antidote to the long hours, strict discipline, and gruelling marches, it may even help to compensate for poor food.
.... 11. There was an ordinance against raising chickens in the residential area, nevertheless, our neighbors had a large flock of hens in their back yard.
.... 12. Alexander Hamilton was a brilliant administrator and executive, always at his best in the realm of practical affairs; Jefferson was a philosopher and an idealist, deeply concerned about the future of the common man.
.... 13. That he was anxious to tell me something, I could sense at once.
.... 14. He had a long, thin face with prominent cheekbones; his graying hair straggled over the tips of his ears.
.... 15. Why should we wash the dishes? I have a great many in the cupboard and still more packed away in the basement.
.... 16. The family consists of a retired railroad engineer, his wife, and a middle-aged daughter; they live next door to my grandparents.
.... 17. The tree swayed slightly under the blows of the axe, and then, with a rending crash, it toppled to the ground.
.... 18. Geology, she vaguely remembered, had something to do with rocks; zoölogy appeared to be mostly concerned with earthworms and frogs.
.... 19. The Pennsylvania Dutch are a thrifty and industrious people, their love of order manifesting itself in their neat, well-tended farms and in their pleasant, substantial homes.
.... 20. Dad walked to a house nearby to telephone for a mechanic; meanwhile I stood guard over the car and our belongings.

To obtain score, multiply number of errors by 5 and subtract total from 100.

SECTION II
Grammar

AGREEMENT OF SUBJECT AND VERB

The verb in every sentence or clause must agree with its subject in person and number. There are three persons: the first person is the speaker; the second person is the person spoken to; the third person is the person or thing spoken of. There are two numbers: the singular and the plural. In all formal use of English the agreement of the verb with its subject must be strictly adhered to; sometimes in colloquial or conversational English exceptions are made to this rule.

1. A verb agrees with its subject in person and number.

I *am* tired.
He *is* the winner.
The book *was* on the table.
They *were* our guests.
These jars *have* no tops.

2. Compound subjects connected by *and* take a plural verb unless the subjects are identical in person or thing or are so closely related as to be singular in idea, in which case a singular verb is used.

Ability and character *are* both essential to success.
The trees and the shrubbery *have been injured* by the drought.
The owner and operator of this lunch stand *is* responsible for maintaining sanitary conditions. (*owner* and *operator* the same person)
The bow and arrow *was* the Indians' favorite weapon. (subject singular in idea)

A singular verb is required with singular subjects preceded by *each*, *every*, and *many a*.

Each candidate and each party manager *has made* a sworn statement of expenses.
Every boy and every girl *is* responsible for his own work.
Many a sigh and many a tear *was spent* over this mistake.

3. Do not allow a modifier of the subject to affect the agreement between the verb and its subject.

WRONG: The purposes of scientific research *was* not always *appreciated* by conservative thinkers.
RIGHT: The purposes of scientific research *were* not always *appreciated* by conservative thinkers. (*purposes* is the subject)
WRONG: A reckoning of all the expenses entailed in these activities *are* to be made by the auditor.
RIGHT: A reckoning of all the expenses entailed in these activities *is* to be made by the auditor. (*reckoning* is the subject)
WRONG: Careful consideration of these very serious matters *have been given* by the committee.

RIGHT: Careful consideration of these very serious matters *has been given* by the committee. (*consideration* is the subject)

4. Do not allow introductory words or phrases, which are often followed by the verb and then the subject, to affect the agreement between the verb and its subject.

WRONG: There *is* a dime and a quarter missing.
RIGHT: There *are* a dime and a quarter missing. (*dime* and *quarter* are the compound subject)
WRONG: There *flies* two of the biggest planes ever built.
RIGHT: There *fly* two of the biggest planes ever built. (*two* is the subject)
WRONG: Out *rushes* three men in search of the burglar.
RIGHT: Out *rush* three men in search of the burglar. (*men* is the subject)
WRONG: In the attic *was* a trunk and an old valise.
RIGHT: In the attic *were* a trunk and an old valise. (*trunk* and *valise* are the compound subject)

5. Words joined to the subject by *as well as, along with, together with, with, including, in addition to, no less than,* and similar expressions do not affect the agreement of the verb with its subject.

The mother, as well as the daughter, *is entered* in the beauty contest.
The instigator, no less than the perpetrator, *is* guilty of the crime.

6. With two or more singular subjects connected by *or, nor,* or *but,* use a singular verb.

The teacher or the janitor always *locks* the windows.
Neither the principal nor the interest *has been paid.*
Not the coach, but the captain, *decides* the plays.

When subjects of different persons or numbers are connected with the correlative conjunctions *either . . . or, neither . . . nor,* the verb agrees in person and number with the nearer subject.

RIGHT: Either you or I *am* wrong.
RIGHT: Either you *are* wrong or I *am.*
RIGHT: Neither the coach nor the players *are* to blame.
RIGHT: Neither the players nor the coach *is* to blame.

The verb agrees with the positive rather than the negative subject introduced by such words as *not, and not, not only . . . but (also).*

RIGHT: The commander, not the soldiers, *was* in danger.
RIGHT: The soldiers, and not the commander, *were* in danger.
RIGHT: Not only the driver but also the other occupants of the car *were injured.*

7. The singular indefinite pronouns as subjects take a singular verb. The following are some of the commonest of these pronouns: *one, anyone, every-*

one (*every one*), *someone, no one, anybody, everybody, nobody, somebody, each, either,* and *neither.*

>   WRONG (or colloquial): Neither of the answers *were* correct.
>   RIGHT: Neither of the answers *was* correct.
>   WRONG (or colloquial): Every one of the prisoners *have been examined.*
>   RIGHT: Every one of the prisoners *has been examined.*

The indefinite pronoun *none* may be either singular or plural, depending upon its meaning in the sentence.

>   RIGHT: None *answers* to this name. (equivalent to *Not one, No one,* or *Nobody*)
>   RIGHT: None of this great fortune *is* now left. (equivalent to *Not any part*)
>   RIGHT: None *are* so blind as those who will not see.
>   RIGHT: None of the animals *have left* their tracks along the shore.

8. Do not allow a verb to be attracted into agreement with a predicate noun.

>   WRONG: The most enjoyable music *were* the symphonies.
>   RIGHT: The most enjoyable music *was* the symphonies. (*music*, not *symphonies*, is the subject)
>   WRONG: His greatest enjoyment *were* memories of his youthful adventures.
>   RIGHT: His greatest enjoyment *was* memories of his youthful adventures. (*enjoyment*, not *memories*, is the subject)
>   WRONG: Weather and terrain *was* the real enemy.
>   RIGHT: Weather and terrain *were* the real enemy. (*Weather* and *terrain* are the compound subject)

9. A verb with a collective noun as its subject is singular if the noun represents a unit, but plural if the noun is thought of in its individual parts.

>   RIGHT: The jury *was* unanimous in its decision.
>   RIGHT: The jury *were divided* in their opinions.
>   RIGHT: Ibsen said that the majority *is* never right.
>   RIGHT: A majority of the delegates *were* farmers.

Such collective names for animals as *cattle, sheep, swine, fish, trout, cod, deer, moose,* and *quail* require a plural verb.

>   RIGHT: The sheep *were grazing* in the pasture.
>   RIGHT: Fish *were* once plentiful in this lake.

10. Supply such auxiliaries as *is, are, was, were, has,* and *have* in the second clause of a compound sentence unless the auxiliary is the same in both clauses.

>   RIGHT: The crop *has been harvested* and the grain *stored.* (not necessary to repeat *has been* before *stored*, for auxiliary the same as in first clause)
>   WRONG: The examination *was given* and the papers *graded.*
>   RIGHT: The examination *was given* and the papers *were graded.*
>   WRONG: The voting places *have closed* and the counting of the votes *begun.*
>   RIGHT: The voting places *have closed* and the counting of the votes *has begun*

11. A relative pronoun having a plural antecedent must have a plural verb.

> WRONG: This is one of the choice tobaccos that *has* to be imported.
> RIGHT: This is one of the choice tobaccos that *have* to be imported. (*tobaccos*, not *one*, is the antecedent of *that*)
> WRONG: She is one of those women who *is* never satisfied.
> RIGHT: She is one of those women who *are* never satisfied. (*women*, not *one*, is the antecedent of *who*)

If the antecedent of the pronoun is in the singular, the verb is in the singular.

> RIGHT: This is the only one of the books that *has* an index. (*one*, not *books*, is the antecedent of *that*)

12. Titles of newspapers, books, plays, poems, pictures, business firms, companies, and the like take a singular verb.

> *The Two Gentlemen of Verona*, written about 1594, *is* a play by Shakespeare.
> "Trees" *is* a poem by Joyce Kilmer.
> Mabley and Carew *is* a department store in Cincinnati, Ohio.

13. Many nouns, plural in form, almost always take a singular verb. Among such words are *news, economics, mathematics, physics, ethics, measles, mumps,* and *whereabouts*.

> Local news *is reported* hourly over this station.
> Mumps *is* primarily a disease of childhood.
> His whereabouts *is known* to only a few persons.

The following nouns may be either singular or plural: *means, politics, wages, alms,* and *amends*.

> Politics *was* the natural expression of his gregarious personality.
> Politics *have corrupted* many weak men.
> Wages *is* a matter of frequent dispute between employer and employee.
> Wages *have been increased* to all workmen receiving less than sixty cents an hour.

The following nouns are almost always construed as plural: *scissors, trousers, riches, acoustics, athletics,* and *tactics*.

> The scissors *were sharpened* by an itinerant mechanic.
> The acoustics of the auditorium *were* good.
> Athletics *are accepted* as a natural part of the life of American youth.

The following foreign plurals require a plural verb: *data, strata, phenomena, alumni,* and *alumnae*.

> All the data *were checked* carefully before publication.
> These phenomena *have been observed* in different parts of the world.

14. Nouns denoting a number, quantity, measurement, mass, price, or time require a singular verb if the subject is considered as a unit.

> Seventy-five dollars *is* the price for this suit.

Seven years *was* the sentence imposed.
Five yards *is* the width of this alley.

In such mathematical expressions as the following, either the singular or the plural verb is correct.

Six times six *is* (or *are*) thirty-six.
Six and six *is* (or *are*) twelve.

A singular noun denoting a part, if modified by an *of*-phrase denoting the whole, is singular if the object of the preposition is singular and plural if the object of the preposition is plural.

Half of the estate *has been consumed* in legal fees.
Half of the potatoes *have rotted*.
A part of the assignment *was* difficult.
A part of the planes *were destroyed*.
Most of the noise *was made* by small boys.
Most of the answers *were* correct.
The rest of the journey *was* easy.
The remainder of the houses *were sold* at public auction.
Ten per cent of his income *is spent* on insurance.
Thirty per cent of the students at this college *are working* their way.

The word *number* preceded by *a* and followed by a plural noun takes a plural verb; if preceded by *the* and followed by a plural noun, it takes a singular verb.

A number of the men *were* absent.
The number of men on a baseball team *is* nine.

15. The expletive *it* is the grammatical subject of the sentence and is followed by a singular verb.

It *is* we who have defended the weak.
It *was* the boys for whom we had been searching.

16. Formal, correct English requires strict adherence to the following rules.
Use *doesn't*, not *don't*, with a subject in the third person and singular number.

He *doesn't want* to play.
The offer *doesn't appeal* to me.

Say "Am I not?" Never say "Aren't I?" or "Ain't I?" There is no contraction for *am not*.

I am right in this, *am* I not?

The plural verbs *are*, *were*, and *have* must be used with the second person, singular number pronoun *you*.

Jane, you *are* (*were*, *have been*) *mistaken*.

Care must be taken to use the correct verb with *kind* and *sort*.

WRONG: This kind *are* no good.
RIGHT: This kind *is* no good.
RIGHT: These kinds *are* no good.
WRONG: This sort *have* blossoms early.
RIGHT: This sort *has* blossoms early.
RIGHT: These sorts *have* blossoms early.

NAME .... DATE .... SCORE ....

6. AGREEMENT OF SUBJECT AND VERB--I

From the forms given in parenthesis choose the correct verb for each sentence and write it in the space at the left.

EXAMPLE:
operate   The man and his wife (operates, operate) a restaurant.

has .... 1. A list of all the supplies needed for the camps (has, have) been made.

is .... 2. I am familiar with many varieties of irises, but this kind (is, are) new to me.

am I not .... 3. I am the first one to turn in a complete set of answers, (am I not, aren't I)?

Doesn't .... 4. (Doesn't, Don't) she have a telephone?

Does .... 5. (Do, Does) either of the boys play the violin?

was .... 6. The news of all the important events (was, were) given at the end of the program.

was .... 7. Each of the letters (was, were) carefully filed in the cabinet.

is .... 8. A lonely boy and his love for a little dog (is, are) the theme for this story.

are .... 9. Some of the better students in the class (is, are) interested in forming a discussion group.

do .... 10. The untidy young man or careless young woman (does, do) not usually succeed in business.

makes .... 11. *The Perils of Pauline* (makes, make) many interesting observations upon the silent movies.

have .... 12. Neither the foreman nor the workmen (has, have) shown much interest in this job.

is .... 13. My favorite reading (is, are) modern novels.

is .... 14. How (is, are) Mr. Johnson and the new store getting along?

is .... 15. What is needed, according to the internationalists, (is, are) frequent and honest exchanges of opinion.

were .... 16. A number of chickens (was, were) running about outside the pen.

was .... 17. The most hotly debated part of the program (was, were) the increases in taxes.

were .... 18. The scissors (was, were) so dull that I could not cut the cloth evenly.

is .... 19. In the front of the house there (is, are) one door and a pair of windows on either side of it.

39

__praise__ 20. Both the producer and the exhibitor (praises, praise) this picture.

__has__ 21. An invoice for new merchandise, including radios, phonographs, and television sets, (has, have) just been received.

__is__ 22. The number of players on a baseball team (is, are) nine.

__are elaborated__ 23. In the first chapter the general problem is stated and in succeeding chapters various phases of the problem (elaborated, are elaborated).

__was__ 24. Thirty per cent of the students (was, were) from rural districts.

__was__ 25. The real reason why he sold the property (was, were) the debts that had accumulated against it.

To obtain score, multiply number of errors by 4 and subtract total from 100.

NAME .... DATE .... SCORE ....

7. AGREEMENT OF SUBJECT AND VERB—II

From the forms given in parenthesis choose the correct verb for each sentence and write it in the space at the left.

EXAMPLE:

are   A number of the strikers (is, are) returning to their jobs tomorrow.

is   1. The approach of the two men to government problems (is, are) much the same.

have   2. Hunches and even accidents, rather than planned research, (has, have) accounted for some of the most remarkable scientific discoveries.

has   3. Neither Mabel nor her sister (has, have) indicated any interest in the new club.

doesn't   4. That price seems rather high, (doesn't, don't) it?

is   5. The chief contribution of the book to agricultural problems (is, are) several chapters devoted to soil conservation.

was   6. The performance which the children enjoyed most (was, were) the acrobats.

were   7. Tin cans, broken glass, and other refuse (was, were) thrown in the ditch.

is   8. Harper and Brothers (is, are) among the oldest American publishers.

do   9. He was one of those unusual persons who never (does, do) the tactless thing.

is   10. The Byrnes picture of Russian tactics in negotiation (is, are) illuminating.

was   11. It surely (was, were) they who originated this plan.

has   12. Neither of these books (has, have) illustrations.

is   13. There (is, are) a pitcher of cider and some doughnuts on the tray.

have been put   14. Your furniture has been thoroughly cleaned and new covers (put, have been put) on two of your chairs.

was   15. Twenty-five dollars (was, were) the regular weekly rent for the summer cottage.

is   16. What this country needs, if it is going to prosper, (is, are) better opportunities for farm boys.

are   17. In many colleges only sixty per cent of the entering freshmen (is, are) graduated.

41

were 18. The alumni of the university (was, were) invited to contribute to the soldiers' memorial.
has 19. It was one of the most remarkable come-backs that (has, have) occurred in the history of baseball.
have 20. There (has, have) been a number of recent inquiries about the price of that house.
knows 21. If neither Sarah nor you (knows, know) the answer, I shall write it on the board.
has 22. Scarcity, as well as the other factors determining prices, (has, have) been considered.
were 23. The data by which she finally proved the case (was, were) amazingly interesting.
_is_ 24. Of the contagious diseases of childhood, measles (is, are) among the most prevalent.
have 25. He is one of a number of remarkable men who (has, have) come out of that unpromising environment.

To obtain score, multiply number of errors by 4 and subtract total from 100.

NAME .... DATE .... SCORE ....

8. AGREEMENT OF SUBJECT AND VERB—III

From the forms given in parenthesis choose the correct verb for each sentence and write it in the space at the left.

EXAMPLE:
was   It (was, were) we who circulated the petition.

were   1. A number of little children (was, were) wandering about in the playgrounds.
am   2. Either you or I (am, are) responsible for this mistake.
were cracked   3. The pitcher was broken and three glasses (cracked, were cracked).
is   4. Neither the parents nor the son (is, are) interested in higher education.
was   5. The house, as well as the outlying buildings, (was, were) razed by the fire.
am   6. Neither Mary nor I (am, is, are) old enough to vote.
were   7. The data on which this report is based (was, were) verified three times.
was   8. Each knife and each fork (was, were) dipped carefully into the sterilizing fluid.
is   9. The committee on nominations (is, are) now ready to file the names for all offices.
needs   10. The back, not the legs of the chair, (needs, need) bracing.
bears   11. *Winds of Doctrine*, written by George Santayana, (bears, bear) the subtitle "Studies in Contemporary Opinion."
doesn't   12. (Doesn't, Don't) he ever return books to the library on time?
was   13. As handled by the Indians, the bow and arrow (was, were) an effective weapon.
was   14. What immediately caught the sympathy of the audience (was, were) the sad smiles of the heroine.
leaves   15. Seven from thirteen (leaves, leave) six.
is   16. Over six hundred miles a minute (is, are) the speed attained by this jet-propelled plane.
are   17. Either the principal or the teachers (is, are) empowered to enforce discipline.
is   18. He said that the average weight of babies at birth (is, are) seven pounds.

43

was 19. In the attic (was, were) a collection of old guns and swords.
_is_ 20. Three dollars a foot (is, are) the price for drilling a well in this kind of soil.
have 21. This is one of the fastest races that (has, have) ever been run on this track.
_is_ 22. Neither of them (is, are) mentioned in the will.
have 23. Each of those who (has, have) sold ten tickets will be given admission free.
was 24. Thirty per cent of the corn crop (was, were) lost because of the early frost.
was 25. The number of persons chosen for this special jury (was, were) thirteen.

To obtain score, multiply number of errors by 4 and subtract total from 100.

NAME .... DATE .... SCORE ....

9. AGREEMENT OF SUBJECT AND VERB—IV

From the forms given in parenthesis choose the correct verb for each sentence and write it in the space at the left.

EXAMPLE:

was   The most entertaining feature of the program (was, were) the sleight-of-hand tricks.

has   1. This is the only one of the switches that (has, have) an automatic control.

was   2. Neither of the bidders (was, were) willing to go beyond ten dollars.

has   3. (Has, Have) everybody been informed of the new time of the meeting?

have been counted   4. The election has been held and all the votes (counted, have been counted).

Doesn't   5. (Doesn't, Don't) she look exactly like her mother?

has   6. Many an opportunity and many a fortune (has, have) been lost by indecision.

was   7. Neither the chief suspect nor the other villainous character (was, were) guilty of the crime.

were   8. The military tactics used by the enemy forces (was, were) daring and confusing.

is   9. The safest feature of this swimming pool for little children (is, are) the numerous guards.

is   10. Ten dollars (is, are) the bond that must be posted for speeding.

places   11. A tabulation of the causes of fires and accidents (places, place) carelessness at the top of the list.

was   12. The best part of the program (was, were) the plantation singers.

were   13. The statistics and popular opinion (was, were) for once in agreement.

is   14. Mathematics (is, are) the most difficult subject I have.

Doesn't   15. (Doesn't, Don't) anyone here know the answer to such a simple question?

threatens   16. If this action is taken, the secretary, along with several other members, (threatens, threaten) to resign.

was   17. According to this plan, eleven years (was, were) the period for paying for this type of house.

fits   18. Either of the dresses (fits, fit) her perfectly.

_is_ 19. In the corner of the yard (is, are) a small arbor and three rustic benches.
seem 20. None of the clocks (seems, seem) to keep exactly the same time.
_is_ 21. Three hundred dollars (is, are) the complete cost for a summer at that boys' camp.
were 22. The acoustics of the studio (was, were) greatly improved by thick curtains.
please 23. Neither this house nor other houses in the neighborhood (pleases, please) me.
_is_ 24. *The Scottish Chiefs*, once among the most popular romances, (is, are) little read today.
was 25. Every letter and every scrap of paper (was, were) read avidly by the detective.

To obtain score, multiply number of errors by 4 and subtract total from 100.

AGREEMENT AND REFERENCE OF PRONOUNS

I. Agreement of a Pronoun and Its Antecedent

A pronoun must agree with its antecedent in gender, person, and number. The case of every pronoun is determined by its use in the sentence or clause in which it stands; in other words, it is independent of its antecedent in the matter of case.

1. A pronoun should agree with its antecedent in gender, person, and number.

>I *who* am older should take the responsibility.
>He *who* is older should take the responsibility.
>They *who* are older should take the responsibility.

If two or more antecedents, singular or plural, are joined by *and*, the pronoun is in the plural; if two singular antecedents are joined by *or* or *nor*, the pronoun is in the singular; if two antecedents, singular or plural, are joined by *or* or *nor*, the pronoun agrees with the nearer.

>RIGHT: Harry and Tom have taken *their* places in the line.
>RIGHT: Mary or Susan has missed *her* cue.
>RIGHT: Neither the auditor nor his assistants were responsible for *their* poor record in tax collections.
>RIGHT: Neither his assistants nor the auditor was responsible for *his* poor record in tax collections.

2. *One, man, person, anyone, everyone, no one, someone, anybody, everybody, nobody, somebody, each, either, neither, kind,* and *sort* are singular, and pronouns referring to these words should be singular.

>WRONG: Everyone must sign *their* own pledge.
>RIGHT: Everyone must sign *his* own pledge.
>WRONG: Neither of the boys were in *their* seats.
>RIGHT: Neither of the boys was in *his* seat.
>WRONG: A person never does *their* best when *they* are in a hurry.
>RIGHT: A person never does *his* best when *he* is in a hurry.

3. Unless precision in reference is necessary, avoid the cumbersome expressions *he or she, his or her*.

>RIGHT: Every man and every woman present must sign *his or her* name to these terms.
>CORRECT BUT AWKWARD: If any person saw the accident, will *he or she* kindly arise?
>SATISFACTORY: If any person saw the accident, will *he* kindly arise?
>BETTER: Will any person who saw the accident kindly arise?

4. Particular attention must be paid to the antecedent of a relative pronoun.

RIGHT: One of the investigators *who* have worked on the case is ready to report. (The antecedent of *who* is *investigators*, hence *have*.)
RIGHT: This is the only one of the roads *that* leads to Midgeville. (The antecedent of *that* is *one*, hence the singular *leads*.)

II. Reference of Pronouns

A second difficulty in the use of pronouns is vague reference. A pronoun may be used with grammatical correctness but be unclear or misleading to the reader or hearer. To correct vague reference in the use of pronouns, the previous noun or some near equivalent may have to be repeated or even the whole sentence recast. Obviously, loose reference of pronouns is incompatible with clear expression of thought.

5. A pronoun should not have two possible antecedents.

VAGUE: Jack told his father that *he* had made a mistake.
VAGUE: Jack told his father of *his* mistake.
CLEAR BUT AWKWARD: Jack told his father that he (Jack) had made a mistake.
CLEAR BUT AWKWARD: Jack told his father that the latter had made a mistake.
CLEAR: Jack said to his father, "I have made a mistake."
CLEAR: Jack said to his father: "You have made a mistake."
VAGUE: The girl chose for her teacher the quotation which *she* liked best.
VAGUE: The girl chose for her teacher *her* favorite quotation.
CLEAR: The girl chose for her teacher the quotation which the teacher liked best.
CLEAR: The girl chose the quotation which she liked best for her teacher.

6. The indefinite use of *they* and *it* should be avoided in formal writing and speaking.

VAGUE: The weather forecasts are often wrong. *They* do not know any more about *it* than the average person does.
CLEAR: The weather forecasts are often wrong. The forecasters do not know any more about the weather than the average person does.
VAGUE: In Holland *they* use wooden shoes extensively.
CLEAR: The Hollanders use wooden shoes extensively.
CLEAR: Wooden shoes are used extensively in Holland.
VAGUE: On the radio *it* says that tomorrow will be colder.
CLEAR: The radio reports that tomorrow will be colder.
CLEAR: Colder weather is predicted for tomorrow by the radio.
COLLOQUIAL: When are *they* going to repair this street?
BETTER: When will this street be repaired?

The impersonal use of *it* in statements about the weather, time, distance, and the like is correct as well as its expletive use.

It rained very hard last night. *It* is getting late. How far is *it* to Pittsburgh?
It is a fact that we have not answered their letters promptly. (expletive use)
It is regrettable that we have neglected them. (expletive use)

7. Avoid referring to a vague or implied antecedent in a previous part of the sentence or in a preceding sentence.

VAGUE: The chief gave us a policeman's whistle, and we are to call *them* if there is any trouble.
CLEAR: The chief gave us a policeman's whistle, and we are to call the police if there is any trouble.
VAGUE: We have covered the bed with mosquito netting. I am sure *they* won't get in to annoy us tonight.
CLEAR: We have covered the bed with mosquito netting. I am sure the mosquitoes won't get in to annoy us tonight.

8. Avoid the use of indefinite *you* and *your*.

VAGUE: Some waters can make *you* sick.
CLEAR: Some waters can make *a person* (or *one*) sick.
CONFUSED: As one approaches the volcano, *you* see smoke curling from the crater.
CLEAR: As one approaches the volcano, *he* sees smoke curling from the crater.
CONFUSED: I believe sociology is valuable because it widens *your* interest in people.
CLEAR: I believe sociology is valuable because it widens *my* (or *one's*) interest in people.

9. Make the pronoun refer to the important noun in the sentence or clause, preferably the subject. Avoid an antecedent in the possessive case if such reference leads to unclearness.

VAGUE: Jack's father entered the army when he was three years old.
CLEAR: When Jack was three years old, his father entered the army.
VAGUE: Then we saw a rabbit's pen which was running around the yard.
CLEAR: Then we saw the pen of a rabbit which was running around the yard.

10. In modern English *which* should not be used of persons except collective nouns signifying a group of persons.

WRONG: The man *which* knocked at our door was a tramp.
RIGHT: The man *who* (or *that*) knocked at our door was a tramp.
RIGHT: The crew *which* saved the ship received decorations.

11. In conversation and informal writing we use *which*, *this*, and *that* with the idea of a preceding clause or sentence as the antecedent. In careful and formal writing and speaking, reference should be to a single word.

VAGUE: Many children do not have their teeth attended to, and their teeth decay. *This* may affect them severely in later life.
CORRECTION: *This neglect* may . . . or *Such carelessness* may . . .
VAGUE: A rattle snake buzzes its rattles when alarmed, *which* warns a person approaching.
ACCEPTABLE: A rattle snake buzzes its rattles when alarmed, *a sound which* warns a person approaching.
PREFERABLE: A rattle snake buzzes its rattle when alarmed. *This characteristic sound* warns a person approaching.
VAGUE: He boasted about his wonderful accomplishments, *which* made him very disagreeable.
ACCEPTABLE: He boasted about his wonderful accomplishments, *an attitude which* made him very disagreeable.

PREFERABLE: He boasted about his wonderful accomplishments. *Such boasting* made him very disagreeable.

12. A pronoun used with a collective noun should be either singular or plural to agree with the idea expressed in the noun.

RIGHT: The committee insisted upon unrestricted use of *its* funds.
RIGHT: The committee took *their* regular seats.

13. The indefinite pronoun *one* need not be followed by *one's* or *oneself*. The correct forms of *he* or *she* satisfy all the requirements of good usage.

PEDANTIC: *One* is liable to slip and hurt *oneself* in *one's* bath.
PREFERABLE: *One* is liable to slip and hurt *himself* in *his* bath.

14. Do not use the reflexive or intensive pronoun *myself* or *I* or *me*.

UNDESIRABLE: My wife and *myself* play professional bridge.
PREFERABLE: My wife and *I* play professional bridge.
UNDESIRABLE: The superintendent asked Mr. Jenkins and *myself* to report.
PREFERABLE: The superintendent asked Mr. Jenkins and *me* to report.

15. If the noun of the phrase following such words as *part, rest, remainder, number*, and the like is singular, the pronoun will be singular; if plural, the pronoun will be plural.

RIGHT: The rest of the picture was boring in *its* repetition.
RIGHT: The remainder of the children will have *their* picnic next week.

16. Avoid ambiguity or misunderstanding by placing a relative pronoun as near as possible to its antecedent.

VAGUE: Prizes are frequently offered by big companies *which* make the winners rich.
CLEAR: Big companies frequently offer prizes *which* make the winners rich.
VAGUE: He admired an old picture in the museum *which* was standing on an easel.
CLEAR: In the museum he admired an old picture *which* was standing on an easel.

17. The possessive pronoun should be used with the gerund. If the emphasis is upon the person and not upon the action, the objective pronoun modified by a participle is used.

RIGHT: I did not like *his* answering my question so curtly. (emphasis on *answering*, a gerund, hence *his*)
RIGHT: I saw *him* talking to John at the corner. (emphasis upon *him*, hence the participle *talking*)

NAME .... DATE .... SCORE ....

10. AGREEMENT OF PRONOUN AND ANTECEDENT—I

From the forms given in parenthesis choose the correct pronoun for each sentence and write it in the space at the left.

EXAMPLE:

his   Everyone will obtain (his, their) equipment at the supply room.

he 1. Many a successful man will tell you that (he, they) might easily have been a failure.
it 2. Although the ball-pointed pen had enormous sales when first introduced, users have not found (it, them) entirely satisfactory.
his 3. We shall get nowhere, if everyone is going to try to have (his, their) own way.
his 4. If anyone asks about this house, tell (him, them) it is not for sale.
it 5. I have little interest in mathematics because I cannot see that (it, they) will be of any use to me in my work.
its 6. Every church should be interested in the spiritual welfare of (its, their) members.
his 7. Neither Tom nor Will showed the proper interest in (his, their) work.
their 8. Both Margaret and Jane developed (her, their) sense of responsibility at the camp.
his 9. Neither the lawyer nor his clients had expected such a ruling in (his, their) case.
its 10. According to modern thinkers a nation must ultimately depend upon force for (its, their) real safety.
he 11. Many an eloquent speaker will confess that (he, they) used to experience fright before audiences.
he 12. If any student wishes to discuss this problem further, will (he, they) come to my office after class?
his 13. Many a person has entered upon (his, their) life work without giving the matter any serious consideration.
him 14. If anybody asks about the lesson for tomorrow, tell (him, them) the assignment is on the board.
his 15. Every player had to submit to a thorough physical examination before being given (his, their) uniform.
its 16. The Human Relations Club holds (its, their) meetings on the first Monday of each month.
his 17. Neither of the young men has yet reached (his, their) majority.

his 18. Some one has left (his, their) car parked in our driveway.
its 19. The grand jury completed (its, their) work in three days.
their 20. Will the members of the club signify (its, their) pleasure in this matter?
_he_ 21. Sometimes a person hardly knows what (he, they) can do to help people in other countries.
his 22. Almost everyone taking that road loses (his, their) way.
his 23. Neither the foreman nor the workmen felt that (his, their) rights were respected by the company.
him 24. I have never seen a person that didn't have some good in (him, them).
its 25. During World War II California had a remarkable growth in (its, their) population.

To obtain score, multiply number of errors by 4 and subtract total from 100.

NAME .... DATE .... SCORE ....

11. AGREEMENT OF PRONOUN AND ANTECEDENT—II

From the forms given in parenthesis choose the correct wording for each sentence and write it in the space at the left.

EXAMPLE:

he loses — It has been said that the average person never values health until (he loses, they lose) it.

it has — 1. This neighborhood store has always occupied the same building, and (it has, they have) established an enviable reputation in the community.

have — 2. The whereabouts of many European relatives (has, have) long been unknown to their American cousins.

was — 3. Each of the injured workmen (was, were) given emergency treatment.

is — 4. In the alumni files (is, are) kept the name, the current address, and the occupation of each graduate of the college.

does his — 5. He is the sort of mechanic who (does his, do their) work in a conscientious way.

its place — 6. When you children are through playing you must put everything back in (its place, their places).

that seems — 7. Every traveler visiting a foreign country discovers many a custom (that seems, that seem) strange to him.

his — 8. Every member agreed to pay (his, their) back dues immediately.

is — 9. It is I who (am, is, are) responsible for these funds; therefore I must have absolute control of them.

is — 10. The phenomena of nuclear physics (is, are) so mystifying that the average layman is terrified about the future.

his — 11. Each person was then asked to take (his, their) seat immediately.

it has — 12. The dealers prefer this type of mixer because (it has, they have) immediately adjustable parts.

his — 13. One or the other of them will surely have to pay for (his, their) carelessness.

were — 14. Bringing up the rear end of the parade (was, were) a mule and three small boys beating a drum.

it is — 15. The rock strata of western Pennsylvania first revealed oil, and (it is, they are) the origin of the world's colossal oil industry.

who kick — 16. James is the only one of the boys (who kicks, who kick) the ball over the goal post.

53

were 17. At the beginning of the game everything was in confusion because there (was, were) more tickets sold than there were seats.

they are 18. The young business man is disturbed about his finances because (it is, they are) very precarious at the present time.

who have 19. This is exactly the kind of job you (who has, who have) dealt with people for years should handle successfully.

he follows 20. Anyone can learn to take good pictures if (he follows, they follow) these simple directions.

who has 21. He is the type of man (who has, who have) so often proved the old adage about success.

it has 22. I enjoy listening to *The Tales of Hoffman;* (it has, they have) some of my favorite melodies.

who is 23. A short conference is helpful to many a student (who is, who are) uncertain about some course.

was 24. Neither time nor work (was, were) spared in making this Home Coming a success.

who salates 25. Pearl Buck is one of the few American writers (who has, who have) received the Nobel Prize.

To obtain score, multiply number of errors by 4 and subtract total from 100.

NAME .... DATE .... SCORE ....

12. REFERENCE OF PRONOUNS—I

Examine each italicized pronoun which appears in the sentences below. If it is incorrect, colloquial, or pedantic, write the preferable form in the space at the left. If it is correct, leave the space at the left blank.

EXAMPLE:

I   John and *myself* were walking down Main Street.

....	1. A number of the automobile manufacturers have announced that *their* new models are already on the assembly lines.
himself	2. This story emphasizes the theme that whatever the cost, one must be true to *one's self*.
a person	3. Most psychiatrists recommend that *you* should have some interest outside the daily routine of a job.
....	4. He showed an almost abnormal interest in *himself*.
....	5. With the heavy snow of the last month, *it* is likely that the winter wheat crop will be saved.
I	6. While you are cutting the grass, John and *myself* will trim the hedge.
who	7. She wrote a courteous letter to the girl *which* had been assigned as her roommate.
his	8. Statistics prove that a person generally joins the same church *your* family attended in the past.
I	9. Since I was lonesome, another fellow and *myself* struck up a conversation in the smoking car.
....	10. As a consequence of the disagreement between James and *him*, the business was listed for sale.
their	11. According to the management, part of the workers had expressed *its* willingness to accept a longer working week.
....	12. The woman *that* wrote the best letter about Satin Soap was to receive a free trip to Hollywood.
a person	13. The dishonest practices of some radio repair shops, especially in the large cities, are enough to convince *you* that there should be some form of regulation in the field of radio servicing.
who	14. Is he the crooner *which* is known to radio audiences as the Texas Cowboy?
flying time	15. *It* is less than four hours' flying time from Chicago to Dallas.
me	16. Between you and *myself*, I regard Frank as the worst driver I have ever seen.

55

.... 17. After winning a prize with his snapshot titled "A Faun at Dawn," Mr. Davis came to regard *himself* as an artist of the first rank.
your .... 18. The more I thought about it, the more I resented *you* asking me why I was wearing that hat.
.... 19. Many scientists advocated setting up a federal commission *which* would control experiments in precipitating rain from the clouds.
The landlord's raising of 20. *His* raising the rents brought immediate objections from the tenants of the apartment building.
their people's 21. With the opening of the Southern highlands to the tourist traffic, a number of the mountain people found that *its* folk songs and handicrafts were profitable assets.
.... 22. *It* rains frequently in Seattle, as in many parts of the Northwest.
.... 23. It was once a business axiom that every man had to look out for *himself*.
me .... 24. The story the tramp told did not sound plausible either to Harry or to *myself*.
they .... 25. The writer of a popular article avoids detailed footnotes, for *it* will be of no interest to the average reader.

To obtain score, multiply number of errors by 4 and subtract total from 100.

NAME .... DATE .... SCORE ....

13. REFERENCE OF PRONOUNS—II

Correct the vague or indefinite reference of pronouns in the sentences below. To make a correction, draw a circle around the inexact pronoun and write your correction in the space at the left. You may correct these errors either by making the pronoun a part of a noun phrase, or by substituting more concrete wording in place of the pronoun. If the passage is free from error, leave the space at the left blank.

EXAMPLES:

a fact which   He answered the questions evasively, (which) aroused the suspicions of the police.

the English   In England the traffic regulations are somewhat different from ours. For example, (they) drive on the left side of the road.

.... 1. After explaining the rule, the instructor went on to list the exceptions, which were seemingly endless.

the physicist 2. The physicist's laboratory is today an exciting place, for (he) stands on the frontiers of a new science.

.... 3. Parkman lived for a time with the Sioux Indians in their crude lodges, and (this) led him to distrust Cooper's picture of "the noble savages."

In recent years we have seen 4. (Recent years have seen) the development of chemical compounds which will help to keep the lawn free from weeds.

This change 5. Several large railroad companies have been replacing their steam locomotives with oil burning diesels. (This) will result in more comfortable travel for passengers and greater economy of operation.

Nancy's suggestion was approved 6. Nancy suggested that the dinner be formal, which was immediately approved by the whole sorority.

a fact which 7. The boys in our algebra class were often unruly, (which) probably explained the chronic ill temper of our instructor.

Macbeth 8. *Macbeth* is a great psychological drama. As the usurper of the Scottish throne, (he) found that there could be no peace for a traitor and a murderer.

because 9. It is still possible to see the whole show, (for) the final performance does not begin until nine o'clock.

the Mexicans 10. In Mexico the period just before Christmas is known as *posada* time; with traditional songs and rituals, (they) go from house to house greeting neighbors and friends.

57

a fact which 11. The modern automobile shifts gears automatically, which eliminates one of the chief worries of the beginning driver.

that 12. Reporters often rack their brains to concoct feature stories which will enliven the front page.

his sister 13. As a boy, he was always up to some mischievous prank like hiding his sister's doll or stealing candy from her.

Mark Twain 14. *The Adventures of Tom Sawyer* is a classic story of American boyhood. He drew heavily upon his own experience to write this engaging narrative.

this habit 15. The thief never left a house without first sampling the contents of the refrigerator. This accounted for his nickname—in police circles—of "Icebox Charlie."

an effort that 16. Then we tried to push the car out of the ditch, which was completely futile.

this circuit 17. During an interview with reporters, the actress announced that this would be her farewell tour.

The Southerners 18. On our trip through the South we especially enjoyed the food. They have a unique way of preparing and serving meals.

the Siamese people 19. In Siam it is a popular sport to put fighting fish together and to watch the combat. In fact, they make wagers on the outcome of such contests.

this practice 20. The instructor always had amusing anecdotes to tell about the writers we were studying, or timely illustrations to explain our reading assignments. This made his classes far from boring.

To obtain score, allow 5 points for each sentence properly corrected and for each sentence identified as correct.

NAME .... DATE .... SCORE ....

14. REFERENCE OF PRONOUNS—III

Revise the following sentences to eliminate vague or ambiguous reference of pronouns. Some of the sentences can be corrected by changes in word order; others will need rephrasing. If the exercise consists of two sentences, rewrite only the sentence involving the error.

EXAMPLES:

One afternoon he caught a five-pound bass on Lake Seneca which they ate for dinner.

One afternoon on Lake Seneca he caught a five-pound bass which they ate for dinner.

A mother can influence a boy's life to a great extent. This may be either good or bad.

This influence may be either good or bad.

1. When the business owned by Johnson's father was threatened with failure, he withdrew from the University.

   When his father's business was threatened with failure, Johnson withdrew from the University.

2. I have just read about a two-faced aluminum owl in *Time* magazine that is designed to frighten starlings away.

   I have just read, in Time magazine, about a two-faced aluminum owl that is designed to frighten starlings away.

3. In the city, parades are so common that they pay no attention to it.

   In the city, parades are so common that the people pay no attention to them.

4. After a supper at the hotel, we went back to the girl's home who was giving the party.

   After a supper at the hotel, we went back to the home of the girl who was giving the party.

5. In the handbook it says that the fan belt should be kept reasonably tight.

   The handbook says that the fan belt should be kept reasonably tight.

59

6. Jane told her aunt that her cookies were delicious.
   Jane said to her aunt, "Your cookies were delicious."

7. There is a red canoe in the loft of the garage that recalls summer days at the lake.
   There is a red canoe in the loft of the garage that makes me recall summer days at the lake.

8. I found a photograph in the attic ~~which~~ *that* Mother had once given to Father.

9. Early in his career Ford aspired to build a low-priced, efficient automobile. This resulted in the famous Model T.
   This aspiration resulted in the famous Model T.

10. Awakened by her neighbor's singing who was working in the garden below, Mrs. Dobbs angrily slammed the window shut.
    The singing of a neighbor, working in the garden below, awakened Mrs Dobbs and she angrily slammed the window shut.

11. In ancient times ~~they~~ *the Romans* believed that the flight of birds might foretell success or failure in battle.

12. ~~Many~~ *Many people* in the audience were restless, ~~which~~ *but* the speaker did not appear to notice *their restlessness*.

To obtain score, allow 8½ points for each sentence properly revised.

60

CASE

Case is that property of a noun or pronoun which shows its relation to the other words in a sentence or clause. Since nouns vary little in form, except the possessive, to indicate case, the real difficulties in the correct use of case in English are with pronouns, which are rather highly inflected.

1. Nouns and pronouns used as the subject of a sentence, as the subjective complement of a sentence, or in apposition with either the subject or the subjective complement are in the subjective case.

The subject of a sentence or clause is in the subjective case.

The *yard* has just been mowed.
We listened to the radio in the afternoon.
The *man who* is alert will find business opportunities.
They did not know *who* took the bicycle.
Who is the next batter?

A noun or pronoun used as a subjective complement is in the subjective case.

The three oldest members were the *committee*.
It was *she* (*he, I, we, they*).
The worst offenders are *those* who disregard the rules.

In colloquial use "It's me" or "It is me" is permissible, but in formal writing and speaking "It is I" is the correct form. There has been a great deal of discussion in recent years about the "correct" form of the pronoun to use as a subjective complement. The so-called modernists defend "It is him," "It is her," "It is us," and "It is them" as correct; the more conservative insist that "It is he," "It is she," "It is we," and "It is they" are right. Each side misses the real point at issue: the problem is not a matter of "correctness" but of level of usage. "It is him" and "It is he" may be equally "correct," the former being informal or conversational, the latter being formal. So the discussion should be directed to the level of usage desired, not to the grammatical correctness of the colloquial forms.

A noun or pronoun in apposition with the subject or the subjective complement is in the subjective case.

Mr. Judd, our *principal*, announced the holiday.
The three winners—*you, Mary,* and *I*—will go to the state contest. (*you, Mary,* and *I* in apposition with the subject *winners*)
We *boys* are ready for the game. (*boys* in apposition with the subject *we*)
They are most pleasant company, her *sister* and *she*. (*sister* and *she* in apposition with the subjective complement *company*)

2. The objective case is used as the direct or indirect object of a verb or verbal (infinitive, participle, or gerund).

> Jane lost her *kittens*, but she found *them* in the cellar.
> We wanted to invite *them* to our party. (*them* object of the infinitive *to invite*)
> Having called *him* before breakfast, we made an early appointment. (*him* object of participle *having called*)
> Ignoring *him* so pointedly was an act of impoliteness. (*him* object of gerund *Ignoring*)
> The coach complimented *Harry* and *me*.
> Where is the guide *whom* we have hired? (*whom* object of *have hired*)
> *Whom* did you see at the meeting? (*Whom* object of *did see*)
> The mailman gave *him* the letter. (*him* indirect object of *gave* = gave to him)
> To tell *them* the truth was difficult. (*them* indirect object of the infinitive *To tell*)
> Having promised *them* complete satisfaction, we considered the matter settled. (*them* indirect object of the participle *Having promised*)
> Telling *them* the truth was difficult. (*them* indirect object of gerund *Telling*)

3. A noun or pronoun used as an objective complement is in the objective case.

> The team elected John *captain*.
> They decided to name the baby *Mary*.
> The judges thought the best orator to be *him*.

4. The subject of an infinitive is in the objective case.

> They asked *us* to come early. (*us* is subject of the infinitive *to come*, and the whole infinitive phrase "us to come early" is the object of *asked*)
> We have arranged for *them* to rent our cottage. (*them* is subject of the infinitive *to rent*, and the whole infinitive phrase "them to rent our cottage" is the object of the preposition *for*)
> This work was done by a man *whom* we know to be trustworthy. (*whom* is subject of the infinitive *to be*, and the whole infinitive phrase "whom to be trustworthy" is the object of the verb *know*)

5. A noun or pronoun used as the object of a preposition is in the objective case.

> The children went for the *milk*.
> There was an understanding between *him* and *me*. (*him* and *me* objects of *between*)
> Here is the girl *whom* you asked about. (*whom* object of *about*)
> All of *us* boys worked in the clean-up campaign. (*us* is object of the preposition *of*, and *boys* is in apposition with *us*)
> *Whom* are you looking for?
> For *whom* are you looking?

6. A noun or pronoun in apposition with any word in the objective case is likewise in the objective case.

> Let's *you* and *me* go to the show. (*Let's* = *Let us*, and *us* is the objective case, subject of the infinitive (*to*) *go*, and *you* and *me* are in apposition with *us*)

> We have already invited them, *her* and her *sister*. (*her* and *sister* are in apposition with *them*, the object of *have invited*)
> The will was contested by two heirs, *him* and his *cousin*. (*him* and *cousin* are in apposition with *heirs*, the object of the preposition *by*)

7. The subjective case of all pronouns is used with all forms of the verb *to be* (*am, is, was, were, have been,* etc.) if the pronoun is the same person or thing as the subject; the objective case is used if the person or thing is not the same as the subject.

> The losers were *she* and *I*. (*she* and *I* = *losers*)
> The murderer was *he* who throughout the story had seemed most innocent. (*he* = *murderer*)
> The culprits were believed to be *they*. (*they* = *culprits*)
> Should you want to be *he?* (*he* = *you*)
> The grangers declared *him* to be the thief. (*him* does not = *grangers*)
> The grangers declared the thief to be *him*. (*him* does not = *grangers*)

8. Especial care must be taken in the use of relative pronouns. The case of a relative pronoun depends upon its use in the clause in which it stands—never upon the case of its antecedent. Parenthetical expressions like *I thought, he said, she believed, they suspected* have no bearing upon the case of the pronouns. Construe the sentence as though such expressions were not present.

> The records were given to the officer *who* was appointed by the president. (*who* is the subject of *was appointed*)
> The records were given to the officer *whom* the president appointed. (*whom* is the object of *appointed*)
> There was no question about *who* deserved the prize. (*who* is the subject of *deserved*, and "who deserved the prize" is the object of *about*)
> There is no question about *whom* they wanted for president. (*whom* is the object of *wanted*, and "whom they wanted for president" is the object of *about*)
> We shall hire *whoever* has the best qualifications. (*whoever* is the subject of *has*, and "whoever has the best qualifications" is the object of *shall hire*)
> We shall vote for *whomever* the committee selects. (*whomever* is the object of *selects*, and "whomever the committee selects" is the object of *for*)
> This is the man *who* they thought would do the work satisfactorily. (*who* is the subject of *would do*. In construing the sentence, omit the parenthetical "they thought" which, as an independent addition to the sentence, governs nothing within the sentence)
> This is the man *whom* the detective said the police wanted. (*whom* is the object of *wanted*, "the detective said" being grammatically independent of the sentence)

9. Comparisons after *than* and *as* in elliptical clauses take the case which the expanded clause would require. You will note that the pronoun is most likely to be in the same case as the word with which it is compared.

> Jack is two inches taller than *I*. (expanded comparison is "than I am" and the comparison is with *Jack*, subject of *is*)

I like her better than *him*. (expanded comparison is "than I like him" and the comparison is with *her*, object of *like*)

I like her better than *he*. (expanded comparison is "than he likes her" and the comparison is with *I*, subject of *like*)

We are not so well prepared as *they*. (expanded comparison is "as they are prepared" and the comparison is with *we*, subject of *are prepared*)

I was planning to invite them as well as *him*. (expanded comparison is "as to invite him" and the comparison is with *them*, object of *to invite*)

10. To form the singular possessive of nouns add *'s* to the singular form of the noun, as: *girl's, lady's, monkey's;* to form the plural possessive of nouns add an apostrophe after the plural form if it ends in *s* but *'s* if the plural form does not end in *s*, as: *girls', ladies', monkeys',* but *men's, children's, oxen's*. If a proper name ends in *s*, an apostrophe or an apostrophe and *s* may be added to form the possessive, as: *Keats', Keats's; Dickens', Dickens's*. The apostrophe must never go back into the name itself, as *Dicken's*, which would be correct only if the man's name were *Dicken*. If a word particularly unpleasant in sound results from adding an apostrophe and *s* to a proper name, the simpler form is to be preferred. Thus *Moses'* laws sound more euphonious than *Moses's* laws; *Hutchins'* presidency at the University of Chicago is preferable to *Hutchins's* presidency at the University of Chicago.

Of inanimate objects the *of*-phrase is used to express possession: the rocker *of the chair*, the door *of the house*. However, certain words of time, distance, measurement, value, price, and many established phrases take the apostrophe: a *week's* wages, a *mile's* distance, a *dollar's* worth, the *heart's* desire, *freedom's* voice.

In compound words or in word groups expressing a single idea, the possessive is added to the last member, as: *mother-in-law's*, the *Queen of Holland's* cabinet.

Use an *of*-phrase of persons to indicate the object of an action.

The *man's* killing excited the neighborhood. (This means that the man did the killing)
The killing *of the man* excited the neighborhood. (This means that the man was killed)

11. To represent joint possession, the apostrophe is used with the last noun; to represent separate possession, the apostrophe is used with each noun.

Tom and Harry's parents came to camp for the week-end. (parents of the two boys the same persons)
Tom's and Harry's parents came to camp for the week-end. (parents of the two boys different persons)
Lord and Taylor's store is in New York City. (one firm)
Gimbel's and Macy's stores are in New York City. (two firms)

12. When words in apposition are in the possessive case, the apostrophe is used with the appositive only.

The inventor Edison's genius manifested itself early.

If the possessive with the appositive results in a clumsy construction, it is best to recast the sentence.

CLUMSY: Herbert Hoover, the former food administrator's, work is still remembered in Europe.
BETTER: The work of Herbert Hoover, the former food administrator, is still remembered in Europe.

13. The possessive personal pronouns (*yours, his, hers, its, ours, theirs*) and the relative and interrogative possessive *whose* never take an apostrophe to express possession.

WRONG: I have found my tennis racket, but I can't find *your's*.
RIGHT: I have found my tennis racket, but I can't find *yours*.
WRONG: There is no name in the book, but I think it is *her's*.
RIGHT: There is no name in the book, but I think it is *hers*.
WRONG: The business has lost *it's* former prosperity.
RIGHT: The business has lost *its* former prosperity.
WRONG: I refuse to admit that your arguments are better than *our's*.
RIGHT: I refuse to admit that your arguments are better than *ours*.
WRONG: Our candidates are more popular than *their's*.
RIGHT: Our candidates are more popular than *theirs*.
WRONG: The man *who's* name is drawn out of the hat will receive five dollars.
RIGHT: The man *whose* name is drawn out of the hat will receive five dollars.
WRONG: *Who's* car is parked in the driveway?
RIGHT: *Whose* car is parked in the driveway?

It's is a contraction of *it is*, never a possessive; *who's* is a contraction of *who is*, never a possessive. The indefinite pronouns require the apostrophe to express the possessive, as: *one's, nobody's, neither's, someone's*.

14. Care must be taken, especially with nouns ending in -*y*, not to use the plural for the possessive.

WRONG: Every citizen is interested in the *countries* welfare.
RIGHT: Every citizen is interested in the *country's* welfare.
WRONG: We tried to protect our *allies* shipping.
RIGHT: We tried to protect our *ally's* shipping. (one ally)
RIGHT: We tried to protect our *allies'* shipping. (more than one ally)

15. Use the idiomatic forms *anybody else's, everybody else's, nobody else's, somebody else's, someone else's*, not the historic forms *anybody's else*, etc., as the possessive of these words.

RIGHT: This is *someone else's* responsibility.
RIGHT: This is my hat; that is *somebody else's*.

16. The possessive case should be used with the gerund.

I am interested in *his* advancing with the company.
We appreciate *their* taking such an interest in the work.

If other words come between the gerund and its modifier or if the construction is a common noun plus a gerund, the possessive is usually omitted.

RIGHT: What was the reason for Miller, the expert, saying such an absurd thing?
RIGHT: The engineer was surprised at his old *locomotive* making only thirty-five miles an hour.
MORE FORMAL: The engineer was surprised at his old *locomotive's* making only thirty-five miles an hour.

NAME .... DATE .... SCORE ....

15. POSSESSIVE CASE WITH NOUNS AND PRONOUNS—I

In the sentences below, supply the correct possessive form for each of the nouns or pronouns given in parenthesis. Write your answers in the spaces at the left.

EXAMPLE:
your   What is the time of (you) appointment?

anybody's 1. I refused to take (anybody) word for it; I wanted to find out for myself.
weeks 2. On Thursday we leave for a two (weeks) vacation in Canada.
somebody else's 3. After reaching home, I realized that I had taken (somebody else) suitcase.
women's 4. Wanted: an alert girl for part-time employment in a (women) dress shop.
its 5. The house needed painting, and (it) roof leaked in several places.
Laurel & Hardy's 6. The audience laughed uproariously at (Laurel and Hardy) clever antics.
son-in-law's 7. Mr. Brady telephoned his (son-in-law) office that morning.
donkey's 8. The (donkey) eyes were sad and reproachful.
his 9. In a radio address he gave the reasons for (he) abdicating the throne.
servants' 10. On the top floor of the brownstone mansion were the (servants) quarters.
Italy's 11. With the Allied successes in the Mediterranean area, (Italy) capitulation was inevitable.
Baker and Smith's 12. One of the oldest firms in the city is (Baker and Smith) department store.
Children's 13. In the window of the bookstore was an attractive display of (children) stories.
stone's 14. The new hotel is but a (stone) throw from the railroad station.
ten dollars' 15. In the fall we bought (ten dollars) worth of seasoned firewood.
Filipino's 16. This article is a (Filipino) account of his experiences as a military scout.
Dr. Haines' 17. I could hear (Dr. Haines) voice booming in the next office.
yours 18. Everyone thought that the anonymous letter was (you).

67

poet Burns's 19. The (poet Burns) songs are known to every loyal Scot.
day's 20. We took enough food for a (day) journey.
week's 21. After a (week) trial, we decided to buy the radio.
W. B. Yeats' 22. (W. B. Yeats) poems have a significant place in Irish literature.
theirs 23. Rival companies tried to prove that our machine was merely an adaptation of (they).
whose 24. Will Rogers was a humorist (who) sayings were quoted in every American household.
his 25. We were amused by (he) mimicking of well-known radio voices.

To obtain score, multiply number of errors by 4 and subtract total from 100.

NAME .... DATE .... SCORE ....

16. POSSESSIVE CASE WITH NOUNS AND PRONOUNS--II

In the sentences below, supply the correct possessive form for each of the nouns or pronouns given in parenthesis. Write your answers in the spaces at the left.

EXAMPLE:

women's — The (women) magazines have a wide circulation in America.

its 1. The Chamber of Commerce will pick new officers at (it) annual election meeting this week.

water's 2. The jungle, thick and impenetrable, reached almost to the (water) edge.

city's 3. It was the (city) worst storm since the blizzard of 1888.

Emperor of Japan's 4. Gulliver visited the (Emperor of Japan) court on one of his fantastic journeys.

whose 5. The banker was a reserved, scholarly man (who) principal hobby was book-collecting.

Barnum & Bailey's 6. Perhaps the most spectacular show of that era was (Barnum and Bailey) great circus.

John Adams' 7. During (John Adams) administration, a war with France was narrowly averted.

yours 8. Do you remember that old, faded-yellow house that stood directly across the street from (you)?

sister Mary's 9. Over Charles Lamb there was always the cloud of his (sister Mary) insanity.

brother-in-law's 10. Acting upon his (brother-in-law) advice, he sold the farm and moved to the village.

hers 11. My room in the dormitory was considerably larger than (she).

anyone else's 12. This must be her writing; I cannot believe that it is (anyone else).

their 13. The property owners of the neighborhood have voiced (they) objection to any changes in the zoning ordinance.

Whose 14. (Who) package is this on the stand?

no one else's 15. Mr. Ward's desk had been ransacked, but (no one else) belongings had been disturbed.

King Henry VII's 16. The Tudor line began with (King Henry VII) accession in 1485.

Firemen's 17. The (Firemen) Picnic, held every summer, is an important social event in our town.

69

sisters'   18. Under his (sisters) constant teasing about his romance, he became sulky and irritable.

ten cents'   19. On her birthday the kindergarten teacher was presented with (ten cents) worth of bubble gum.

your   20. Did you receive a telegram from (you) father yesterday afternoon?

three months'   21. After serving abroad, he returned to the States on a (three month) furlough.

their   22. The judge then asked the lawyers for the defense to present (they) witnesses.

Gilbert and Sullivan's   23. *The Mikado* is one of (Gilbert and Sullivan) famous operettas.

Tom's and Frank's   24. Over the mantel was a portrait of (Tom and Frank) mother.

soprano's   25. Because of the (soprano) illness, the concert will not be given this evening.

To obtain score, multiply number of errors by 4 and subtract total from 100.

NAME .... DATE .... SCORE ....

17. MISTAKES WITH POSSESSIVE PRONOUNS—III

Draw a circle around any pronoun incorrectly used or any word mistakenly used for a pronoun and write the correct word in the margin on the left. If the sentence is correct as it stands, let the space remain blank.

EXAMPLE:

its   I want to show you the house that had (it's) roof blown off.

his 1. Like the character in this story, everybody has ~~their~~ daydreams of wealth, fame, or heroism.
their 2. Pontiac and his Indian warriors met with stubborn resistance in ~~they're~~ siege of Detroit.
C 3. The conductor told the old lady that the next stop would be hers.
Whose 4. ~~Who's~~ radio is blaring at this time of night?
It's 5. ~~Its~~ amazing to learn that the play *Uncle Tom's Cabin* has been performed many thousands of times.
they're 6. By this time ~~their~~ probably returning from the show.
their 7. Too much time was wasted in the meeting by ~~them~~ quibbling over minor issues.
C 8. As usual, the newspapers are suggesting that everyone should do their Christmas mailing early.
C 9. The life of a commercial pilot may be rather strenuous, but it's never dull.
You're 10. ~~Your~~ very kind to do this errand for me.
whose 11. My father, ~~who's~~ curiosity was now aroused, went downstairs to investigate the noise.
you're 12. If ~~your~~ looking for a summer cottage, you may be interested in ours.
C 13. I had no ticket for the game, but she gave me her's.
there's 14. According to the familiar adage, ~~theirs~~ no fool like an old fool.
who's 15. ~~Whose~~ coaching the freshman squad this fall?
ours 16. There were many beautiful floats in the parade, but ~~our's~~ had the most original idea.
himself 17. I stopped and offered my help, but he wanted to change the tire ~~hisself~~.
there's 18. Some geologists believe that ~~theirs~~ no reason for predicting a sudden depletion of our oil reserves.
Its 19. On the corner was a brightly lighted restaurant, ~~it's~~ neon sign commanding us to "Eat."

~~themselves~~ 20. Few people are able to see ~~theirselves~~ as others see them.
her 21. Any woman interested in serving as a Red Cross aide should leave ~~their~~ name and address at the town hall tomorrow.
his 22. I deeply resented ~~him~~ rebuking me in the presence of customers.
yours 23. My English class meets at the same time as ~~your's~~.
C 24. At the customs barrier, no one was allowed to proceed unless their luggage had been inspected.
C 25. "It's a case of mistaken identity, your honor," the man said firmly.

To obtain score, multiply number of errors by 4 and subtract total from 100.

NAME .... DATE .... SCORE ....

18. CASE OF PRONOUNS—I

Draw a circle around any errors in the case forms of the pronouns used in the sentences below. In every instance of error, write the proper case form in the space at the left. If no error occurs in the sentence, leave the space blank.

EXAMPLE:

whom   Is that the girl (who) I saw at your house yesterday?

.... 1. Was it them, by any chance, whom you passed on the road this morning?

.... 2. At the national convention, the club was represented by two delegates—Mr. Rowley and I.

.... 3. The shop foreman told George and me to report for work the following Monday.

.... 4. Please inform whomever handles the advertising that we wish to reserve space in the November issue.

.... 5. The Italian Renaissance is especially remembered for its brilliant achievements in art and literature.

.... 6. Of the possible candidates, Gregory Peck was the actor who I believed had the best chance of winning the Academy Award.

.... 7. As for your mother and I, we want to stay home this evening.

.... 8. How could anyone be expected to know whom invented the rocking chair?

.... 9. By him flying faster than 740 miles an hour, man has learned to travel faster than sound.

.... 10. Dr. Roberts, a big and friendly man, had a jovial greeting for whomever came to his office.

.... 11. After the November elections, the Republicans of the city found theirselves in possession of only four of the nine council seats.

.... 12. The senior counselors—Tom, Paul, and me—were in charge of athletics at the camp.

.... 13. The city manager ordered him to submit his resignation immediately.

.... 14. Since he was standing idly by the counter, I took he to be a clerk.

.... 15. At Chancellorsville the Confederates lost General "Stonewall" Jackson, who's leadership had meant much to the South.

73

.... 16. The traffic policeman never seemed irritated by us saluting him every time we passed the corner.
.... 17. Have you had word as to who your roommate will be?
.... 18. It was him, more than anyone else, who persuaded me to go to college.
.... 19. I admit that I have had less training, less experience, than he.
.... 20. It should be the goal of the country to put good medical service within reach of whoever needs such service.
.... 21. Nobody suspected that it was she who had put salt in the sugar bowl.
.... 22. Between you and I, this store has been losing money during the past year.
.... 23. With the encouragement of the principal, seven of us boys announced that we would start a school orchestra.
.... 24. The committee voted to divide the scholarship between two contestants—John and she.
.... 25. Let's go to the show at the Capitol—you and me.

To obtain score, multiply number of errors by 4 and subtract total from 100.

NAME .... DATE .... SCORE ....

19. CASE OF PRONOUNS—II

Draw a circle around any error in the case forms of the pronouns used in the sentences below. In every instance of error, write the proper case form in the space at the left. If no error occurs in the sentence, leave the space blank.

EXAMPLE:

me   Everyone except John and (I) had left the dormitory.

1. This sports editor states that golf is experiencing it's greatest boom in years.
2. He will probably ask the secretary or me to look up the records of the case.
3. That afternoon, all the players except he reported for practice at the usual time.
4. On the desk is a pile of scratchy old records which the musical souls like Jean and I are fond of playing over and over.
5. My brother and I look so much alike that people often take him to be me.
6. The song was a popular success, but its gloominess caused it to be banned from the radio.
7. Our's are reputable products, backed by years of manufacturing experience.
8. Because my brother was smaller than me, he escaped such chores as mowing the lawn and firing the furnace.
9. This is the man whom, I venture to predict, the critics will name as the outstanding author of the year.
10. When I was a child, my parents would not have tolerated me using such expressions as "ain't" and "guy."
11. On the station platform were two policemen, an elderly gentleman, and us.
12. To we who had known the big excursion boat, the story of the fire brought a touch of sadness.
13. The Chamber of Commerce will be glad to send maps and information to whomever may be interested in visiting this region.
14. Most of the girls want her to be named chairman of the committee on entertainment.
15. At the close of the play, us actors appeared on the stage for several curtain calls.
16. Deliver this message to whoever you find at the house.

.... 17. Since the elm tree was near their property, it shaded them rather than we.
.... 18. Roger was the one who the seniors had chosen as the student most likely to succeed.
.... 19. Mayor Dudley is a man who, I honestly believe, we may rely upon for sound, progressive ideas.
.... 20. The landlord asked three families—the Browns, Williamses, and we—to vacate our apartments before the first of September.
.... 21. It is rumored that the factory will move elsewhere, but between you and me, there is no truth in the story.
.... 22. Later, when the telephone started ringing, I thought it to be she.
.... 23. At the election meeting to be held next spring, you may nominate whoever you choose.
.... 24. For several days the nation wondered whom the next governor of Georgia would be.
.... 25. We have our little disputes, Mother and me, but we are really the best of friends.

To obtain score, multiply number of errors by 4 and subtract total from 100.

NAME ....DATE ....SCORE ....

20. CASE OF PRONOUNS—III

Draw a circle around any error in the case forms of the pronouns used in the sentences below. In every instance of error, write the proper case form in the space at the left. If no error occurs in the sentence, leave the space blank.

EXAMPLE:

me   They have elected the three of us—you, Harry, and (I.)

.... 1. Commuters like you and me will find the new schedule more convenient.
.... 2. Do you follow the baseball scores as closely as him?
.... 3. If there is good skating at the pond, let's you and I go over.
.... 4. I suggest that we let Mary and her choose the menu.
.... 5. I suggested that Mary and her should choose the menu.
.... 6. It was not the teachers who demanded better lighting; it was us students.
.... 7. The clown bowed solemnly to Martha and she.
.... 8. The teacher evidently thought the gigglers to be us girls sitting in the last row.
.... 9. It is an old saying that them who look for trouble will generally find it.
.... 10. The lane between the two houses is a driveway for the Joneses and us.
.... 11. Why on earth did you take him to be I?
.... 12. I never expected that the new conductor of the symphony orchestra would be he.
.... 13. Never for one moment did I think it was she.
.... 14. Everyone completed the assignment except him and I.
.... 15. I grant that it could have been him.
.... 16. At a sporting event, most of us Americans will cheer earnestly for the underdog.
.... 17. Last summer his uncle and him went to Minnesota on a fishing trip.
.... 18. Mother wanted us boys to wash the windows and put up the screens.
.... 19. After her and I began strumming the keys, the others gathered around the piano.
.... 20. The Bakers and we had Thanksgiving dinner together.

.... 21. We grew up together, John and I.
.... 22. The principal then ordered Will and I to sweep up the broken glass.
.... 23. For we Texans, the story of the Alamo is the classic example of pioneer heroism.
.... 24. If I am not mistaken, there is some resemblance between you and she.
.... 25. Who the gods would destroy, they first make mad.

To obtain score, multiply number of errors by 4 and subtract total from 100.

21. CASE OF PRONOUNS—IV

Draw a circle around any error in the case forms of the pronouns used in the sentences below. In every instance of error, write the proper case form in the space at the left. If no error occurs in the sentence, leave the space blank.

EXAMPLE:

whoever Accept a contribution from (whomever) willingly offers to help.

.... 1. Whom are you writing this letter to?
.... 2. Did you see either of them, he or his wife, at the Paradise Grill last evening?
.... 3. Near the cashier's desk stood a short, swarthy man who we took to be the owner.
.... 4. The governor will not tell us reporters who he favors for the judgeship.
.... 5. It being she who related the story, we did not know how much was fact and how much was fiction.
.... 6. I shall recommend whomever I think is most deserving.
.... 7. Whomever I recommend will almost certainly receive the appointment.
.... 8. Naturally we respect the opinion of a man who we know to be an expert in his field.
.... 9. The children suspected the tall, gangling Santa Claus was him.
.... 10. The children suspected the tall, gangling Santa Claus to be him.
.... 11. Whoever you select will have my approval and support.
.... 12. She is the singer whom I predicted would make a name for herself.
.... 13. William Harvey was an English physician who history credits with important discoveries about the circulation of the blood.
.... 14. Could it have been they whom we saw on the dock yesterday?
.... 15. Everyone knows who he will ask to be his partner.
.... 16. Whom did I hear they were inviting as chaperons?
.... 17. The people should pick as their leader whomever they believe ranks highest in statesmanship and practical wisdom.
.... 18. Whom have I seen walk with that long, swinging stride?

79

.... 19. He is the umpire who the players charge is unfair.
.... 20. He is the umpire who the players accused of unfairness.
.... 21. As for Uncle Harry and we, Tuesday evening would be the most convenient time for the dinner.
.... 22. The district manager will gladly interview whoever is interested in this kind of work.
.... 23. Who do you think was here for the game today?
.... 24. Who do you think I saw at the game today?
.... 25. The contract will be awarded to whoever makes the lowest bid.

To obtain score, multiply number of errors by 4 and subtract total from 100.

MOOD AND TENSE

The following discussion treats only of some common uses of the subjunctive mood and of some common errors in the use of tenses, especially in the sequence of tenses.

I. THE SUBJUNCTIVE MOOD

The subjunctive mood today is used neither so frequently nor so precisely as in the past. In fact, in conversation and in informal writing, it has been almost superseded by the indicative mood. However, it still has uses, especially in formal discourse, that give an accuracy and subtlety of meaning not obtainable by the indicative mood. A few of the more common uses of the subjunctive mood will be considered.

1. In formal discourse, the subjunctive mood should be used to express a condition contrary to fact.

> RIGHT: If I *were* she, I should accept the offer.
> RIGHT: *Were* he honest, he would have paid this bill.
> RIGHT: If there *be* ample time, why are you hurrying?
> RIGHT: If she *have* an alibi, now would be the time to present it.
> RIGHT: If they *be* our friends, they would come to our aid.

2. In formal writing and speaking, use the subjunctive mood to state a condition that is strongly improbable or to make a statement that expresses a high degree of doubt, uncertainty, or supposition.

> RIGHT: If the weather *were* controllable, each person would want weather suited to his own advantage or pleasure. (strongly improbable)
> RIGHT: I do not believe that they *be* friends of ours. (doubt)
> RIGHT: If the weather *be* clear tomorrow, we shall start on the trip. (uncertainty)
> RIGHT: If money *were* equally divided, it would not remain so for any length of time. (supposition)

3. The subjunctive mood is used to express a wish, a regret, a request, a command, or necessity.

> RIGHT: I hope that I *be* as successful as you when I am thirty. (wish)
> RIGHT: Oh, that honesty *were* more revered. (regret that it is not)
> RIGHT: *Be* so kind as to forget that remark. (request)
> RIGHT: I demand that you *be* here on time. (command)
> RIGHT: It is obligatory that I *be* notified. (necessity)

4. The subjunctive mood is used after *as if* and *as though*.

> RIGHT: He acted as if he *were* guilty.
> RIGHT: This board looks as though it *were* rotten.

5. The subjunctive mood has certain conventional uses as in resolutions, parliamentary motions, legal phraseology, and also in prayers.

RIGHT: *Be* it resolved, enacted, proclaimed, etc.
RIGHT: I move that the request *be* denied.
RIGHT: It is voted that every member *pay* his dues monthly.
RIGHT: We recommend that the officer *take* such precautions as are necessary.
RIGHT: The committee proposes that Mr. Judd *be* dropped from membership.
RIGHT: *Be* Thou ever present, O God.
RIGHT: God *bless* us every one.

II. Tense

6. The present tense is used to state a general truth.

WRONG: The ancients knew that ocean water *was* salty.
RIGHT: The ancients knew that ocean water *is* salty.
WRONG: Scientists discovered that the Anopheles mosquito *carried* malaria.
RIGHT: Scientists discovered that the Anopheles mosquito *carries* malaria.
WRONG: He started an argument by saying man *was* an animal.
RIGHT: He started an argument by saying man *is* an animal.
WRONG: Galileo believed that a heavy body *fell* no faster than a light one.
RIGHT: Galileo believed that a heavy body *falls* no faster than a light one.
RIGHT: Aristotle believed that a heavy body *fell* faster than a light one. (past tense right, for statement not true)

7. The past tense is used of an action completed in the past; the present perfect tense is used of an action begun in the past but continued to the time of writing or speaking. For instance, "I *worked* at this job for ten years" means that I do not work at it now; "I *have worked* at this job for ten years" means that I am still working at this same job.

WRONG: I *have locked* the garage an hour ago.
RIGHT: I *locked* the garage an hour ago.
WRONG: He *has quit* his job last week.
RIGHT: He *quit* his job last week.
WRONG: They *have taken* their vacation early in the summer.
RIGHT: They *took* their vacation early in the summer.
WRONG: *Have* you *painted* your house last spring?
RIGHT: *Did* you *paint* your house last spring?
WRONG: *Did* you *write* the letter yet?
RIGHT: *Have* you *written* the letter yet?
WRONG: I *have written* him three times last month.
RIGHT: I *wrote* him three times last month.
WRONG: We *have ordered* goods from you frequently before your merger.
RIGHT: We *ordered* goods from you frequently before your merger.

8. The past perfect tense should be used to indicate an action that was completed before some other past action.

WRONG: On the floor he spread the skin of a leopard which he *killed*.
RIGHT: On the floor he spread the skin of a leopard which he *had killed*.

WRONG: He attributed the pain in his stomach to the green apple which he *ate*.
RIGHT: He attributed the pain in his stomach to the green apple which he *had eaten*.
WRONG: He was now boasting about the wonderful vegetables from the garden which he *planted*.
RIGHT: He was now boasting about the wonderful vegetables from the garden which he *had planted*.
WRONG: On Christmas morning I received the watch which I always *wanted*.
RIGHT: On Christmas morning I received the watch which I *had* always *wanted*.

9. Do not use a variety of tenses for action in the same time. The relation of tenses must be logical and consistent. Even the historical present (sometimes used to express graphic or intense action or feeling) should not be introduced abruptly into a series of past tenses.

WRONG: He *walked* slowly down the road, *stops* suddenly to observe a beautiful butterfly, *makes* a futile attempt to catch it, and then *went* on his way as though nothing *happened*.
RIGHT: He *walked* slowly down the road, *stopped* suddenly to observe a beautiful butterfly, *made* a futile attempt to catch it, and then *went* on his way as though nothing *had happened*.
MIXED TENSES: In *rushes* Mary and *looks* about wildly, but the people in the lobby of the hotel simply *stared* at her.
BETTER: In *rushed* Mary and *looked* about wildly, but the people in the lobby of the hotel simply *stared* at her.
BETTER: In *rushes* Mary and *looks* about wildly, but the people in the lobby of the hotel simply *stare* at her.

The historical present may be very effective, especially if the occasion seems to justify a change in tenses.

HISTORICAL PRESENT: Slowly the clock ticked the long night away. Mrs. Lincoln had been gently led from the room—there was little hope that the President would regain consciousness. At last the dawn filtered in around the drawn curtains. Almost by intuition those at the bedside knew that the end had come. In the silence Stanton *stands* up and *speaks* those immortal and peculiarly inspired words, "Now he belongs to the ages." (student theme)

10. Avoid using perfect infinitives in place of present infinitives. Remember that the present infinitive expresses the same time as the main verb (whether that verb be present, past, or past perfect), and a perfect infinitive indicates time *before* that of the main verb.

RIGHT: We intend (intended or had intended) *to spend* a week there.
RIGHT: It is unusual for primitive people *to have made* such artistic drawings.
RIGHT: I should like *to have had* this opportunity twenty years ago.
RIGHT: He is too young *to have voted* in 1924. (infinitive refers to time before that of *is*)
RIGHT: He was too young *to vote* in 1924. (infinitive and verb refer to same time)

11. A present participle or a present gerund indicates time simultaneous with that of the main verb; a perfect participle or a perfect gerund indicates time antecedent to that of the main verb.

> WRONG: *Playing* golf all morning, I want to relax this afternoon.
> RIGHT: *Having played* golf all morning, I want to relax this afternoon.
> WRONG: I expect to make more money after *having acquired* a college education.
> RIGHT: I expect to make more money after *acquiring* a college education.

NAME .... DATE .... SCORE ....

22. THE SUBJUNCTIVE MOOD—I

Supply for each of the following sentences the correct subjunctive form of the verb to be. *Write your answer in the space at the left.*

EXAMPLE:
were   If I .... you, I should follow the doctor's advice.

be 1. It is urgent that he .... informed at once.
were 2. The man shouted as if he .... angry.
were 3. .... I taking such a trip, this is the route I should probably follow.
be 4. Far .... it from me to tell you what courses you should choose.
were 5. If the house .... in a more favorable location, it would be a good investment.
were 6. .... the color of the soil any indication of its fertility, soil analysis would not be as important as it is.
be 7. For best results, it is essential that the printed instructions .... followed carefully.
were / be 8. Even if it .... not true, the story of the wolf-child has been widely publicized as fact.
were 9. From the deck of the boat it looked as though the city skyline .... moving.
be 10. The Lord .... merciful unto us.
be 11. It has been moved and seconded that a special committee .... appointed to study the matter.
were 12. He knew he had to hurry if he .... to be on time for his class at eight o'clock.
be 13. If this .... justice, then I have no understanding of the law.
were 14. How I wish that she .... here!
be 15. The physician is subject to call at any time, ... it day or night.
were 16. .... he here, we could finish the work promptly.
be 17. If these figures .... correct, the college has doubled its enrollment in the past ten years.
be 18. To assure complete safety in driving, it is necessary that the lights and brakes .... inspected periodically.
were 19. .... I a postman, I should dread the approach of the Christmas season.

be .... 20. If this store is to build up patronage, it is necessary that every clerk .... courteous and obliging.

be .... 21. .... that as it may, I am determined to carry out my original plans.

were .... 22. Even if I .... wealthy, I should want to live as simply as possible.

be .... 23. If we are to understand our economic system, it is necessary that we .... aware of the problems confronting both labor and management.

be .... 24. Baseball is a sport which appeals to most men, ... they young or old.

was .... 25. The dog acts as though he .... nervous.

To obtain score, multiply number of errors by 4 and subtract total from 100.

23. THE SUBJUNCTIVE MOOD—II

The following sentences call for subjunctives other than forms of the verb to be. *You should be able to determine from the context of each passage what verb will be acceptable. Write your answer in the space at the left.*

EXAMPLE:

make   If one wants to stay at this hotel during the summer months, it is advisable that he .... his reservations well in advance.

1. Is it essential to her happiness that she .... to the movies three or four times a week?
2. When he looks for a new job, it will be required that he .... the names of his previous employers.
3. The committee arranging for the picnic asks that everyone .... his own dishes and silver.
4. Her husband insists that she .... a new hat on Easter Sunday.
5. Long .... the King.
6. Is it customary that the new President .... the oath of office in the presence of the Chief Justice?
7. One of the requirements for the degree is that every candidate .... a reading knowledge of at least one foreign language.
8. If he wishes to go home on Thursday, it will be necessary that he .... the final examination early.
9. After fining him twenty-five dollars and costs for speeding, the judge advised that he .... more carefully in the future.
10. I suggested that he .... the matter over before making his decision.
11. Heaven .... that he should think me his enemy.
12. If he wishes to make a good record in his studies, it is important that he .... to concentrate.
13. Mr. Dowling looked amused when the doctor recommended that he .... golf as a means of relaxation.
14. The motion before us is that the club .... the resignation of William Lewis, who is moving to another city.
15. If the living room is to have plenty of sunlight, it is essential that it .... a window facing south.
16. It is important that she .... the earlier train if she wishes to be there on time.

.... 17. The instructor suggested that each student .... a theme describing a recent experience.

.... 18. The landlord required that he .... the rent on the first of each month.

.... 19. Who advised that he .... the kitchen walls a bright shade of pink?

.... 20. Earl West, chairman of the local March of Dimes campaign, urges that everyone .... generously.

To obtain score, multiply number of errors by 5 and subtract total from 100.

NAME .... DATE .... SCORE ....

24. CHOOSING THE CORRECT TENSE

From the forms given in parenthesis, choose the appropriate tenses for the sentences below. Write your answers in the spaces at the left.

EXAMPLE:

had been   When the first complete volume of his plays was published, Shakespeare (was, had been) dead for seven years.

.... 1. I (talked, have talked) with him at the bank only yesterday.

.... 2. (Did you see, Have you seen) the eclipse of the moon last Thursday?

.... 3. (Raising, Having raised) the window, she leaned out and began to shake the dust mop energetically.

.... 4. How amazing it seems for the early Arabians to (know, have known) as much about the sciences as they did.

.... 5. He pushed his way through the crowd, boarded the bus, and (settles, settled) himself for the long ride home.

.... 6. This story tells how two young men, on a walking trip, stop at a Devonshire farm. While there, one of them (falls, fell) in love with a pretty country girl.

.... 7. After (carrying, having carried) the magazines from the attic, where they (gathered, had gathered) dust for
....   years, he proceeded to arrange and classify them.

.... 8. The monkey leaped upon his master's shoulder, waved his tiny cap, and then (hides, hid) his face as though he
....   (has seen, had seen) an evil spirit.

.... 9. In the sixteenth century there was a widely accepted theory that a worm (causes, caused) the toothache.

.... 10. As Lincoln ends his short address, there (is, was) only a light ripple of applause, as though he (has made, made)
....   little impression on the vast audience.

.... 11. A lone plane came into view and flew in lazy circles above the village; then it (disappears, disappeared) as
....   suddenly as it (came, had come).

.... 12. The townspeople wished to establish a park which (will, would) honor those who had served in the war.

.... 13. (Jacking, Having jacked) up the car, you must next loosen the bolts holding the wheel.

.... 14. Isn't he too old to (be, have been) in college only five years ago?

89

_____ 15. Among the curios was a Japanese saber which he (found, had found) along the roadside near Manila.
_____ 16. The lecturer presented impressions that he (received, had received) on a recent tour of Europe.
_____ 17. The Department of Agriculture recently announced that paint (lasts, lasted) longer on the north side of a house than on the south side.
_____ 18. He intended to (go, have gone) home yesterday.
_____ 19. As I picked up the broken pieces, I recalled the old saying that haste (makes, made) waste.
_____ 20. I should like to (see, have seen) the play *Oklahoma* the last time it (was, has been) here.

To obtain score, multiply number of errors by 4 and subtract total from 100. (The above exercises provide for twenty-five answers.)

PROBLEMS IN THE USE OF CERTAIN VERBS

This lesson will treat of certain verbs which are frequently misused and of the basic principle in the correct use of the so-called strong verbs.

Although *shall* and *will*, as well as *should* and *would*, no longer conform to the complicated and largely theoretical rules given in some grammars and handbooks, there are a few basic distinctions that should be observed in formal writing.

1. To express simple futurity, use *shall* in the first person and *will* in the second and third persons. To express intention, promise, choice, determination, command, or threat, use *will* in the first person and *shall* in the second and third persons.

> I *shall* be tired at the end of the day. (simple future)
> He *will* deliver the milk in the morning. (simple future)
> I *will* build this house according to my own ideas. (intention)
> We *will* pay this account in full at the end of the month. (promise)
> I *will* take this one. (choice)
> We *will* defeat this measure in one way or another. (determination)
> You *shall* do exactly what I say. (command)
> He *shall* pay dearly for this. (threat)

If the idea of intention or willingness is implied in some other word in the sentence, I *shall* or we *shall* is correct, as the following: "I shall be pleased to receive such an honor" (*pleased* implies willingness); "We shall be happy to visit you" (*happy* implies intention).

In informal speech and writing, *I will* and the contraction *I'll* are used almost to the exclusion of *I shall*.

2. Generally, *should* and *would* follow the uses of *shall* and *will*. However, use *should* for all persons to express condition, expectation, or obligation; use *would* for all persons to express a wish, a customary action, or a repeated occurrence.

> If he *should* win the prize, he would accept it modestly. (condition)
> The letter *should* reach us by Tuesday. (expectation)
> James *should* take more pains with his work. (obligation)
> *Would* that I had wings. (wish)
> Every evening I *would* take a walk around the block. (customary action)
> Whenever we passed her house, we *would* knock on Miss Butler's door and run. (repeated occurrence)

3. *May* expresses permission, possibility, purpose, or wish. *Can* expresses ability or possibility.

May I have another piece of cake? (permission)
The letter *may* come tomorrow. (possibility)
Read carefully so that you *may* understand fully. (purpose)
May you always be as happy as you are this minute. (wish)
How fast *can* you take dictation? (ability)
This mistake *can* be rectified easily. (possibility)

Might and *could* parallel the uses of *may* and *can* rather closely.

4. *Lie*, *sit*, and *rise* are intransitive verbs; the action in the verb therefore is complete in itself. These verbs do not take an object and are not used in the passive voice. *Lay*, *set*, and *raise* are transitive verbs; the action described in them is exerted on something else: on an object when these verbs are in the active voice and on the subject when they are in the passive voice.

Lie (*lying*), *lay*, *lain* means "to recline," "to be situated," or "to be inactive." *Lay* (*laying*), *laid*, *laid* means "to put," "to place," "to cause to lie."

I *lie* down for a little nap each afternoon.
The book is *lying* on the table.
He *lay* in a coma for an hour yesterday.
A spirit of hopelessness had *lain* over the people.
Our boundary line *lay* to the right.
This field has *lain* fallow for many years.
They will *lay* a walk out to the street. (*walk* is object of *will lay*)
The generals are *laying* careful plans for the enemies' defeat. (*plans* is object of *are laying*)
James *laid* his books on the porch. (*books* is object of *laid*)
A foundation for the house was *laid* by the workmen. (passive voice, subject acted upon)

One exception should be noted: *lay* is used intransitively of fowls. "Hens do not *lay* so well in cold weather" is idiomatic English and correct.

Sit, *sat*, *sat* means "to rest," "to be seated." *Set*, *set*, *set* means "to place," "to put," "to cause to sit or stand," "to adjust," or "to arrange."

I usually *sit* by the window to enjoy the sun.
He *sat* under that tree last night.
You have *sat* in this chair before.
She *set* the baby in a high chair. (*baby* is object of *set*)
He *set* that pail on the steps last night. (*pail* is object of *set*)
The record has been *set* by the champion. (passive voice, subject acted upon)
He *set* the clock back an hour. (*clock* is object of *set*)
The usher *set* the chairs in order. (*chairs* is object of *set*)

A few intransitive uses of *set* should be noted: "This cement *sets* in an hour"; "The sun *sets* at 6:43 today"; "We *set* out for the long trek home"; "The hot days of Indian summer will *set* in next month"; "He *set* to work with renewed energy." These idiomatic uses of *set* of the sun or moon, of hardening substances like cement or plaster, of starting or beginning, and of applying oneself are correct.

Rise, rose, risen means "to go up," "to reach a higher level or position."
Raise, raised, raised means "to lift up," "to elevate," "to cause to rise."

I *rise* at 7:00 A. M.
An angry grumble *rose* from the crowd.
He has *risen* in the world.
They *raised* the flag higher. (*flag* is object of *raised*)
The funds have been *raised* by the committee. (passive voice, subject acted upon)

5. In strong or irregular verbs the past tense and the past participle are often different. This difference leads to many illiterate mistakes in using such verbs. No auxiliary may be used with the past tense of a verb. *Has, have,* and *had* and all forms of the verb *to be* necessary to form the passive voice must be added to the past participle.

WRONG: He *done* some repair work in his spare time.
RIGHT: He *did* some repair work in his spare time.
WRONG: This neglect has certainly *went* on for a long time.
RIGHT: This neglect has certainly *gone* on for a long time.
WRONG: I *seen* him only last night.
RIGHT: I *saw* him only last night.
WRONG: They *come* yesterday.
RIGHT: They *came* yesterday.
WRONG: I have often *swam* across that stream.
RIGHT: I have often *swum* across that stream.
WRONG: The work was *began* last week.
RIGHT: The work was *begun* last week.
WRONG: The tree has *fell* right across the driveway.
RIGHT: The tree has *fallen* right across the driveway.
WRONG: He *drunk* the dipper of water in three gulps.
RIGHT: He *drank* the dipper of water in three gulps.

The principal parts of the more commonly used verbs are given in the Outline of Inflections at the back of the book. Consult this list when you are in doubt.

6. The correct verb form must be used with the auxiliary.

WRONG: He always *has* and always *will be* an interesting person.
RIGHT: He always *has been* and always *will be* an interesting person.
WRONG: He still *thinks*, as he always *has*, that he will be successful.
RIGHT: He still *thinks*, as he always *has thought*, that he will be successful.
RIGHT: He always *has been* and *is* now *considered* a successful man.

7. Certain verbs need special attention to guard against mistakes in their use.
The past tense of *pay, lay,* and *say* is *paid, laid,* and *said,* not *payed, layed,* and *sayed.*

I *paid* (never *payed*) the telephone bill.
She *laid* (never *layed*) her purse on the seat.

The third person, singular number, indicative mood of verbs ending in *-y* preceded by a consonant ends in *-ies: cries*, not *crys; tries*, not *trys; replies*, not *replys*.

The past tense of *lead* is *led;* of *choose* is *chose;* of *burst* is *burst*, not *bursted*.

>Washington *led* his troops to the frontier.
>He *chose* his friends carefully.
>Yesterday an airplane *burst* into flames near our house.

In formal writing and speaking, *doesn't*, not *don't*, is used in the third person, singular number, indicative mood.

>He *doesn't* (not *don't*) take as much interest in his work as he did formerly.

Omit *got* when *has, have,* or *had* adequately expresses the idea, and do not use *have got* in the sense of *must*.

>I *have* (not *have got*) a pain in my shoulder.
>He *must* (not *has got to*) account for the money.

Do not use *leave* for *let* or *allow; enthuse* for *be enthusiastic* or *have enthusiasm; suspicion* for *suspect; claim* for *assert* or *maintain; drug* for *dragged; dove* for *dived; use* for *used; ask* for *asked; suppose* for *supposed*.

>*Let* (not *Leave*) me cut the cake.
>*Allow* me to help you (not *Leave* me help you) with your coat.
>He *was enthusiastic* (not *enthused*) over the offer.
>We *suspected* (not *suspicioned*) him from the first.
>I *maintain* (not *claim*) that he is dishonest.
>The car *dragged* (not *drug*) the child a block.
>He *dived* (not *dove*) from a high cliff.
>I *used* (not *use*) to see him every evening.
>John *asked* (not *ask*) his employer for an increase in salary.
>The pickle dish was *supposed* (not *suppose*) to be of sterling silver.

25. PROBLEMS IN THE USE OF CERTAIN VERBS—I

Shall and *Will, Should* and *Would*

Each of the sentences immediately following is to be completed with shall or will. Select in each instance the verb which seems appropriate to a formal style and write this verb in the space at the left.

EXAMPLE:

will   There .... be a meeting of the Kiwanis Club next Tuesday noon.

will ✗   1. We .... probably see the Grand Canyon and Yellowstone Park during our trip.
will   2. Next month the new library building .... be formally dedicated.
will   3. If I be allowed to choose, I .... take geology instead of the course in chemistry.
will   4. It is difficult to tell how successful the play .... be.
shall   5. In the yard was a sign which read: "There .... be no trespassing on this property."
will ✗   6. I am determined that this situation .... not continue.
will   7. The opening address .... be made by the president of the association.
shall   8. If you do not pay this bill, you .... hear from me again.
will   9. During February someone .... announce that he has seen the first robin.
will   10. He .... undoubtedly read this new book on foreign trade problems.
shall   11. We .... be glad to make an estimate of the cost of insulating your house.
will   12. At the electrical show there .... be a complete display of household appliances.
shall ✗   13. I .... take not a cent less than the figure I have named.

Each of the sentences immediately following is to be completed with should or would. Select in each instance the verb which seems appropriate to a formal style and write this verb in the space at the left.

would   14. .... that I had never seen this house!
would   15. Whenever we needed directions, we .... invariably ask someone who was a stranger in the city.
should   16. The train .... arrive at 7:58 this evening.

95

would 17. When we had finished skating, we .... go back to the Williamses for sandwiches and cocoa.
should 18. .... you need my help, be sure to send for me.
should 19. On a busy day like this, the store .... have more clerks.
would 20. .... that I had never said such a ridiculous thing!
should 21. If you .... be going to the post office, please mail this letter for me.
would 22. Just when we needed it most, the car .... refuse to start.
should 23. Helen admits that she does not study as hard as she ....
would 24. Our spaniel .... often growl or bark while asleep.
would 25. Upon inquiry, we found that the stores .... not open until nine-thirty.

To obtain score, multiply number of errors by 4 and subtract total from 100.

NAME ....DATE ....SCORE ....

26. PROBLEMS IN THE USE OF CERTAIN VERBS—II

May and Can, Might and Could

Each of the sentences immediately following is to be completed with may or can. Select in each instance the verb which seems appropriate to a formal style and write this verb in the space at the left.

EXAMPLE:
may I suppose that there .... be some truth in what he says.

May 1. .... I congratulate you on your new position.
Can 2. There's an old saying that faith .... move mountains.
May 3. We plan to install an oil furnace, no matter what it .... cost.
Can 4. .... you identify most of the birds of this locality?
Can 5. I shall go to Chicago tonight if I .... get a reservation.
may 6. Since it is snowing hard, the bus .... be late.
may 7. .... I use your telephone?
may 8. It .... require from ten days to two weeks to make delivery on this order.
can 9. .... you tell me the source of this quotation?
may 10. I am taking this route in order that we .... avoid the business section.
Can 11. .... you make out what this word is?
can 12. The mechanism is so simple that with a few instructions anyone .... operate it.
May 13. .... I have a glass of water?
can 14. I do not see how he .... listen to such trash as these records.

Each of the sentences immediately following is to be completed with might or could. Select in each instance the verb which seems appropriate to a formal style and write this verb in the space at the left.

could 15. The voice sounded vaguely familiar, but I .... not tell whose it was.
could 16. A placard on the wall stated that the firm .... not be held responsible for lost articles.
might 17. For a time, it was feared that the whole block .... be destroyed by the fire.
could 18. .... you understand the cockney dialect in that English picture?

97

could / might 19. We asked the farmer whether we .... hold the picnic on his land.
might 20. Believing that they .... come while we were away, we left the key at the house next door.
could 21. The boat, which was upturned on the shore, was so heavy that I .... not lift it.
could 22. The doctor promised that he would come as soon as he ....
might 23. The students did not realize to what extent their actions .... reflect upon the school.
could 24. The speaker replied that in the light of present conditions he .... not predict the future of Germany.
could 25. Jim felt certain that he .... pass the test for an operator's license.

To obtain score, multiply number of errors by 4 and subtract total from 100.

NAME .... DATE .... SCORE ....

27. PROBLEMS IN THE USE OF CERTAIN VERBS—III

Lie and *Lay*, *Sit* and *Set*, *Rise* and *Raise*

Choose the correct form of lie *or* lay *for each of the sentences immediately following. Write your answers in the blank spaces at the left.*

EXAMPLE:

lying   The old dog was .... in the sun.

lay .... 1. As we stood in the observation tower, we marveled at the scene which .... below us.

lies .... 2. The Gulf of California, into which the Colorado River empties, ... in the northwestern part of Mexico.

laid .... 3. The barber carefully .... my glasses on the shelf where he kept his razors.

lay .... 4. A huge yellow cat .... on the window seat.

laid .... 5. At the dinner table, places had been .... for ten persons.

lain .... 6. The chocolates had .... in the showcase so long that they had turned gray.

lain .... 7. After lunch, he had .... down on the sofa for a few minutes' rest.

laying .... 8. The masons have started .... a stone wall along the edge of the drive.

lying .... 9. .... in ambush, the Indians await the coming of the stagecoach.

Choose the correct form of sit *or* set *for each of the sentences immediately following. Write your answers in the blank spaces at the left.*

sat .... 10. At baseball games, we have always .... in the bleachers, shouting until we are hoarse.

sit .... 11. Let's .... at the counter this time.

sets .... 12. One of the advantages of this enamel is that it .... rapidly, giving a hard, lustrous finish.

sit .... 13. We invited them to come in and .... down.

set .... 14. I forgot to .... my watch by the time signals this morning.

set .... 15. Every night we had to change the linen and .... the tables for breakfast.

sets .... 16. The manufacturer allows for a reasonable margin of profit when he .... the price of an article.

sets .... 17. The Palmer house, shaded by giant elms, ... far back from the street.

99

Choose the correct form of rise *or* raise *for each of the sentences immediately following. Write your answers in the blank spaces at the left.*

....risen.... 18. Wages have ...., to be sure, but prices have also moved upward.
....rise.... 19. Promptly at 8:30, the curtain will .... for the opening scene of the play.
....raising.... 20. The landlord sent us a notice that he was .... the rent.
....rises.... 21. Before you can bake the bread, you must wait until the dough ....
....rose.... 22. Henry Ford was a man who .... from obscurity to become one of the nation's industrial leaders.
....raise.... 23. By releasing this catch, you can .... the hood of the car.
....rising.... 24. Smoke was .... from the chimneys on that crisp winter morning.
....raised.... 25. Many of the local merchants have .... objections to the plan for installing parking meters.

To obtain score, multiply number of errors by 4 and subtract total from 100.

NAME _____ DATE _____ SCORE _____

28. PROBLEMS IN THE USE OF CERTAIN VERBS—IV

Lie and *Lay*, *Sit* and *Set*, *Rise* and *Raise*

Examine each of the sentences below for errors in the use of lie *and* lay, sit *and* set, rise *and* raise. *Draw a circle around any error and give the correct form in the space at the left. If the form given in the sentence is correct, leave the space at the left blank.*

EXAMPLE:

sit   Would you like to (set) in this chair?

laid   1. The house is (lain) out in a T-shape design, with the principal rooms facing south.
sets   2. The vase, which is a family heirloom, (sits) on a low mahogany stand.
rose   3. When the speaker asked for questions from the audience, a number of hands were (risen).
sitting 4. After (setting) in the waiting room for two hours, he was finally admitted to the doctor's office.
_____   5. Over a ten-year period the earnings of the company rose steadily.
set   6. Next week, with the schools closing for the long vacation, hundreds of families will (sit) out for the mountains or the seashore.
raised 7. The number of unsolved crimes has (risen) serious question as to the efficiency of the police department.
_____   8. After the airplane had been discovered, a rescue party set out for the scene of the mishap.
sitting 9. We were (setting) too far back from the stage to have a good view of the actors' faces.
lay   10. Indifferent to the passing automobiles, the dog (laid) asleep in the middle of the street.
risen 11. Through his energy and tireless ambition, he had (rose) to a position of considerable importance.
_____ 12. His assignment as ambassador to Great Britain had laid heavy responsibilities upon him.
_____ 13. Tonight the sun will set at about seven o'clock.
raised 14. The conductor bowed to the audience, turned to face the orchestra, and (rose) his baton.
lies   15. If the motor fails to idle properly, the trouble probably (lays) with the carburetor.
sit   16. Couldn't we straighten out this matter if we were to (set) down and talk things over?

.... 17. Year after year, the town has raised money for the support of the summer opera program.
lying .... 18. As I entered the dentist's office, I noticed the shiny instruments which were laying on the shelf near the chair.
.... 19. When the danger of frost has passed, we can set out the tomato plants.
rises .... 20. Whenever a major disaster occurs, the Red Cross always raises to the emergency.
.... 21. Fire broke out on the *Normandie* as the huge ship was lying at anchor in New York.
rose .... 22. He raised from his chair and walked slowly toward the window.
sets .... 23. The oldest child sits an example which the younger ones will invariably follow.
.... 24. The waitress had laid the tray on the stand and was preparing to serve us.
.... 25. Higher wages have raised the general standard of living in this country.

To obtain score, multiply number of errors by 4 and subtract total from 100.

NAME .... DATE .... SCORE ....

29. PROBLEMS IN THE USE OF CERTAIN VERBS—V

Past Tense and Past Participle, Correct Form with Auxiliary

Draw a circle around each faulty or incomplete verb in the sentences below, and write the correct form in the space at the left. If there is no mistake in the sentence, leave the space at the left blank.

EXAMPLES:

gone — I did not know until today that Harry had (went).
has been — John never (has) and never will be a co-operative person.

....	1. When she saw that the balloon had burst, the child started to cry.
began	2. She overcame her shyness and (begun) to take part in social affairs.
will think	3. I thought then, as I always (will), that a sport should be played for the fun of it.
were	4. At the garage I was told that the brake linings are nearly (wore) out.
ran	5. He polled a large number of votes every time he (run) for council.
have stolen	6. The paper carried the story of a man who had (stole) a school bus and driven to Florida.
ridden	7. I was ashamed to admit, in that company of Westerners, that I had never (rode) on a horse.
....	8. We boys had often (swum) in a pond near the abandoned stone quarry.
bought	9. On the kitchen table was an enormous pile of groceries that Mother had just (boughten).
gone	10. He later regretted that he had not (went) to college.
....	11. He does not and will not consider himself a candidate for the office.
rung	12. Nobody knew who had (rang) the school bell that evening.
....	13. As the boat moved toward the dock, the deckhand flung a rope to a man waiting below.
gave	14. I happen to know that she (give) ten dollars for the hat she is wearing.
made	15. Our firm always has and always will (make) a product of superior quality.
....	16. The picture had evidently been taken many years earlier.
swam	17. When he saw that he could not overtake the boat, the dog turned about and (swum) back to shore.

_____did_____ 18. He never done an honest day's work in his entire life.
_____ _____ 19. The cat had sprang at him so quickly that poor Duke had been taken completely unawares.
_____brought_____ 20. When we were ready to eat, we found that we had not brung any butter.
_____ _____ 21. During the lunch hour he had drunk a glass of milk and nibbled at some crackers.
_____have agreed_____ 22. I never have and never will agree that cats are more intelligent than dogs.
_____came_____ 23. My brother come back from Japan with interesting yarns about his experiences in the service.
_____no had_____ 24. He had climbed the tree and shook the branches to bring down the fruit.
_____rode_____ 25. We had ridden slowly through the canyon, which was indescribably beautiful.

To obtain score, multiply number of errors by 4 and subtract total from 100.

NAME .... DATE .... SCORE ....

30. PROBLEMS IN THE USE OF CERTAIN VERBS—VI

Past Tense and Past Participle, Correct Form with Auxiliary

Draw a circle around each faulty or incomplete verb in the sentences below, and write the correct form in the space at the left. If there is no mistake in the sentence, leave the space at the left blank.

EXAMPLES:

rang The janitor (rung) the school bell every morning at eight o'clock.

has thought He still thinks, as he always (has), that his farm is the best in the county.

.... 1. We cannot and will not support a wavering, indecisive foreign policy.
.... 2. For this cake you need four egg yolks, which should be thoroughly beat.
.... 3. The lecturer expressed the opinion that the American Indian originally come from Asia.
.... 4. In a friendly scuffle with George I had tore my coat.
.... 5. The explosion had occurred when someone had thrown kerosene into a laundry stove.
.... 6. Many persons cannot sleep if they have drank coffee before retiring.
.... 7. Our free press always has and always will be the safeguard of our democratic society.
.... 8. Next, a fine cherry cupboard had been put up for sale, and I had bidden twenty-five dollars for it.
.... 9. With the drop in commodity prices, some believed that a recession had began.
.... 10. The tree expert swang from one branch to another as nimbly as a monkey.
.... 11. I intend to study after I have eaten my lunch.
.... 12. On the witness stand, the manufacturer stated that he had neither given nor seeked any personal favors in his relations with government officials.
.... 13. Before the party ended, we had gathered around the piano and sang our favorite songs.
.... 14. This advertisement shows the plight of a man whose collar has shrunk.
.... 15. She seen him put his finger on the scales as he weighed the meat.

.... 16. As he drove along the new highway, he noted that tourist camps and filling stations had sprang up everywhere.
.... 17. This maple tree, which we set out only a few years ago, has growed very rapidly.
.... 18. Until help reached them, the would-be sailors had clung to their overturned boat.
.... 19. On her way to school she had slipped and fell on the icy street.
.... 20. We always have and always will offer the lowest prices to be found anywhere.
.... 21. I am impressed now, as I have been many times before, by the friendliness of these people.
.... 22. After washing the socks, he wrang them out and put them on the line.
.... 23. On the sands of Kitty Hawk, North Carolina, the Wright brothers had flew the first airplane.
.... 24. On the wall of the castle hung a tapestry showing a medieval hunting scene.
.... 25. As a young man, he had borrowed some money and went into business for himself.

To obtain score, multiply number of errors by 4 and subtract total from 100.

NAME .... DATE .... SCORE ....

31. PROBLEMS IN THE USE OF CERTAIN VERBS—VII

Miscellaneous Errors

Examine carefully each italicized verb form in the sentences below. If the verb is faulty, give the correct form in the space at the left. If the verb is correctly used, leave the space at the left blank.

EXAMPLE:

used   He *use* to send me a card every Christmas.

.... 1. When he rose to speak, his mind went blank and he could not remember what he was *suppose* to say

.... 2. If one speaks in a colorless monotone, he quickly *looses* the attention of his listeners.

.... 3. A young woman *claimed* the necklace which was found in the theater yesterday.

.... 4. Did you get a receipt when you *payed* the bill?

.... 5. Even as late as August, 1939, some experts *claimed* that Germany would not go to war.

.... 6. Jane *has got* a keen mind and a pleasing personality.

.... 7. He merely glanced at the newspaper and then *laid* it on the seat beside him.

.... 8. At six o'clock I was *awaken* by the sound of the milk truck.

.... 9. I *have got to* write a few letters this afternoon.

.... 10. *Leave* me take your coat and hat.

.... 11. Whatever he undertakes, he *tries* to do it well.

.... 12. A noted explorer, Admiral Byrd *lead* several expeditions to the Antarctic.

.... 13. Everyone *is enthused* about the new advances in television.

.... 14. I shall not know his plans until he *replys* to my note.

.... 15. He was so fond of argument that he often *choose* to defend an unpopular point of view.

.... 16. People sometimes wondered why this man had *choosen* to enter politics.

.... 17. Having seen no one enter or leave the house, the neighbors *suspicioned* that something was wrong.

.... 18. To my annoyance, the sack had *burst* and its contents had spilled onto the sidewalk.

.... 19. The first drops of rain began to fall as we *drug* the canoe onto the beach.
.... 20. After several of our chickens had been killed, we *layed* a trap for the marauder.
.... 21. The plumber told us that a water pipe in the basement had *busted*.
.... 22. I heard a thud above my head, as if someone had *throwed* a piece of metal at me.
.... 23. He came into the drug store and *ask* for a bottle of cough medicine.
.... 24. We watched the hawk as it circled in the air and then *dived* toward its prey.
.... 25. This watch *don't* keep accurate time.

To obtain score, multiply number of errors by 4 and subtract total from 100.

NAME .... DATE .... SCORE ....

32. PROBLEMS IN THE USE OF CERTAIN VERBS—VIII

Miscellaneous Errors

Draw a circle around each incorrect verb in the sentences below, and write the correct form in the space at the left. If the sentence contains no error, leave the space at the left blank.

EXAMPLE:

led   Theodore Roosevelt (lead) an adventurous life.

1. When we heard a low, rumbling sound, we suspicioned that a tire was flat.
2. If anyone else applys, tell him that the position has been filled.
3. As I was about to leave, the salesman ask whether I wished to look at anything else.
4. He feels that he has got to leave college in order to help his father.
5. You must let me carry some of your luggage.
6. He was so accustom to the noises of the factory that he could immediately detect any break in the rhythm of the machines.
7. This train goes to Boston, don't it?
8. We may be able to fill your order in a few days if you will leave me take your name and address.
9. Scientists are enthused about the possibilities of the new 200-inch telescope on Palomar Mountain.
10. Her pride injured, the child had burst into tears.
11. The moment the whistle blew, the workmen layed down their tools.
12. It was the first time he had ever ridden in a jeep.
13. We boys use to set traps along the river bank, for muskrats were numerous in that region.
14. I have got no suggestion to make at this time.
15. He had just fell asleep when he was awakened by a pounding at the door.
16. A boiler had blown up, disabling the ship.
17. Our basketball team has been beaten only twice this season.
18. The site for the new city hall has not yet been choosen.

.... 19. Although he has a fairly good position, office work don't appeal to him.
.... 20. He has got a severe head cold today.
.... 21. The instructor looked amused when we brung our suitcases to the classroom.
.... 22. Whenever he tries to say anything, she always interrupts him.
.... 23. The defenders of Pearl Harbor never suspicioned that a Japanese attack was imminent.
.... 24. Many persons claim that goats can live on a diet of tin cans, but biologists scoff at this ridiculous belief.
.... 25. Small boys dived for coins which the ship's passengers tossed into the water.

To obtain score, multiply number of errors by 4 and subtract total from 100.

PROBLEMS WITH MODIFIERS

Adjectives and adverbs are both modifiers—the basic, grammatical difference between them is *what* they modify. An adjective modifies or limits a noun or, rarely, a pronoun. An adverb modifies a verb or verbal, an adjective, or another adverb. The following sentences illustrate the use of these two modifiers.

The shabby and *neglected* house belonged to Mr. Thompson. (adjectives in the attributive position before the noun)
The house, *shabby* and *neglected*, belonged to Mr. Thompson. (adjectives *shabby* and *neglected* in the appositive position after the noun)
Mr. Thompson's house was *shabby* and *neglected*. (adjectives used as subjective complements)
Time had left Mr. Thompson's house *shabby* and *neglected*. (adjectives used as objective complements)
The mountain stream flowed *swiftly*. (adverb modifies *flowed*)
Flowing *swiftly*, the mountain stream sparkled in the sun. (adverb modifies the verbal *flowing*)
The mountain stream had a *very* swift current. (adverb modifies the adjective *swift*)
The mountain stream flowed *very* swiftly. (adverb modifies the adverb *swiftly*)

1. Do not use an adjective to modify a verb. This error is most likely to occur with such adjectives as *good, bad, sure, fine, real*, and the like.

WRONG: He did *good* in the preliminaries.
RIGHT: He did *well* in the preliminaries.
WRONG: You type very *bad* (or *poor*).
RIGHT: You type very *badly* (or *poorly*).
WRONG: I *sure* want to pass this course.
RIGHT: I *surely* want to pass this course.
WRONG: You did *fine* in the play.
RIGHT: You did *well* (or *splendidly*) in the play.
WRONG: I am *real* surprised to see you.
RIGHT: I am *really* (or *indeed*) surprised to see you.
WRONG: He came back *quick*.
RIGHT: He came back *quickly*.
WRONG: You could do this work *easy*.
RIGHT: You could do this work *easily*.
WRONG: You can turn this *easier* with a wrench.
RIGHT: You can turn this *more easily* with a wrench.
WRONG: I can sweep this room as *easy* as I can get out the vacuum cleaner.
RIGHT: I can sweep this room as *easily* as I can get out the vacuum cleaner.
WRONG: The mill has been running *steadier* this year.
RIGHT: The mill has been running *more steadily* this year.

2. Do not use an adjective to modify an adjective or adverb.

WRONG: *Most* any cook book will give you that recipe.
RIGHT: *Almost* any cook book will give you that recipe.
WRONG: *Most* every town has a bank.
RIGHT: *Almost* every town has a bank.
WRONG: *Most* all men prize liberty.
RIGHT: *Almost* all men prize liberty.
WRONG: He came back *right* quickly.
RIGHT: He came back *very* quickly.
WRONG: It's *awful* hot this afternoon.
RIGHT: It's *very* (or *exceedingly*) hot this afternoon.
WRONG: He did *some* better today.
RIGHT: He did *somewhat* better today.
WRONG: The storm was *terrible* destructive.
RIGHT: The storm was *terribly* destructive.

3. Modifiers after all forms of the verb *to be, become, appear, seem, look, feel, taste, smell, sound, remain, grow, prove,* and some others are adjectives if they describe the subject of the sentence. In other words, they are subjective complements.

RIGHT: I feel *bad*. (in reference to health or spirits, never *badly*)
RIGHT: I feel *good* this morning. (in reference to health or spirits)
RIGHT: I feel *well* (or *ill*). (in reference to health)
RIGHT: The rose smells *sweet*. (*sweetly* would imply that the rose could smell)
RIGHT: That cough sounds *alarming*. (not *alarmingly*)
RIGHT: The rock remained *immovable* (not *immovably*)

If the modifier describes the action of the verb, an adverb should be used.

RIGHT: He looked *frantically* around the room. (tells how he looked)
RIGHT: The fox smelled the bait *cautiously*. (tells how he smelled)
RIGHT: These words shall remain *everlastingly*. (tells how long the words remain)
RIGHT: He felt *nervously* in his pocket for the key. (tells how he acted)

4. If the modifier describes the object of a verb, an adjective is used, in other words, an objective complement; if the modifier describes the action in the verb, an adverb is used.

RIGHT: He held his voice *firm*. (firm voice)
RIGHT: He spoke the words *firmly*. (how he spoke)
RIGHT: He pressed the stencil *tight* against the wax. (tight stencil)
RIGHT: He held the child *tightly* in his arms. (how he held)
RIGHT: He poured the cup *full*. (full cup)
RIGHT: He spoke his mind *fully*. (how he spoke)

5. Especial care must be taken in the use of the comparative and the superlative degree of adjectives and adverbs.

Do not use a form of the comparative or superlative adjective or adverb that is not recognized by correct usage.

WRONG: She was the *beautifullest* girl in the show.
RIGHT: She was the *most beautiful* girl in the show.
WRONG: Since he was late, he walked *more fastly*.
RIGHT: Since he was late, he walked *faster*.

Do not use a double comparative or a double superlative adjective or adverb.

WRONG: Great rumbles of thunder rolled *more nearer* all the time.
RIGHT: Great rumbles of thunder rolled *nearer* all the time.
WRONG: This act was the *most noblest* example of heroism I ever knew.
RIGHT: This act was the *noblest* example of heroism I ever knew.

Do not use the comparative or the superlative of words which express absolute qualities. Among such words are the following: *universal, dead, square, round, parallel, final, unique, fatal, perfect, supreme, omniscient,* and many others.

WRONG: He seems to be a *most omniscient* man.
RIGHT: He seems to be an *omniscient* man.
WRONG: That poison is the *fatalest* one.
RIGHT: That poison is *fatal*.

When two persons or things are compared, use the comparative degree of the adjective; when more than two persons or things are compared, use the superlative degree of the adjective.

RIGHT: This is the *better* dog of the two.
RIGHT: This is the *best* dog in the kennels.
RIGHT: Mary is *taller* than her sister, but she is not the *tallest* girl in the class.

In using the comparative degree, the person or thing must be excluded from the class with which he or it is compared.

WRONG: John D. Rockefeller was richer than any man in America.
RIGHT: John D. Rockefeller was richer than any *other* man in America.
WRONG: The Bible is more widely read than any book.
RIGHT: The Bible is more widely read than any *other* book.

In using the superlative degree, the person or thing must be included within the class with which he or it is compared.

WRONG: Cleveland is the largest of any city in Ohio.
RIGHT: Cleveland is the largest of *all* cities in Ohio.
RIGHT: Cleveland is the largest city in Ohio.
WRONG: Shakespeare is the greatest of any genius in English literature.
RIGHT: Shakespeare is the greatest of *all* geniuses in English literature.
RIGHT: Shakespeare is the greatest genius in English literature.

In all formal writing and speaking, comparisons and intensive statements should be completed. Words that clarify or complete comparisons must not be omitted.

AMBIGUOUS: She liked Mrs. Jenkins better than her mother.
CLEAR: She liked Mrs. Jenkins better than her mother *did*.
AMBIGUOUS: The eye-sight of a cat is many times more powerful than a man.
CLEAR: The eye-sight of a cat is many times more powerful than a *man's* (or *that of a man*)
INCOMPLETE: He is the *most* unreliable person.
COMPLETE: He is the most unreliable person that I know.
INCOMPLETE: This movie is *more* satisfying.
COMPLETE: This movie is more satisfying than the one we saw last week.
INCOMPLETE INTENSIVE: It was *such* a bargain.
COMPLETE: It was such a bargain that I couldn't resist it.
INCOMPLETE INTENSIVE: This book is *so* interesting.
COMPLETE: This book is so interesting that I cannot put it down.

If the second part of a comparison gives an incorrect form for completing the first comparison, the first comparison must be expanded to completeness.

WRONG: Lincoln was one of the noblest, if not the noblest, man of the nineteenth century.
RIGHT: Lincoln was one of the noblest *men*, if not the noblest man, of the nineteenth century.
WRONG: This cake is as good, if not better than, the ones I bake.
RIGHT: This cake is as good *as*, if not better than, the ones I bake.
BETTER: This cake is as good as the ones I bake, if not better.

6. If a noun used as an adjective results in an awkward or misleading combination, change the modifying noun to a phrase.

CLUMSY: He is a *military correspondence* specialist.
BETTER: He is a specialist *in military correspondence*.

7. The articles (*a, an, the*) must be repeated to show separate modification.

RIGHT: *A* red and white parasol was in the window. (one parasol)
RIGHT: *A* red and *a* white parasol were in the window. (two parasols)
RIGHT: *The* superintendent and foreman is responsible for working conditions. (one person)
RIGHT: *The* superintendent and *the* foreman are responsible for working conditions. (two persons)

8. A number of minor errors in the use of adjectives and adverbs must be guarded against.

Do not use the pronoun *them* as an adjective. Use *these* or *those*.

WRONG: I want no more of *them* wormy apples.
RIGHT: I want no more of *those* wormy apples.

These and *those* must not modify *kind* or *sort*, but *kinds* or *sorts*.

WRONG: *These* kind of people will always cause trouble.
RIGHT: *This* kind of people will always cause trouble.

RIGHT: *These* kinds of people will always cause trouble.
RIGHT: *That* sort of rumor should be disregarded.

Avoid using *this here* and *that there*.

WRONG: *This here* one is yours, but *that there* one is mine.
RIGHT: *This* one is yours, but *that* one is mine.

Do not use *that* for the adverb *so*.

WRONG: He was *that* angry he could scarcely talk.
RIGHT: He was *so* angry that he could scarcely talk.

Use *from*, not *than*, after *different* and *differently*.

WRONG: His real motives were different *than* his stated ones.
RIGHT: His real motives were different *from* his stated ones.
WRONG: There is no sense in his acting differently *than* the others.
RIGHT: There is no sense in his acting differently *from* the others.

Do not use *kind of* and *sort of* for the adverbs *somewhat* and *rather*.

WRONG: She was *kind of* upset.
RIGHT: She was *somewhat* upset.
WRONG: He was *sort of* particular.
RIGHT: He was *rather* particular.

The article *a* or *an* must not be used after *kind of* or *sort of*.

WRONG: He is a *kind of an* impersonator. (If he is *an* impersonator, he is not a *kind of an* impersonator)
RIGHT: He is a *kind of* impersonator.
WRONG: This is a *sort of a* combustion engine. (If it is *a* combustion engine, it is not a *sort of a* one)
RIGHT: This is a *sort of* combustion engine.

The double negative should be guarded against. This mistake is easily avoided when both words are clearly negative. It is with such words as *only, hardly, scarcely, but*, with which the negative idea is more subtle, that errors are likely to occur.

WRONG: I *don't* want *none* of these dresses.
RIGHT: I *don't* want *any* of these dresses.
WRONG: He *won't hardly* speak to me.
RIGHT: He *will hardly* speak to me.
WRONG: They *wouldn't* do *nothing* to encourage the boy.
RIGHT: They *would* do *nothing* to encourage the boy.
RIGHT: They *wouldn't* do *anything* to encourage the boy.
WRONG: He *hadn't scarcely* any time to prepare his lesson.
RIGHT: He *had scarcely* any time to prepare his lesson.
WRONG: She *couldn't* help *but* think of her friend.
RIGHT: She *couldn't* help thinking of her friend.

WRONG: I do *not* doubt *but* that he is trying.
RIGHT: I do *not* doubt that he is trying.
WRONG: Mr. Trumble *hadn't never* been in an airplane before.
RIGHT: Mr. Trumble *hadn't ever* been in an airplane before.
RIGHT: Mr. Trumble *had never* been in an airplane before.

NAME .... DATE .... SCORE ....

33. PROBLEMS WITH MODIFIERS—I

Identifying Adjectives and Adverbs

Determine whether each italicized word in the exercises below is an adjective or an adverb, and whether it is correctly used in the sentence. If it is correctly used, identify it as an adjective or as an adverb by writing it in the proper space at the left. If it is incorrectly used, give the required word in the proper space at the left.

EXAMPLES:

ADJECTIVE	ADVERB	
prompt		You must be *prompt* in reporting for work.
	promptly	You must answer his letter *prompt*.

ADJECTIVE   ADVERB

1. He never appears until the dishes are *near* done.
2. Everyone says that she plays the piano *good*.
3. It was *sure* cold when I got up this morning.
4. The story was *timely* and amusing.
5. The procession moved *slowly* up the street.
6. According to the old saying, the grass is always *greener* on the other side of the fence.
7. We can do the work *easy* if we have the proper tools.
8. I believe that *most* every student has a radio in his room.
9. The old gentleman would always bow *courteous* to us whenever we passed him on the street.
10. The merchandise in the store was arranged *neat*.
11. Explorers report that the natives of the island are *friendly*.
12. His voice sounds *husky*.
13. Cutting out the intricate pattern was *real* difficult.
14. You should not feel *badly* because of such a trifling error.
15. He is so well informed that he can talk on *most* any subject.
16. He can repair the radio *easier* if you take it to his shop.
17. In laundering the shirts, make the starch *thick*.

ADJECTIVE   ADVERB

.... 18. When planting your vegetables, make the rows *straight*.
.... 19. If he expects to win the scholarship, he must study *hard*.
.... 20. The food being delicious, we ate *heartier* than usual.
.... 21. Despite unfavorable rumors, the stock market remains *firm*.
.... 22. For some reason, the time always seemed to pass *quicker* in the mornings.
.... 23. The house looks *shabby*.
.... 24. The molasses cookies taste *good*.
.... 25. The young woman was dressed quite *fashionable*.

To obtain score, multiply number of errors by 4 and subtract total from 100.

NAME .... DATE .... SCORE ....

34. PROBLEMS WITH MODIFIERS—II

Using Adjectives and Adverbs Correctly

From the forms given in parenthesis choose the correct modifier for each sentence below. Write your answer in the space at the left.

EXAMPLE:

rather — We were (kind of, rather) weary after our swim.

1. After taking the medicine he felt (some, somewhat) better.
2. Of the two houses this is the (larger, largest).
3. The styles of today are much different (than, from) those of twenty years ago.
4. A Swedish and (Dutch, a Dutch) freighter were anchored in the harbor.
5. I (sure, surely) intend to see that picture.
6. He is typically (rather, sort of) slow in making up his mind.
7. If the carpenter works (steady, steadily) at the job, he can finish the repairs in a week.
8. Because of the extremely dry summer, the farmers are (sort of, somewhat) worried about their crops.
9. Quinine is one of the most (common, universal) remedies for malaria.
10. The fables suggest that there is no (slyer, more slyer) animal than the fox.
11. Do you believe that there is any truth in (them, those) rumors?
12. The novel brings out the idea that there is no offense (worse, worser) than the ingratitude of children.
13. *The Return of the Native* is as (good, good as), if not better than, Hardy's later novels.
14. During the German occupation, the French remained (staunch, staunchly) in their conviction that they would regain their freedom.
15. Their living room is (so, very) attractive.
16. During his lecture Dr. Stone paced (nervous, nervously) back and forth.
17. Even though the war had ended, the situation in Europe remained (tense, tensely).
18. It is (real, very) kind of you to offer your assistance.

.... 19. Mount Everest is the highest of (any mountain, all mountains) in the world.
.... 20. The Whites live in (that, that there) brick house at the end of the street.
.... 21. Robert Frost is better known than (any, any other) American poet.
.... 22. The milk in this glass tastes (sour, sourly).
.... 23. Before ordering Venetian blinds, be sure to measure the windows (exact, exactly).
.... 24. (This, These) kind of shoes will be popular this season.
.... 25. For ideal croquet, the lawn should be rolled (smooth, smoothly).

To obtain score, multiply number of errors by 4 and subtract total from 100.

NAME .... DATE .... SCORE ....

35. PROBLEMS WITH MODIFIERS—III

Using Adjectives and Adverbs Correctly

From the forms given in parenthesis choose the correct modifier for each sentence below. Write your answer in the space at the left.

EXAMPLE:

well   Don't you think that he plays the piano (good, well)?

.... 1. Which is the (larger, largest) vessel, the *Queen Mary* or the *Queen Elizabeth?*

.... 2. He promised to write home as (frequent, frequently) as he could.

.... 3. There is an American Express office in (most, almost) every European city.

.... 4. The automatic washing machine is perhaps the (usefullest, most useful) appliance that has recently been developed.

.... 5. I am (indeed, sure) grateful to you for granting my request.

.... 6. The trunk was so heavy that the two of us could (scarcely, not scarcely) lift it.

.... 7. Where did I put (them, those) road maps that we used on our trip?

.... 8. Mrs. Dopp was (rather, kind of) scornful of her husband's attempts at cooking.

.... 9. The dog evidently hadn't (ever, never) encountered a porcupine before.

.... 10. (This, These) kind of fish can be found only in tropical seas.

.... 11. This idea is (so, absolutely) ridiculous.

.... 12. An old stone tower in Newport, Rhode Island, is one of the most (unique, unusual) relics of an earlier America.

.... 13. By the time we arrived at the farm, dinner was (most, almost) ready.

.... 14. I feel more (secure, securely) in my mind when I know that the house is locked.

.... 15. The prospects for a settlement of the dispute are (some, somewhat) brighter today.

.... 16. This room seems (very, awful) cold.

.... 17. Chicago is the largest of (any city, all cities) on the Great Lakes.

.... 18. It would be difficult to say which was the (worse, worst) in its effect upon London—the Great Plague of 1665, or the Great Fire of the following year.
.... 19. After the new manager came, the store began to look (neater, more neatly).
.... 20. The blue grapes taste (juicier, more juicily) than the white ones.
.... 21. In its basic principle, the turbine is a (sort of, sort of a) windmill.
.... 22. I should answer the question (thus, thusly).
.... 23. As a soldier he had acquired the habit of talking (respectful, respectfully) to his superiors.
.... 24. Garrick was one of the (best, best actors), if not the best actor, of the eighteenth century.
.... 25. Many believe that the city-manager plan is more efficient than (any, any other) form of municipal government.

To obtain score, multiply number of errors by 4 and subtract total from 100.

DANGLING AND MISPLACED MODIFIERS

I. Dangling Modifiers

1. Avoid the use of dangling adjectives and adverbs.

DANGLING ADJECTIVES: *Red, yellow,* and *blue,* the little girl admired the flowers.
RIGHT: The little girl admired the red, yellow, and blue flowers.
RIGHT: The little girl admired the flowers, which were red, yellow, and blue.
DANGLING ADJECTIVES: The woods were frequented by many visitors, *cool* and *shady.*
RIGHT: The cool and shady woods were frequented by many visitors.
DANGLING ADVERB: *Personally,* horse racing is an intensely interesting sport.
ACCEPTABLE: Horse racing is an intensely interesting sport to me personally.
BETTER: Personally, I think horse racing is an intensely interesting sport.
DANGLING ADVERB: *Individually,* prizes stimulate the members' interest.
RIGHT: Members, individually, have their interest stimulated by prizes.

2. Infinitive, participial, gerundive, and prepositional phrases must not be loosely or illogically related to the rest of the sentence. Usually the wrong relation is to the subject of the sentence.

To correct such dangling modifiers, you may change the subject of the sentence, or the phrase itself may be expanded into a subordinate clause.

DANGLING INFINITIVE PHRASE: *To read books intelligently,* attention must be given to details.
RIGHT: To read books intelligently, one must give attention to details.
RIGHT: If one wishes to read books intelligently, he must give attention to details.
RIGHT: To read books intelligently requires that attention be given to details.
DANGLING PARTICIPIAL PHRASE: *Thumbing rides for a whole day,* Boston was finally reached.
RIGHT: Thumbing rides for a whole day, the hitchhiker finally reached Boston.
RIGHT: After he had thumbed rides all day, Boston was finally reached.
BETTER: After he had thumbed rides all day, he finally reached Boston.
DANGLING GERUNDIVE PHRASE: *By pressing this little button,* the ironing-board comes out of the wall.
RIGHT: By pressing this little button, one lets the ironing-board come out of the wall.
RIGHT: When one presses this little button, the ironing-board comes out of the wall.
DANGLING PREPOSITIONAL PHRASE: *After that narrow escape,* the mountain roads seemed even more frightful.
RIGHT: After that narrow escape, we found the mountain roads even more frightful.
RIGHT: After we had that narrow escape, the mountain roads seemed even more frightful.

3. Participial phrases of result, which usually come at the end of a sentence should not loosely modify the thought of the entire sentence but should modify the subject of the sentence.

LOOSE: He was a very excitable person, *often causing him to stutter.*
BETTER: He was a very excitable person, and this nervous condition often caused him to stutter.
BETTER: He was such an excitable person that he was often caused to stutter.
LOOSE: The picture was in a shadow, *thereby making it unclear.*
BETTER: A shadow clouded the picture, thereby making it unclear.
LOOSE: A short-cut can be taken, *thus lessening the time.*
BETTER: We can take a short-cut, thus lessening the time.

4. Do not use *due to, owing to,* and *caused by,* unless they have a logical noun or pronoun to modify.

COLLOQUIAL: *Due to* an accident, he was late to work.
RIGHT: *Because of* an accident, he was late to work.
RIGHT: His being late to work *was due to* an accident.
COLLOQUIAL: We have not filled your order, *owing to* a shortage in certain articles.
RIGHT: We have not filled your order *on account of* a shortage in certain articles.
RIGHT: We have not filled your order because there has been a shortage in certain articles.
COLLOQUIAL: The road was blocked, *caused by* a wash-out.
RIGHT: The road was blocked *because of* a wash-out.
RIGHT: A wash-out caused the road to be blocked.

5. In formal writing the loose use of *which* with the preceding part of the sentence as a vague antecedent should be avoided.

COLLOQUIAL: He was industrious, *which* accounted for his rapid advancement.
CORRECT BUT PEDANTIC: He was industrious, *which fact* accounted for his rapid advancement.
CORRECT BUT PEDANTIC: He was industrious, *a fact* (or *characteristic*) *which* accounted for his rapid advancement.
BETTER: He was industrious, and it was this industry which accounted for his rapid advancement.

6. Avoid dangling elliptical clauses. If an elliptical clause is used, the subject of the main clause should also be the subject of the elliptical clause. If the clauses have different subjects, the elliptical clause should be expanded to completeness.

WRONG: When three months old, my father bought this house.
RIGHT: When I was three months old, my father bought this house.
WRONG: While practising the piano, the doorbell rang.
RIGHT: While I was practising the piano, the doorbell rang.
RIGHT: While practising the piano, I heard the doorbell ring.
WRONG: When ill, the physician should be called.
RIGHT: When ill, one should call a physician.
RIGHT: When one is ill, a physician should be called.

II. MISPLACED MODIFIERS

As a rule, a modifier should be placed close to the word it modifies, and the word modified should preferably be an important word in the sentence.

7. An adverb should be as close as possible to the word it modifies.

WRONG: I *only* want to buy three oranges.
RIGHT: I want to buy *only* three oranges.
WRONG: I *only* took this course for the credit it gives.
RIGHT: I took this course *only* for the credit it gives.
WRONG: She was *even* disliked by her own relatives.
RIGHT: She was disliked *even* by her own relatives.
WRONG: I *scarcely* know a thing about him.
RIGHT: I know *scarcely* a thing about him.
WRONG: The secretary was *not* appointed by the president but by the committee.
RIGHT: The secretary was appointed *not* by the president but by the committee.
WRONG: I *merely* wanted to see him, not to bother him.
RIGHT: I wanted *merely* to see him, not to bother him.
WRONG: I *hardly* consider it probable.
RIGHT: I consider it *hardly* probable.
WRONG: I *never* anticipate having a fortune.
RIGHT: I do *not* anticipate *ever* having a fortune.
WRONG: This is the largest factory I *almost* ever saw.
RIGHT: This is *almost* the largest factory I ever saw.
WRONG: This is the shrewdest bargain I *nearly* ever drove.
RIGHT: This is *nearly* the shrewdest bargain I ever drove.
WRONG: Do you *ever* expect this stock to advance?
RIGHT: Do you expect this stock *ever* to advance?
WRONG: We *just* have ice delivered three times a week.
RIGHT: We have ice delivered *just* three times a week.
WRONG: He tried to push the door open *hard*.
RIGHT: He tried *hard* to push the door open.

8. So-called squinting modifiers lead to probable misunderstanding of the sentence. The grammatical and ideational word to which the "squinter" is attached must be clear. The following are examples of squinting adverbs.

VAGUE: They were told *repeatedly* to buy low-priced stocks.
CLEAR: They were *repeatedly* told to buy low-priced stocks.
CLEAR: They were told to buy low-priced stocks *repeatedly*.
VAGUE: The workman who had been injured *recently* quit his job.
CLEAR: The workman who had *recently* been injured quit his job.
CLEAR: The workman who had been injured quit his job *recently*.

Squinting prepositional phrases may lead to a misunderstanding of the writer's or speaker's meaning.

WRONG: *At the age of nine,* my mother gave me a wrist watch.
RIGHT: At the age of nine, I was given a wrist watch by my mother.
RIGHT: When I was nine years old, my mother gave me a wrist watch.
WRONG: Truth *beyond question* stands high among the virtues.
RIGHT: Beyond question, truth stands high among the virtues.
WRONG: Many states have made it possible for injured workmen to be cared for *by establishing compensation laws.*
RIGHT: Many states, by establishing compensation laws, have made it possible for injured workmen to be cared for.

125

Of the pronouns, the relative is most likely to "squint." The pronoun should be placed close to its antecedent.

CONFUSED: He picked some fruit from the old apple tree, *which* he ate in a hurry.
CLEAR: From the old apple tree he picked some fruit, *which* he ate in a hurry.
CONFUSED: Mrs. Jamison finally bought an old farm house from a real estate dealer *that* she had always admired.
CLEAR: From a real estate dealer Mrs. Jamison finally bought an old farm house *that* she had always admired.
CONFUSED: A man was discovered in the alley by a policeman *who* was thought to be a thief.
CLEAR: A man *who* was thought to be a thief was discovered in the alley by a policeman.
CONFUSED: We walked up to a little house *that* peeped out from the trees and went in.
CLEAR: We walked up to a little house that peeped out from the trees; then we went in.
CLEAR: After we had walked up to a little house that peeped out from the trees, we went in.

NAME .... DATE .... SCORE ....

36. DANGLING MODIFIERS—I

Revise the following sentences to eliminate dangling constructions. Make such changes in wording as may be necessary.

EXAMPLE:
Before going to the show, this letter must be finished.
Before I go to the show, this letter must be finished.

1. Being a quarrelsome dog, my father always kept Felix on the leash during their walks together.
   My father always kept Felix, being a quarrelsome dog, on the leash during their walks together.

2. Looking out of our hotel window, a snow-capped mountain could be seen in the distance.
   A snow capped mountain could be seen in the distance by looking out of our hotel window.

3. When ordering tickets by mail, a self-addressed envelope should be enclosed.
   A self addressed envelope should be enclosed w/ the order when ordering tickets by mail.

4. During our talk I learned that Tony was an orphan, which came as a surprise to me.
   Coming as a surprise to me, during our talk I learned that Tony was an orphan.

5. Walking into the library, a statue of Lincoln can be seen in the corridor.
   When one walks into the library, a statue of Lincoln can be seen.

6. The streets were slippery, which led to several accidents.
   The streets being slippery led to several accidents.

7. By taking the ferry, the trip can be shortened by several miles.

8. While ~~climbing~~ *I was* climbing the ladder to the porch roof, a wasp stung me.

9. ~~If~~ *When* buying a used automobile, a 90-day guarantee should be demanded.

10. The flight was delayed due to low clouds and poor visibility.

11. After trimming the paper to the desired width, it is rolled and wrapped for shipping.
    After being trimmed to the desired width, the paper is rolled and wrapped for shipping.

12. ~~Being~~ *Because I was* a large child, the conductor looked questioningly at my half-fare ticket.

To obtain score, allow 8½ points for each sentence correctly revised.

128

NAME .... DATE .... SCORE ....

37. DANGLING MODIFIERS—II

Write brief sentences which will complete the beginnings or endings listed below. Make sure that your finished sentence does not contain a dangling construction.

EXAMPLE:

To prepare for a diplomatic career   one should acquire a knowledge of foreign languages.

1. Perching on the edge of the desk ....

2. .... due to hay fever.
3. Taking the *Daily Times* from his pocket ....

4. Running to catch the bus ....

5. Submitting his resignation ....

6. Personally, ...
7. To make an interesting snapshot ....

8. Upon entering the store ....
9. While staying in Boston ....

10. .... which I regard as impractical.
11. When taking an examination ....

12. To be a good reporter ....

13. When excavating for the new building ....

14. When a small child ....

129

15. ....
   .... thus confirming our suspicion.

16. Counting my change ....
   ....

17. .... due to the pilot's negligence.

18. .... which always amused me.

19. When driving in city traffic ....
   ....

20. By insulating the walls of the house ....
   ....

To obtain score, allow 5 points for each sentence correctly completed.

NAME ....DATE ....SCORE ....

38. MISPLACED MODIFIERS—I

Revise each of the sentences below to eliminate any confusion or obscurity resulting from the faulty placement of modifiers. Make such changes in ordering or punctuation as you deem necessary, but do not alter the actual phrasing of the sentence.

EXAMPLE:
I only have fifteen minutes between trains.
I have only fifteen minutes between trains.

1. We bought some chairs at the second-hand store which we later took to our summer camp.
   At the second-hand store we bought some chairs which we later took to our summer camp.

2. It was the hardest work we had almost ever done.
   It was almost the hardest work we had ever done.

3. In 1896 Bryan attempted to win the Presidency unsuccessfully on the Democratic ticket.
   In 1896 Bryan unsuccessfully attempted to win the Presidency on the Democratic ticket.

4. She used the berries in making the pie that we picked yesterday.
   She used the berries that we picked yesterday in making the pie.

5. The store owner tried to overtake the thief who fled down the street in vain.
   The store owner tried in vain to overtake the thief who fled down the street.

6. He placed the glove on the counter that he had found in the doorway.
   He placed the glove that he had found in the doorway on the counter.

131

7. She scarcely spends any time on her studies.
   She spends scarcely any time on her studies.

8. When it is finished, this dormitory will house approximately four hundred students alone.
   When it is finished, this dorm, alone, will house approximately four hundred students.

9. We only know a few facts about Shakespeare's early life.
   We know only a few facts about Shakespeare's early life.

10. Father settled himself comfortably in the big chair breathing a sigh of relief.
    Father, breathing a sigh of relief, settled himself comfortably in the big chair.

11. A miniature colonial house stands on the corner lot, which serves as a real estate office for the new development.
    A miniature colonial house, which serves as a real estate office for the new development, stands on the corner lot.

12. We had to stand in line to get seats at the show for twenty minutes.
    We had to stand in line for twenty minutes to get seats at the show.

To obtain score, allow 8½ points for each sentence correctly revised.

NAME .... DATE .... SCORE ....

39. MISPLACED MODIFIERS—II

Revise each of the sentences below to eliminate any confusion or obscurity resulting from the faulty placement of modifiers. Make such changes in ordering or punctuation as you deem necessary, but do not alter the actual phrasing of the sentence.

EXAMPLE:
She left the book on the sofa that was to be returned to the library.
She left on the sofa the book that was to be returned to the library.

1. The instrument was displayed in a pawnshop window which he was very anxious to buy.

2. We hardly bought any of the souvenirs.

3. The gray-haired man who was dictating casually nodded at me as I entered the office.

4. The severe damage to the trees was not caused by high wind but by a heavy coating of ice.

5. We gave the old magazines to a junk dealer that had been lying in our basement.

6. He states that he is not returning to America until the war ends in one of his letters.

7. He was the dreamiest person I probably ever knew.

   ....

8. An old-fashioned piano stood in one corner of the recreation room which had several broken keys.

   ....

   ....

9. He found a revolver in the desk that bore a German trademark.

   ....

   ....

10. The new radio system which was installed in police cars recently has helped to solve crimes promptly.

    ....

    ....

    ....

11. For Sale: A 1947 Packard sedan to settle an estate with low mileage.

    ....

    ....

12. This evening Miss Wilks, home economics expert, will give a talk on meatless menus at the Y.W.C.A.

    ....

    ....

    ....

To obtain score, allow 8½ points for each sentence correctly revised.

PROBLEMS WITH CONNECTIVES

There are two kinds of connectives in English: conjunctions and prepositions.

Conjunctions are of two classes. The co-ordinate conjunctions (*and, but, or, nor*) join words, phrases, and clauses of equal rank. Subordinate conjunctions, expressing time, place, condition, purpose, result, cause, reason, concession, manner, comparison, and degree, join dependent clauses to independent or main clauses.

A preposition controls a noun or pronoun as its object, and the preposition and its object and any modifiers of the object form a prepositional phrase, which has the function of an adjective or an adverb in the sentence. Prepositions may be simple, as: *about, above, across, after, against, along, among, at, before, behind, below, beneath, by, down, during, except, for, from, in, into, of, off, on, over, through, till, to, toward, under, until, up, upon,* and *with;* or they may be compound, as: *according to, as for, as to, because of, in accordance with, in spite of, instead of, on account of,* and *with regard to.*

1. When using co-ordinate conjunctions, keep the sentence elements parallel. Especially avoid the *and who* and *and which* construction, unless there is a preceding *who* or *which* in the sentence with which to form a parallel construction.

POOR: He was very *tall* and *of great strength.*
BETTER: He was very *tall* and *strong.*
POOR: He *bought* an old house, and *it was remodeled* by him.
BETTER: He *bought* an old house and *remodeled* it.
POOR: All applicants for this work must be intelligent, tactful, and *have good health.*
BETTER: All applicants for this work must be intelligent, tactful, and *healthy.*
BETTER: All applicants for this work must have intelligence, tact, and good health.
POOR: James Colton won most of the games, *and who* was the youngest player on the team.
BETTER: James Colton, who was the youngest player on the team, won most of the games.
BETTER: Although James Colton was the youngest player on the team, he won most of the games.
POOR: He inherited the property from his grandmother, *and which* had been in the family for over a hundred years.
BETTER: He inherited the property *which* had belonged to his grandmother *and which* had been in the family for over a hundred years.
BETTER: The property, *which* he inherited from his grandmother, had been in the family for over a hundred years.

2. Correlative conjunctions, as *either . . . or, neither . . . nor, both . . .*

and, not only . . . but also, whether . . . or, should be used in logical pairs. For instance, *neither . . . or* would be incorrect.

>   WRONG: He was *neither* tall *or* handsome.
>   RIGHT: He was *neither* tall *nor* handsome.

Nor is usually used in the second part of a compound sentence if *not* has been used in the first part.

>   RIGHT: He is *not* satisfied with his present position, *nor* does he like the town in which he lives.
>   RIGHT: The middle and lower classes are *not* invited to membership in the club, *nor* is this policy likely to be changed.

When the parallel parts of the sentence are short and the negative idea of *not* in the first part readily carries over into the second part, *or* is often used.

>   RIGHT: I will *not* speak *or* write to such a person.
>   RIGHT: He did *not* see *or* hear a thing.

3. Especial care must be exercised in the use of certain of the subordinate conjunctions.

As, since, and *while* must not be used ambiguously.

>   RIGHT: *As* I ate my dinner, events of the morning kept running through my mind. (idea of time clearly intended)
>   RIGHT: *As* I was in a hurry, I took a subway. (idea of cause or reason clearly intended)
>   AMBIGUOUS: *As* the rain fell mercifully upon the parched fields, the farmers rejoiced. (may be either time or reason)
>   CLEAR: *When* (or *While*) the rain fell mercifully upon the parched fields, the farmers rejoiced. (time intended)
>   CLEAR: *Because* the rain fell mercifully upon the parched fields, the farmers rejoiced. (cause or reason intended)
>   AMBIGUOUS: *Since* he has a new car, he travels a great deal.
>   CLEAR: Ever since he has had a new car, he travels a great deal.
>   CLEAR: *Because* he has a new car, he travels a great deal.
>   RIGHT: *While* James practised his music, the children outside kept calling him. (time clearly intended)
>   AMBIGUOUS: *While* the baby was very young, it learned to like orange juice. (may be either time or concession)
>   CLEAR: *When* the baby was very young, it learned to like orange juice.
>   CLEAR: *Although* the baby was very young, it learned to like orange juice.

Originally, *while* meant "at the same time that." However, its concessive use, equivalent to *although,* and even its adversive use, equivalent to *whereas,* are approved by many modern authorities.

>   ACCEPTABLE: *While* styles frequently change, conservative colors are always in good taste.
>   PREFERABLE: *Although* styles frequently change, conservative colors are always in good taste.

ACCEPTABLE: We usually have a surplus of crops, *while* China usually has a deficiency in food.
PREFERABLE: We usually have a surplus of crops, *whereas* China usually has a deficiency in food.

The loose use of *while* for the co-ordinate conjunctions *and* and *but* should be avoided.

WRONG: Mary is the prettier, *while* Susan is the smarter.
RIGHT: Mary is the prettier, *but* Susan is the smarter.
WRONG: Behind him lay an unsatisfactory past, *while* before him lay an uncertain future.
RIGHT: Behind him lay an unsatisfactory past, *and* before him lay an uncertain future.

In formal writing or speaking do not use *like* as a conjunction. Use *as, as if, as though*, or *that*.

COLLOQUIAL: Many natural phenomena are not mysteries to us *like* they were to ancient peoples.
FORMAL: Many natural phenomena are not mysteries to us *as* they were to ancient peoples.
COLLOQUIAL: It looks *like* we may have a shower.
FORMAL: It looks *as if* (or *as though*) we may have a shower.
WRONG: He feels *like* he should make some amends.
RIGHT: He feels *that* he should make some amends.

If should be used to express a condition; *whether* should be used in an indirect question.

WRONG: I do not know *if* he will come.
RIGHT: I do not know *whether* (or *that*) he will come.

Do not use *so* for *so that*.

WRONG: He brushed his clothes carefully *so* he would present a neat appearance.
RIGHT: He brushed his clothes carefully *so that* he would present a neat appearance.

Do not use *than* for *when* or *before*.

WRONG: The cannon had hardly been fired *than* the enemy started to retreat.
RIGHT: The cannon had hardly been fired *when* the enemy started to retreat.
WRONG: We had scarcely started to eat breakfast *than* it was time to leave.
RIGHT: We had scarcely started to eat breakfast *before* it was time to leave.

Do not use *as* for *that* or *whether*.

WRONG: I do not know *as* I shall receive the nomination.
RIGHT: I do not know *that* (or *whether*) I shall receive the nomination.

Do not use *when* for *if*.

WRONG: *When* jellies are sufficiently sweetened, they will not spoil.
RIGHT: *If* jellies are sufficiently sweetened, they will not spoil.

Do not use *where* for *although* or *whereas*.

WRONG: *Where* most men used to wear straw hats in summer, only a few do so now.
RIGHT: *Although* (or *Whereas*) most men used to wear straw hats in summer, only a few do so now.

Do not use *except* or *without* for *unless*.

WRONG: I cannot hear *except* I sit up front.
RIGHT: I cannot hear *unless* I sit up front.
WRONG: You will miss the bus *without* you hurry.
RIGHT: You will miss the bus *unless* you hurry.

Do not use *immediately* or *directly* for *as soon as*.

WRONG: *Immediately* he started fiddling, the dancers' feet began to move.
RIGHT: As soon as he started fiddling, the dancers' feet began to move.

4. Do not use superfluous prepositions. Note that the thought is redundantly expressed by the unneeded prepositions in the following sentences.

He jumped *off* (not *off of*) the wagon.
They *ended* (not *ended up*) the game in a hurry.
We have *finished* (not *finished up*) the dishes.
Mr. Harrison *settled* (not *settled up*) the bill.
He *ascended* (not *ascended up*) the ladder.
This peculiar odor is *inside* (not *inside of*) the house.
Do not throw the ball *outside* (not *outside of*) the yard.
Where have they gone? (not *gone to?*)
Where is my fountain pen? (not *pen at?*)
I do not *remember* (not *remember of*) any such remark.
All the boys (not *All of the boys*) wore uniforms.

5. Do not omit prepositions necessary to ideational or grammatical completeness.

INCOMPLETE: He was looking for a healthful and inexpensive *place to live*.
COMPLETE: He was looking for a healthful and inexpensive *place in which to live* (or *place to live in*).
INCOMPLETE: You will find somebody about the place *whom you can give it*.
COMPLETE: You will find somebody about the place *to whom you can give it* (or *whom you can give it to*).
INCOMPLETE: These prefabricated houses are sold *by* mail order as well as stores.
COMPLETE: These prefabricated houses are sold *by* mail order as well as *by* (or *at*) stores.
INCOMPLETE: Poisons are used *for* rats as well as gophers.
COMPLETE: Poisons are used *for* rats as well as *for* gophers.
WRONG: He had a liking and took a deep interest *in* chemistry.
CORRECT: He had a liking *for*, and took a deep interest *in*, chemistry.
BETTER: He had a liking *for* chemistry and took a deep interest *in* it.
WRONG: I said that small colleges are different, not preferable *to* large universities.
RIGHT: I said that small colleges are different *from*, not preferable *to*, large universities.
WRONG: This action is contrary and not compatible *with* the public interest.

CORRECT: This action is contrary *to*, and not compatible *with*, the public interest.
BETTER: This action is contrary *to* the public interest and not compatible *with* it.

6. Certain prepositions need special attention to insure their correct use. *Between* is used of two; *among* is used of more than two.

RIGHT: The contest lay *between* Mary and Ellen.
RIGHT: An excellent spirit existed *among* the boys on the team.

In denotes position; *into* denotes movement to or entering.

RIGHT: An old tree stood *in* the yard.
RIGHT: The car is *in* the garage.
RIGHT: He drove the cow *into* the stable.
RIGHT: He jumped *into* the water.

Beside means "at the side of"; *besides* means "in addition to."

RIGHT: Place this vase *beside* the other one.
RIGHT: Two others made speeches *besides* the president.

Do not use the preposition *of* for *have*, as in *could of, would of, might of, may of, must of, ought to of*.

He *must have* (not *must of*) taken it.

Do not use the compound preposition *on account* or *on account of* as a subordinate conjunction to introduce a clause.

WRONG: We had to walk fast *on account of* it was getting dark.
RIGHT: We had to walk fast *because* it was getting dark.
RIGHT: We had to walk fast *on account of* approaching darkness.

Avoid using *inside of* for *within* in reference to time, *outside of* for *aside from, different than* for *different from*, and *in back of* for *behind*.

He will be back *within* (not *inside of*) an hour.
Aside from (not *Outside of*) a few unexcused absences your record is good.
Your present themes are very *different from* (not *different than*) the ones you used to write.
We stood *behind* (not *in back of*) a policeman.

There is an increasing tendency to use *due to* as a compound preposition. In formal writing and speaking, *due* must be construed as an adjective, usually a predicate complement, and must modify a noun or pronoun.

COLLOQUIAL: We ran off the road *due to* a curve.
RIGHT: We ran off the road *because of* a curve.
RIGHT: Our running off the road *was due to* a curve.

7. Prepositions must be used idiomatically, as shown in the following list: acquit *of;* adapt *to;* adequate *to* (not *for*); agree *to* (a thing) and *with* (a person); angry *at* (a thing) and *with* (a person); arrive *at* (not *to*); *as regards* or *in regard to* (not *as regards to*); averse *to;* blame him *for it*, not blame it *on* him; capable *of;* careful *to;* charge *with* (a crime); compare *with* (when set side by side to show similarities) and *to* (when presented as something similar); compensate *for;* concentrate *on* or *upon;* concerned *with;* confer *with;* consist *of;* contrast *to;* correspond *to;* depend *on;* desirous *of;* deter *from;* differ *from* (something) and *with* (a person); free *from* (not *of*); identical *with* (not *to*); independent *of* (not *from*); in search *of* (not *for*); listen *to* (not *at*); motive *for;* oblivious *of* (not *to*); part *from* (a person) and *with* (a thing); possessed *of* (not *with*); prefer and preferable *to;* prevail *against* (=withstand), *over* (=conquer), *on* (=to persuade); reconcile *with* or *to;* resentment *of;* reverse *of* (not *to*); stay *at* (not *to*) home; suited or suitable *to* (not *for*); superior *to* (not *than*); susceptible *of* (proof) and *to* (infection); sympathy *with;* synonymous *with* (not *to*); *to* (not *of*) no avail; treats *of* (not *on*) diseases; wait *for* (a person or thing) and *on* (=to serve a person); warn *of* or *against;* with a view *to* (not *for*).

NAME .... DATE .... SCORE ....

40. PROBLEMS WITH CONNECTIVES—I

Using Co-ordinate and Correlative Conjunctions Properly

Revise the following sentences to eliminate errors arising from the careless or inexact use of co-ordinate or correlative conjunctions. In your revision make sure that the conjunctions used are correct in form, that they occupy the right position in the sentence, and that they join parallel sentence elements.

EXAMPLES:

That salesclerk was neither obliging nor of courteous manner.

That salesclerk was neither obliging nor courteous.

Jim Tyler played end on the team and won All-American honors, and who came from Chicago.

Jim Tyler, who came from Chicago, played end on the team and won All-American honors.

1. He was neither a logical thinker nor could he talk convincingly.

2. The rotation of crops will not only help the soil but a better yield will result.

3. In our preliminary training we learned about waiting on customers and how to make out different kinds of sales slips.

4. Aunt Mabel had white hair, a rosy complexion, and was blue-eyed.

5. The police believed that the letter was the work either of a crank, or he was a practical joker.

6. The advertising posters for the campaign were large, colorful, and of clever design.

7. The ending of the story was neither well-motivated or of any force.

8. Clym, the hero of the novel, is a sensitive and visionary young man, and who falls in love with a vain, self-centered girl.

9. The room was cluttered with pictures and bric-a-brac, and which looked thoroughly Victorian.

10. At the beginning of the story Gulliver tells of his study at Cambridge, how he practiced surgery in London, and how he began his travels.

To obtain score, allow 10 points for each sentence correctly revised.

NAME .... DATE .... SCORE ....

41. PROBLEMS WITH CONNECTIVES—II

Using Co-ordinate and Correlative Conjunctions Properly

Revise the following sentences to eliminate errors arising from the careless or inexact use of co-ordinate or correlative conjunctions. In your revision make sure that the conjunctions used are correct in form, that they occupy the right position in the sentence, and that they join parallel sentence elements.

EXAMPLES:

The old-time tenement houses were unsightly, poorly ventilated, and of flimsy construction.

The old-time tenement houses were unsightly, poorly ventilated, and flimsily constructed.

The personnel director hoped to improve relations between the management and the employees and that he could put an end to the constant bickering.

The personnel director hoped to improve relations between the management and the employees and to put an end to the constant bickering.

1. The campers from the city were taught how to swim, how to cook their own meals, and the identification of common flowers and trees.

2. Radar instruments, uncanny in their ability to detect obstacles ahead or below, have made travel safer both on the sea and air.

3. John Keats worked as a surgeon's apprentice and studied medicine for six years, and who later became one of England's greatest poets.

143

4. After leaving college he either plans to be an accountant or sell insurance.

   ....

   ....

5. The hotel clerk could neither offer me a room or could he tell me where I might find one.

   ....

   ....

6. In this company the workers are rewarded for their initiative and not how long they have served.

   ....

   ....

7. The child was so frightened that he neither would look at us or speak.

   ....

   ....

8. The novels of H. G. Wells are entertaining, imaginative, and are written well.

   ....

   ....

9. The puppet shows were colorful and ingeniously staged, and which always attracted large crowds of children.

   ....

   ....

10. Business experts declined to either find gloom in the situation nor to prophesy an oncoming depression.

    ....

    ....

To obtain score, allow 10 points for each sentence correctly revised.

NAME .... DATE .... SCORE ....

42. PROBLEMS WITH CONNECTIVES—III

Choosing the Right Conjunctions

Examine each italicized connective used in the sentences below and decide whether it is appropriate to a formal English style. If the conjunction is inexact or colloquial, write the preferred form in the space at the left. If the conjunction is correctly used, leave the space at the left blank.

EXAMPLE:

as if   It looks *like* the Cardinals will win the pennant again this year.

.... 1. After March 31, one cannot drive his automobile *without* he has obtained the new license plates.

.... 2. The auctioneer looked *as if* he were insulted when he received an opening bid of only one dollar.

.... 3. *Immediately* she saw the puppy, the girl wanted her parents to buy it.

.... 4. He left the house at seven o'clock *so* he would be on time for the meeting.

.... 5. He does not know *if* he will accept the appointment.

.... 6. No sooner had he entered the office *than* everyone began working feverishly.

.... 7. *Since* he has traveled abroad, he has strongly advocated the program for European aid. (*Time relationship intended*)

.... 8. He cannot read *except* he holds the book close to his eyes.

.... 9. We feel *that* the bond issue for a new library building should be approved at the election.

.... 10. He ate *like* he had not tasted food for several days.

.... 11. His head bowed, the old man walked slowly *as though* he were absorbed in thought.

.... 12. We had driven scarcely a mile *than* the motor again stalled.

.... 13. This bill will automatically become law *unless* it is vetoed by the President.

.... 14. *While* he was performing the trick, the magician kept up a steady flow of talk.

.... 15. My employer did not give me a vacation in August *like* he promised to do.

.... 16. *As* it appeared that the fire could not be checked, the captain gave orders to abandon ship. (*Time relationship intended*)
.... 17. He will not sell the store *without* he receives an exceptionally good offer.
.... 18. We do not know *as* we will make the trip this year.
.... 19. *When* one is a baseball enthusiast, he scans the sports page as a matter of habit.
.... 20. I left a note on his desk *so* he would know I had called.

To obtain score, multiply number of errors by 5 and subtract total from 100.

NAME ....DATE ....SCORE ....

43. PROBLEMS WITH CONNECTIVES—IV

Choosing the Right Conjunction

Examine each italicized connective used in the sentences below and decide whether it is appropriate to a formal English style. If the conjunction is inexact or colloquial, write the preferred form in the space at the left. If the conjunction is correctly used, leave the space at the left blank.

EXAMPLE:

as   I never saw anyone else who could throw a baseball *like* he could.

.... 1. The candidates were making extravagant promises *like* office-seekers invariably do.

.... 2. *When* they are stored in a cool, moist place, Baldwin apples will keep through the winter.

.... 3. Two weeks later, she returned to the store to ask *if* the dress might be exchanged for another.

.... 4. It is the policy of this newspaper not to print a letter to the editor *without* the writer signs his name.

.... 5. The schools are to be closed Friday *so* the teachers may attend a convention.

.... 6. *As* I had not seen him for years, I could not recall his name.

.... 7. *Since* he had a part in the high school play, he has wanted to take up acting as a profession. (*Time relationship intended*)

.... 8. In many European countries the first-class railroad coaches have upholstered seats, *while* the third-class coaches have only wooden benches.

.... 9. *Directly* I heard the fire siren, I tried to remember whether I had closed the drafts on the furnace.

.... 10. I do not know *as* the picture is worth seeing.

.... 11. One of Poor Richard's sayings is that we eat to please ourselves, *while* we dress to please others.

.... 12. The baseball game had scarcely got under way *when* the rain began to fall.

.... 13. In this state a driving permit will not be issued to anyone under eighteen *except* his parents sign the application.

.... 14. The instructor wanted to know *whether* anyone in the class had read *Tom Jones*.

.... 15. *As* the party chairman predicted an overwhelming victory in November, the delegates responded with loud applause. (*Time relationship intended*)
.... 16. The explosion sounded *like* it came from the oil refinery at the north end of the town.
.... 17. A red sky at night is generally taken as a sign of fair weather, *while* a red sky in the morning indicates rain.
.... 18. *Where* golf was once regarded as a rich man's diversion, it has now become one of the most popular sports in America.
.... 19. News stories are impersonal and objective, *whereas* editorials generally reflect the writer's opinion or prejudice.
.... 20. We stayed at home that evening *so* we might listen to the election returns.

To obtain score, multiply number of errors by 5 and subtract total from 100.

NAME .... DATE .... SCORE ....

44. PROBLEMS WITH CONNECTIVES—V

Using Prepositions Correctly

Choose, from the forms given in parenthesis below, the wording that is suitable to a formal style. Write each answer in the space provided at the left.

EXAMPLE:

into   We got out of the car and walked (in, into) the restaurant.

.... 1. We were forced to make a long detour (because, on account of) a bridge on the main highway was being repaired.

.... 2. Can you tell me where the doctor (is, is at)?

.... 3. After shifting into second gear, we (descended, descended down) the steep incline.

.... 4. Many factories were closing (because of, due to) a shortage of coal.

.... 5. The thief must (have, of) gained entrance to the building through a basement window.

.... 6. Do you subscribe to any magazines (beside, besides) *Time* and *Harper's?*

.... 7. It was nine o'clock before the postmaster (finished, finished up) sorting the letters.

.... 8. The traveling Chautauqua shows were designed for popular education as well as (entertainment, for entertainment).

.... 9. If he had not changed his course, he could (of, have) taken his degree this year.

.... 10. While we stood at the corner, we saw a large carton fall (off, off of) a passing truck.

.... 11. (Aside from, Outside of) a few temporary housing units, the college has undertaken no building program since the close of the war.

.... 12. He was always (opposed, opposed to), and spoke vehemently against, a retail sales tax.

.... 13. No one is permitted to sell fireworks (inside, inside of) the city limits.

.... 14. The responsibility of editing the magazine will be divided (among, between) us two.

.... 15. Mary suggested that we go (in, into) the music shop to hear some new records.

149

.... 16. On the train an old lady sat down (beside, besides) me and began to tell me of her troubles.
.... 17. The present-day television receiver is considerably different (from, than) its predecessor of a few years ago.
.... 18. At the symphony concert we sat only two rows (behind, in back of) you.
.... 19. My answer to the question is altogether different (from, than) yours.
.... 20. The mechanic promised to have the car ready (inside of, within) a week.
.... 21. He had several old suits, but he did not know anyone to give (them, them to).
.... 22. The treasure hunt, which occupied most of the evening, (ended, ended up) at Carters' house.
.... 23. This place is not especially attractive, but it is a comfortable house to (live, live in).
.... 24. I do not (recall, recall of) locking the door of the garage.
.... 25. The speakers on the program will debate this issue: What is the basis for a lasting peace (among, between) the nations of the world?

To obtain score, multiply number of errors by 4 and subtract total from 100.

NAME .... DATE .... SCORE ....

45. PROBLEMS WITH CONNECTIVES—VI

Using Prepositions Correctly

Choose, from the forms given in parenthesis below, the wording that is suitable to a formal style. Write each answer in the space provided at the left.

EXAMPLE:

behind   I was unable to see the stage because I sat (behind, in back of) a post.

.... 1. If you keep a record of expenditures, you will always know where your money (goes, goes to).

.... 2. (Because, On account of) it was getting cold in the room, we built a fire in the grate.

.... 3. The post-war housing program was seriously hampered (because of, due to) a scarcity of lumber and materials.

.... 4. Louis Pasteur could not (have, of) made his remarkable discoveries without his stubborn perseverance and his devotion to science.

.... 5. The merchants of the village have announced that they will (close, close up) their stores on Wednesday afternoons through the summer months.

.... 6. The policy of the United States today is (consistent, consistent with), not contrary to, the principles laid down in the Monroe Doctrine.

.... 7. Do you (remember, remember of) any announcement as to the time of the examination?

.... 8. It is only human to regard our own problems as different (from, than), and more important than, those of other people.

.... 9. After sweeping the front steps, Mrs. Jones went (in, into) the house.

.... 10. (Aside from, Outside of) a slightly warped cover, the book was in perfect condition.

.... 11. The danger of forest fires has increased (due to, on account of) the extremely dry weather.

.... 12. Which accommodations did you (ask, ask for), an inside or an outside stateroom?

.... 13. In seventeenth century England, the long struggle (among, between) King Charles and the Parliament finally led to the Civil War.

.... 14. Milk of magnesia is available in liquid form as well as (tablets, in tablets).
.... 15. Can you suggest some responsible person whom I may rent my (house, house to)?
.... 16. Does anyone (beside, besides) us know about this "secret" berry patch?
.... 17. The new tax schedule promises reductions for the low-income brackets as well as (persons, for persons) over sixty-five.
.... 18. On the sidewalk (outside, outside of) the hardware store were several new bicycles, an array of garden tools, and some lawn chairs.
.... 19. Outwardly, at least, it appeared that cordial and friendly relations prevailed (among, between) the teachers at the school.
.... 20. Do you know where the janitor (is, is at)?
.... 21. Mr. Laski's new book is a (commentary, commentary on), and an evaluation of, American democracy.
.... 22. This essay points out some of the main distinctions (among, between) wit and humor.
.... 23. (All, All of) the councilmen voted in favor of the motion.
.... 24. Have you any glasses (beside, besides) these?
.... 25. The prowler was captured in an alley (behind, in back of) our house.

To obtain score, multiply number of errors by 4 and subtract total from 100.

NAME .... DATE .... SCORE ....

46. PROBLEMS WITH CONNECTIVES—VII

Choosing Idiomatic Prepositions

Supply, in the space provided at the left, the preposition which will correctly complete each of the sentences below. Make sure that the preposition conforms to idiomatic usage.

EXAMPLE:

with   The traffic officer charged him .... reckless driving.

.... 1. Why doesn't his wife prevail .... him to throw away that battered old hat?

.... 2. The growing child must adapt himself .... new situations as they arise.

.... 3. The school building, which was erected fifty years ago, is hardly adequate .... the demands of the present community.

.... 4. During his concert, the violinist appeared quite oblivious .... the large crowd which filled the auditorium.

.... 5. Mr. Thorpe paced nervously back and forth as he waited .... his train.

.... 6. Reversing the decision of a previous trial, the court today acquitted the man .... first-degree murder charges.

.... 7. The islanders depend .... the ferry boat for their mail and provisions.

.... 8. Their search for a path leading up the mountain was .... no avail.

.... 9. Chanticleer, the vain and pompous rooster of medieval fiction, was quite susceptible .... flattery.

.... 10. Is the word *diffident* synonymous .... *timid*?

.... 11. The girl who waited .... us appeared listless and bored as she jotted down our order.

.... 12. I have just finished reading an article which treats .... the need for more specialized military training in the armed services.

.... 13. Even in his later years, when his fame as a writer was established, Goldsmith was never free .... debts.

.... 14. Most farmers in the state would be averse .... any bill permitting the sale of colored margarine.

.... 15. Company officials stated that they were seeking new capital with a view .... expanding the plant facilities.

.... 16. Northern Canada, where our cool air masses originate, has been compared .... a gigantic refrigerator.

	17.	The inflationary tendencies after World War I compare, in many respects, ... similar trends following the recent war.
....	18.	Her dress is identical .... the one Mary North was wearing at the tea.
....	19.	The town consists .... a general store, two filling stations, and a few scattered houses.
....	20.	The ridicule heaped upon his invention did not deter Robert Fulton .... carrying out his plans for a successful steamboat.
....	21.	The police withheld formal charges until they were possessed .... the necessary evidence.
....	22.	As a roofing material, copper is regarded as superior .... other metals.
....	23.	We enclose a cheque for fifty dollars to compensate .... the damage to your car in the collision.
....	24.	Instead of taking an automobile trip, the Culps will stay .... home this summer.
....	25.	Fly-fishing is altogether different .... fishing with a thread-line spinner.

To obtain score, multiply number of errors by 4 and subtract total from 100.

47. PROBLEMS WITH CONNECTIVES—VIII

Choosing Idiomatic Prepositions

Supply, in the space provided at the left, the preposition which will correctly complete each of the sentences below. Make sure that the preposition conforms to idiomatic usage.

EXAMPLE:

for   What were his motives .... committing such a crime as that?

1. Her husband timidly suggested that perhaps the dress was not suited .... a woman of her years.
2. The judge warned him .... appearing in court again on a similar offense.
3. In what respects does FM differ .... the earlier method of radio broadcasting?
4. It is a common belief that in the art of cooking, the British are inferior .... the French.
5. This book is concerned .... the author's experiences as a missionary in China.
6. Can you explain the method by which you arrived .... your answer?
7. The union leaders conferred .... the mine operators about the terms of a new contract.
8. Although I do not always agree .... him, I find him an entertaining speaker.
9. In awed silence, we children listened .... the story of the headless horseman.
10. Your itinerary through the Western states was almost the reverse .... ours.
11. The branch factory is capable .... assembling one hundred cars a day.
12. Many German artists, finding themselves out of sympathy .... the Nazi regime, sought refuge in other lands.
13. The number on the back of the book will correspond .... the number in the library cataloguing system.
14. The prosecutor reminded the jury that the defendant's story was not susceptible .... proof.
15. In the classic essay *On Liberty*, Mill sets forth the methods by which truth and freedom will prevail .... tyranny.

155

16. On the dunes near Kitty Hawk, North Carolina, the Wright brothers found a terrain suitable .... their requirements.
17. Dr. Stair was angry .... Jim Kendall when he learned of the cruel hoax.
18. The novel *Oliver Twist* reflects the author's humanitarian sympathy, his resentment .... social injustice.
19. Harry is desirous .... securing an internship in a Baltimore hospital.
20. Bastille Day, a national holiday in France, corresponds .... our own Independence Day.
21. Life in the dormitory, he reflected, would be preferable .... his solitary existence in a rooming house.
22. An expedition was organized to explore the Amne Machin range of China in search .... a peak higher than Mount Everest.
23. The medieval manor, a self-sustaining unit, was independent .... the outside world.
24. With swing music filling the room, he found it impossible to concentrate .... his theme.
25. Because of its sentimental associations, she was reluctant to part .... the brooch, which had originally belonged to her grandmother.

To obtain score, multiply number of errors by 4 and subtract total from 100.

PROBLEMS WITH CLAUSES

In the following discussion and examples the word *clause*, as has usually been the case in this book, refers to the subordinate part of a complex sentence. Clauses are used as nouns, adjectives, or adverbs. The three kinds of clauses and their various uses will be treated briefly.

Noun clauses have most of the uses of nouns in the subjective and objective case. The following words introduce noun clauses: *that, how, why, if, whether, lest* (with verbs expressing fear), *when, where, who, whom, which, what, whoever, whomever, whatever.* Representative uses of noun clauses are shown in the following sentences.

Whether he will buy the property is doubtful. (subject of sentence)
When they will come is not certain. (subject of sentence)
Where the new house should be placed on the site is causing heated discussion in the family. (subject of *is causing*)
How she could make ends meet puzzled the anxious mother. (subject of *puzzled*)
Why he was not promoted puzzles everyone. (subject of *puzzles*)
That he was a good man was recognized even by his enemies. (subject of *was recognized*)
His not being on time is *what angered them*. (subjective complement)
The rumor *that they were married* spread through the village. (apposition with the subject *rumor*)
What the prisoner confessed having been recorded, the police returned the prisoner to his cell. (ablative absolute)
He said *that he would help on Saturday*. (object of *said*: indirect discourse)
He said, "I will help on Saturday." (object of *said*: direct discourse)
They asked *how we repaired the car so quickly*. (object of *asked*)
The people inquired *why the council had passed such an ordinance*. (object of *inquired*)
He feared *lest he slip from the cliff*. (object of *feared*)
Give *whoever is first* a prize. (indirect object of *give*)
As a prize the winner was given *whatever he wanted*. (retained object after verb in the passive voice)
You may name the club *whatever is appropriate*. (objective complement)
He was amazed at *what he saw*. (object of preposition *at*)
They resented the suggestion *that they had not paid their share*. (apposition with *suggestion*, the object of *resented*)
This car is not worth *what the dealer asks*. (adverbial objective)

Adjective clauses are introduced by the relative pronouns *who, whose, whom, that, which, what, as,* and by the words *when, where, why, whence, whither.* The italicized words in the following sentences are adjective clauses.

Mr. Turner, *who has been our neighbor for years,* has decided to move to Texas. (a non-restrictive adjective clause modifying *Mr. Turner*)
A man *whose attention is not focused on his driving* is dangerous to others on the road. (restrictive adjective clause modifying *man*)
A person *whom you can trust* is a great satisfaction. (restrictive adjective clause modifying *person*)
This is the letter *that I have been expecting.* (adjective clause)
They refinished the old chair *which they had bought at an auction.* (adjective clause)
This is the camp *where I spent my vacation.* (clause modifies *camp*)
Twilight is the time *when I like to meditate.* (clause modifies *time*)
Persons lost in a woods frequently return to the place *whence they started.* (clause modifies *place*)

Adverbial clauses are introduced by conjunctions of time (*after, as, before, since, till, until, when, whenever, while*), of place (*where, wherever, whence, whither*), of condition (*if, unless, provided that*), of purpose (*that, so that, in order that*), of result (*so that, such . . . that*), of cause or reason (*because, since, as*), of concession (*though, although, even if, even though*), of manner (*as if, as though*), of comparison or degree (*as . . . as, so . . . as, than*), and of contrast (*whereas*). The italicized words in the following sentences are adverbial clauses.

I went *wherever I chose.* (adverbial clause of place and modifies *went*)
Before I planted the seeds, I soaked them in water. (adverbial clause of time and modifies *soaked*)
He will agree to the terms *if you do not press him too urgently.* (adverbial clause of condition and modifies *will agree*)
He moved nearer to the front *so that he might hear better.* (adverbial clause of purpose and modifies *moved*)
They were greatly disturbed *because there were signs of an approaching tornado.* (adverbial clause of cause or reason and modifies *were disturbed*)
I will do this for you *although I honestly do not believe you deserve it.* (adverbial clause of concession and modifies *will do*)
My roommate is taller *than I am.* (adverbial clause of comparison and modifies the adjective *taller*)
The man worked with such energy *that others could not keep up with him.* (adverbial clause of result and modifies the adjective *such*)
Cement posts last longer *than wooden ones do.* (adverbial clause of comparison and modifies the adverb *longer*)
He is not so energetic *as he used to be* (adverbial clause of comparison and modifies the adverb *so*)

1. Do not use adverbial clauses in sentences which grammatically require noun clauses.

WRONG: The reason for his pale complexion is *because he works indoors all the time.* (an adverbial clause used as a subjective complement)
RIGHT: The reason for his pale complexion is *that he works indoors all the time.* (a noun clause rightly used as a subjective complement)

WRONG: *Because you do not know the rules* does not exclude you from playing. (an adverbial clause wrongly used as the subject of *does exclude*)
RIGHT: The fact that *you do not know the rules* does not exclude you from playing. (a noun clause in apposition with *fact*, the subject of *does exclude*)
RIGHT: Your not knowing the rules does not exclude you from playing.
WRONG: A sortie is *when a plane makes a single trip to a target*. (an adverbial clause used as a subjective complement)
RIGHT: A sortie is a single trip made by a plane to a target.
WRONG: A biped is *where an animal has two legs*. (an adverbial clause used as a subjective complement)
RIGHT: A biped is an animal having two legs.
WRONG: In the society news I read *where Miss Mullins is engaged to be married*. (an adverbial clause used as the object of *read*)
RIGHT: In the society news I read *that Miss Mullins is engaged to be married*. (a noun clause, object of *read*)

2. Clumsy sentences often result from the use of an independent sentence element instead of a subordinate noun clause.

AWKWARD: *I cut my finger* is what accounts for my poor writing.
CLEAR: The fact that *I cut my finger* accounts for my poor writing.
CLEAR: A cut in my finger accounts for my poor writing.
AWKWARD: The greatest damage done by the falling tree was *it broke the glass in the sun parlor*. (an independent sentence)
CLEAR: The greatest damage done by the falling tree was *that it broke the glass in the sun parlor*. (a noun clause used as a subjective complement)
CLEAR: The greatest damage done by the falling tree was *to break the glass in the sun parlor*. (the noun clause reduced to an infinitive phrase, also a subjective complement)

3. All that you previously learned under Case must be applied in using the correct pronoun in noun and adjective clauses.

WRONG: *Who they called in the emergency*, I do not know. (a noun clause, object of *do know*, but *Who* should be *Whom* as the object of *called*)
RIGHT: *Whom they called in the emergency*, I do not know.
WRONG: There is the man *who they took to be me*. (adjective clause)
RIGHT: There is the man *whom they took to be me* (*whom*, the objective case, subject of the infinitive *to be*)
WRONG: This is the man *whom they suspect was passing worthless checks*. (adjective clause)
RIGHT: This is the man *who they suspect was passing worthless checks*. (*who* is the subject of *was passing*—the parenthetical *they suspect* has no grammatical bearing upon the sentence)

Review the text of the lesson on Case if you have any difficulty with the subjective and objective use of pronouns.

4. A very common error is the use of *but what* or *but that* for *that* to introduce clauses after verbs of doubting or expressions of uncertainty.

WRONG: I do not doubt *but that* (or *but what*) he resented the remark.
RIGHT: I do not doubt *that he resented the remark.* (a noun clause, the object of *do doubt*)
WRONG: I am not certain *but what* he paid the bill.
RIGHT: I am not certain *that* he paid the bill. (an adverbial clause, modifying the adjective *certain*)
RIGHT: I am uncertain about his having paid the bill.

NAME ....DATE ....SCORE ....

48. PROBLEMS WITH CLAUSES—I

Revise the sentences below to correct errors in the use of clauses. Make certain that every part of your revised sentence is grammatically sound.

EXAMPLE:
A "dud" is when a shell or a bomb does not explode.
A "dud" is a shell or a bomb which does not explode.

1. Near the scene of the attempted holdup, the police captured a man whom they believe was an accomplice in the affair.
   The police captured a man near the scene who they believe was an accomplice in the attempted holdup.

2. The Browns are moving to California is the reason why they are selling their household goods at auction.
   The Browns are selling their household goods at auction because they are moving to California.

3. A dromedary is when a camel has only one hump.
   A dromedary is a camel which has only one hump.

4. We do not question but what you intend to pay the bill as soon as you can.
   We do not question the fact that you intend to pay the bill as soon as you can.

5. The worst effect of the flood was it rendered hundreds of families homeless.
   The worst effect of the flood rendered hundreds of families homeless.

6. A filibuster is when an attempt is made by long speeches or other tactics of delay to block legislation.
A filibuster is made to block legislation by long speeches or other tactics of delay.

7. Who the director will choose to play the leading rôle, no one can guess.

8. My understanding is that a "pancake" is when the airplane makes a flat landing after it has levelled off just above the ground.
My understanding of a pancake is the flat landing of an airplane after it has levelled off just above the ground.

9. Paul was a boy who his teachers, honest and considerate though they were, could not understand.
Paul's teachers, honest and considerate though they were, could not understand him.

10. His reason for selling the business was because his health was failing.
His reason for selling the business was his failing health.

11. This article reveals Handel's "Messiah" was composed in just twenty-four days.
This article reveals the composing, in just thirty-four days, of Handel's "Messiah".

12. Because an individual graduates from high school does not mean that he will succeed in college.
Graduation from high school does not mean that an individual will succeed in college.

To obtain score, allow 8½ points for each sentence correctly revised.

NAME .... DATE .... SCORE ....

49. PROBLEMS WITH CLAUSES—II

Revise the sentences below to correct errors in the use of clauses. Make certain that every part of your revised sentence is grammatically sound.

EXAMPLE:
In the market reports I have noticed where the price of wheat is rising.
In the market reports I have noticed that the price of wheat is rising.

1. He is fond of elaborate gestures and flowery language is what marks him as an old-fashioned orator.

   His fondness for elaborate gestures and flowery language marks him as an old-fashioned orator.

2. It is the Duryea brothers whom this writer contends should be credited with the invention of the first gasoline-driven automobile.

   This writer contends that the Duryea brothers should be credited with the invention of the first gasoline-driven automobile.

3. India has an acute shortage of doctors is the reason for the public health problem in that country.

   The reason for India's public health problem is the country's acute shortage of doctors.

4. In typesetting, a "widow" is when an incomplete line appears at the top of a page.

   In typesetting, a widow is an incomplete line which appears at the top of a page.

5. In a recent news account, I have read where slave traffic still flourishes in the Arabian peninsula.

   I read in a recent news account that slave traffic still flourishes in the Arabian peninsula.

6. On the second or third ballot, when the "favorite sons" have been eliminated, is when the voting trend becomes decisive.

   The voting trend becomes decisive on the second or third ballot, when the "favorite sons" have been eliminated.

7. Mercury is a silvery fluid is the reason for its early designation as quicksilver.

   The reason for the early designation of Mercury as quick silver was its silver fluidity.

8. I learned from a feature article where the qualifying tests for a London cab driver are perhaps harder than for any other occupation in Britain.

   I learned from a feature article, that the qualifying tests are perhaps harder for a London cab driver, than for any other occupation in Britain.

9. He wanted to drive to California was his excuse for buying a new car.

   His excuse for buying a new car, was that he wanted to drive to California.

10. The reason why I dislike most modern furniture is because it looks as if it had been made from discarded orange crates.

    I dislike most modern furniture because it looks as if it had been made from discarded orange crates.

11. Radio furnishes an easy source of entertainment accounts for the neglect of reading in the typical home.

    Radio, which furnishes an easy source of entertainment, accounts for the neglect of reading in the typical home.

12. I do not doubt but what a knowledge of Latin would be useful to a doctor or a lawyer.

    I do not doubt that a knowledge of Latin would be useful to a doctor or a lawyer.

To obtain score, allow 8½ points for each sentence correctly revised.

WORDS MISUSED FROM SIMILARITY OF SOUND OR MEANING

Accept means "to take something offered"; *except*, as a verb, means "to leave out," "to exclude," "to omit."

> We will *accept* any reasonable bid.
> All persons over forty-five are *excepted* from military service.

Access means "admission to"; *excess* means "overabundance," "superfluity."

> Every employee had *access* to the president.
> There was such an *excess* of potatoes that prices were low.

Adapt means "to make suitable," "to adjust"; *adopt* means "to take by choice as one's own."

> He *adapted* himself to the new conditions.
> We shall *adopt* a new policy at our next meeting.
> They *adopted* a baby only six weeks old.

Advice is the noun; *advise* is the verb.

> He would not listen to *advice*.
> I *advise* you to come early.

Affect means "to influence," "to move," and also "to pretend," "to assume as one's own"; *effect* means "to cause," "to produce," "to procure," "to accomplish." As a noun, *effect* means "result," "outcome."

> The damp atmosphere *affected* his health.
> The blow *affected* his hearing.
> The emotional speech *affected* the audience.
> She *affected* a cultured accent.
> The medicine *effected* a cure.
> They hope to *effect* an understanding.
> The *effect* of the drug soon wore off.
> That combination of colors gave a peculiar *effect*.

Aggravate properly means "to make worse," "to increase in severity." It is only colloquially that it is used in the sense of "to irritate," "to annoy," "to disturb."

> His hasty suggestions only *aggravated* the tense situation.

All ready means "wholly or completely prepared"; *already* means "previously."

> We found the equipment *all ready*.
> It was *already* dark when we arrived.

All together signifies "collectively in a group"; *altogether* means "wholly," "completely," "entirely."

> Now let us pull *all together*.
> It is *altogether* improbable that he will acquiesce.

Angel is used in religious associations; *angle* is used in mathematics.

> An *angel* of the Lord descended unto him.
> These lines make an *angle* of forty-five degrees.

Altar is the noun; *alter* is the verb.

> The children knelt at the *altar*.
> Will you *alter* this suit for me?

Balance should not be used for *rest* or *remainder*.

> Take the *rest* (or *remainder*, not *balance*) of the supplies for yourself.

Born means "brought forth," "given birth to"; *borne* means "carried," "sustained."

> Lincoln was *born* in a log cabin.
> This courage is *born* of desperation.
> They have *borne* great tribulations.

Canvas is the noun; *canvass* is the verb.

> The awning was made of *canvas*.
> We shall *canvass* the entire town for contributions.

Capital refers to the city in which a government is situated; *capitol* refers to the building in which the government is carried on.

> Springfield is the *capital* of Illinois.
> Many state *capitols* have huge domes.

Coarse is the adjective; *course* is the noun.

> This *coarse* cloth will do for sun-parlor curtains.
> He pursued a hazardous *course* in his business dealings.

Complexioned, not *complected*, is the right word.

> Mr. Jones is a light-*complexioned* (not -*complected*) man.

A *complement* is that which fills out to a recognized or established amount or whole; a *compliment* is a courteous expression of appreciation or good will.

> You must now find the *complement* of this angle.
> She received many *compliments* on her singing.

Conscience is the noun; *conscious* is the adjective.

> The human being seems to be endowed with a *conscience* which distinguishes between right and wrong.

He remained *conscious* throughout the operation.

Contemptible refers to that which merits contempt; *contemptuous*, to that which exhibits contempt.

That was a *contemptible* thing to do.
He answered the suggestion with a *contemptuous* sneer.

Continual is applied to that which is repeated in close succession; *continuous*, to that which is unbroken in time, surface, or space.

The *continual* honking of the automobile horns annoyed him.
The pouring of the water over the dam made a *continuous* hum.
A circle is a *continuous* line all points of which are equally distant from the center.

Council refers to a body of persons gathered for consultation or governing procedures; *counsel* refers to advice given by another or a legal consultant who gives advice; *consul* refers to a representative of a nation in a foreign country.

The town *council* met every Thursday evening.
The adviser offered the boy good *counsel*.
He would not sign the confession before he saw his *counsel*.
Our *consul* at Liverpool is Mr. Hendricks.

Credible means "worthy of belief"; *creditable* means "deserving of praise," "meritorious"; *credulous* means "unsuspecting," "gullible."

You gave a very *credible* account of these peculiar happenings.
The star gave a *creditable* performance of the difficult part.
He was so *credulous* that he believed everything he heard.

A *desert* is a wild, waste region; a *dessert* is a pastry, pudding, or the like, usually served at the end of a meal.

Hot winds blew over the *desert*.
They served ice cream and cake as the *dessert*.

Disinterested means "impartial," "free from ulterior motive"; *uninterested* means "not taking an interest in."

That he acted with entirely *disinterested* purpose was finally believed.
Jack became increasingly *uninterested* in his work.

Dying means "expiring"; *dyeing* means "coloring."

Thousands were *dying* from starvation.
Dyeing cloth is a particular kind of work.

Each other is preferably restricted to an exchange between two; *one another* is used of an interchange between more than two.

Jane and Mary told *each other* many secrets.
Love ye *one another*.
The councilmen consulted *one another* before the vote was taken.

Eminent means "high in renown or esteem"; *imminent* means "threatening," "ominous."

> Robert E. Lee was an *eminent* soldier.
> Everyone believed that a war was *imminent*.

Expect means "to look forward to," "to hope." It refers to events in the future. Its use for *suppose* or *think* is colloquial.

> I *expect* a remittance by tomorrow morning.
> I *suppose* you were terribly frightened.

Extra should not be used for *unusually*.

> There was an *extra* charge for dancing.
> She was an *unusually* bright girl.

Farther is used of physical or measurable distance; *further* is used of degree or quantity.

> Ours is the *farther* house. (adjective)
> Let us have no *further* discussion about this matter. (adjective)
> I can walk *farther* than you can. (adverb)
> Do you wish to discuss this matter *further*? (adverb)

Fewer is used of number; *less* is used of quantity, amount, or degree.

> *Fewer* cars are on the road after midnight.
> *Less* money is in circulation during a depression.

Formerly refers to time in the past; *formally* refers to conventional or polite ceremony.

> They *formerly* lived here.
> We had never been *formally* introduced.

Forth is the adverb; *fourth* is the adjective and noun.

> He went *forth* to battle.
> The *fourth* juror was not convinced.
> A *fourth* of his income was given to charities.

Healthy means "possessing health"; *healthful* means "conferring or promoting health."

> He is a very *healthy* child.
> Colorado has an unusually *healthful* climate.

Human is applied to what is characteristic of man; *humane* is applied to the kindly or sympathetic manifestations of man's nature.

> *Human* nature remains surprisingly unchangeable.
> There are societies that insure *humane* treatment to animals.

Imply means "to suggest"; *infer* means "to draw a conclusion."

You *imply* that I have not tried hard enough.
I *infer* that you do not wish to consider my proposal.

That is *ingenious* which exhibits a high degree of skill or originality; that is *ingenuous* which is simple or naïve.

Edison was an *ingenious* man.
The old man was as *ingenuous* as a child.

Instance means "example"; *instant* means "a moment," "an infinitesimal point in time."

An *instance* of his carelessness was his not acknowledging my letter.
It all happened in an *instant*.

Its is the third person, neuter, possessive personal pronoun. No personal pronoun takes an apostrophe to denote possession. *It's* is a contraction of *it is*.

The car had slackened *its* speed.
The dog had a thorn in *its* foot.
It's time to go.
I know *it's* asking a great deal of you.

Last is applied to that which is final, especially in an order or series; *latest* is applied to that which is nearest in order of time.

This is the *last* book Thomas Wolfe wrote.
This is the *latest* edition of the paper.

Later is applied to that which comes after in time; *latter* is applied to the second of two or, more loosely, to the closing part of a whole.

A *later* dispatch confirmed the report.
The *latter* part of the book became more interesting.

Learn means "to acquire knowledge"; *teach* means "to impart knowledge."

A bright child soon *learns* to read.
He will *teach* you how to repair radios.

Likely refers to that which is possible or probable; *liable* is used of that which makes one responsible in law or of that which holds the possibility of undesired result.

You will *likely* meet him down town.
You may be *liable* for damages if that walk is not repaired.
One is *liable* to slip on the ice.

Lose means "to become separated from unintentionally"; *loose* means "to free," "to untie," and as an adjective "to be free," "to be unfastened."

Do not *lose* these keys.
Loose the string a little so that the blood will circulate.
My shoestring is *loose*.

Luxuriant means "profuse in growth"; *luxurious* means "exhibiting or ministering to luxury."

> The *luxuriant* foliage in the tropics aided snipers.
> He was a man of *luxurious* tastes.
> The meal was *luxurious* enough to please a gourmet.

Moral refers to recognized standards of conduct or character; *morale* is the spirit or tone of a group.

> His sermons were likely to be little *moral* talks.
> A nation must keep up its *morale* in time of war.

Notorious is used of what is *famous* in an unfavorable way.

> Captain Kidd was a *notorious* pirate.
> Confucius was a *famous* philosopher.

Observance is the act of heeding or commemorating that which is prescribed by duty or custom; *observation* is the act of noting or marking carefully.

> The *observance* of Washington's birthday is nation-wide.
> Patient *observation* is necessary to a scientist.

Persecute means "to treat harshly or cruelly, usually without justifiable cause"; *prosecute* means "to punish by due legal processes."

> Dictators usually *persecute* the weak.
> He was *prosecuted* for running a gambling house.

Personal refers to that which is one's own; *personnel* designates a body or group of persons engaged in a common undertaking or business.

> This is my *personal* property.
> The entire *personnel* of the company maintained a high morale.

That is *practical* which produces sound or efficient results; that is *practicable* which may be done or accomplished but may or may not be profitable.

> This *practical* invention will make him wealthy.
> Putting tunnels under rivers did not at first seem *practicable*.

Principle is a rule or standard. *Principal*, as a noun, is a sum of money which draws interest, or a school official; as an adjective, it means "chief," "outstanding," "foremost."

> This is a fundamental *principle* in mechanics.
> He is a man of *principle*.
> I will pay both the *principal* and the interest.
> Our *principal* gave out the school prizes.
> The *principal* reason for his failing is carelessness.

Prophecy is the noun; *prophesy* is the verb.

This *prophecy* finally came true.
He likes to *prophesy* dreadful things that may happen.

Quiet is an adjective; *quite* is an adverb.

The streets were *quiet* after midnight.
You are *quite* mistaken, I can assure you.

Respectfully is said of that which is done with consideration or courtesy; *respectively* refers to each in the order named.

He bowed *respectfully* to the old lady.
Harry and James are five and three years old *respectively*.

Do not use *locate* for *settle* or *become situated in*.

He hopes to *settle* (not *locate*) in Denver.

Site means "place," "location"; *cite* means "to give as a reference," "to quote."

This *site* will be laid out for suburban homes.
He *cited* a similar case in law.

Stationary means "fixed," "immovable"; *stationery* means "writing materials for correspondence."

The cellar has *stationary* wash tubs.
His initials are engraved on his *stationery*.

Suit is an outfit of clothes or a legal process; *suite* is a combination of rooms for a definite purpose or furniture for a specified room.

His *suit* was too big for him.
He brought *suit* against his neighbor.
All first-class hotels have a bridal *suite*.
They bought a dining-room *suite*.

Care must be exercised in the use of *there*, an adverb and expletive, and *their*, the third person, plural possessive pronoun.

Plant the nasturtiums *there*. (adverb of place)
There was a dispute among the members. (expletive)
Their house is larger than ours. (possessive pronoun)

The preposition *to* must not be used for the adverb *too*. The adverb *too* means (1) "very," "extremely," "exceedingly," "more than enough"; (2) "also," "likewise," "in addition."

He went *to* the store. (preposition)

This hat is *too* big. (adverb)
He, *too*, had secret ambitions. (adverb)

Weather is a noun; *whether* is a conjunction.

The *weather* has been unusually pleasant.
I do not know *whether* we shall have the party or **not**.

NAME .... DATE .... SCORE ....

50. WORDS MISUSED FROM SIMILARITY OF SOUND OR MEANING—I

From the forms given in parenthesis choose the correct word for each sentence and write it in the space at the left.

EXAMPLE:

suite   Mrs. Jones purchased a new dining room (suit, suite).

....   1. From 1861 until 1865, William Dean Howells served as the American (consul, council, counsel) at Venice.

....   2. You may have your monogram printed on this (stationery, stationary) for a slight additional charge.

....   3. The Bedouins are a nomadic people living on the (desert, dessert) in Africa or Asia.

....   4. He was kept awake by the (continual, continuous) barking of dogs in the neighborhood.

....   5. I cannot believe that anyone would tell such a (contemptuous, contemptible) lie.

....   6. When he was a young man, Franklin (located, settled) in Philadelphia.

....   7. The seismograph is an (ingenious, ingenuous) device for recording the intensity and approximate location of earthquakes.

....   8. The excursion vessel was making her (last, latest) trip of the summer season.

....   9. George Westinghouse was an (eminent, imminent) American inventor.

....   10. The roof lines converge to form an (angel, angle) of ninety degrees.

....   11. Some people are (credible, creditable, credulous) enough to pay fabulous prices for "paste diamonds" or synthetic jewelry.

....   12. By the time they reached the park, the picnic tables were (all ready, already) taken.

....   13. Nearly a million Americans, it is said, anxiously awaited the fulfillment of William Miller's (prophecy, prophesy) that the world would end on October 22, 1844.

....   14. The mayor recommended that (farther, further) study be made of the question of a municipal electric plant.

....   15. Horace Greeley's (advice, advise)—"Go West, young man"—became a famous slogan.

....   16. Her painful burns will (learn, teach) her to be more cautious about sun bathing.

173

.... 17. After studying a case, a lawyer is prepared to (cite, site) opinions handed down by the courts in similar instances.
.... 18. The blackberries are (liable, likely) to be plentiful this season.
.... 19. Scientists have long debated whether (human, humane) life can exist on Mars.
.... 20. As a result of the Dutch elm disease countless trees were (dyeing, dying).
.... 21. At the beginning of the war, the atom bomb would not have been deemed a (practicable, practical) weapon.
.... 22. Whaling was once the (principal, principle) industry of many New England towns.
.... 23. Jim told the salesman that he wished to buy a double-breasted blue (suit, suite).
.... 24. Beneath the dome of the United States (Capital, Capitol) at Washington is a huge rotunda with a copper ceiling.
.... 25. The (loose, lose) shutter kept banging against the house with an annoying regularity.

To obtain score, multiply number of errors by 4 and subtract total from 100.

NAME ....DATE ....SCORE ....

51. WORDS MISUSED FROM SIMILARITY OF SOUND OR MEANING—II

From the forms given in parenthesis choose the correct word for each sentence and write it in the space at the left.

EXAMPLE:

affects The presence of chlorine (affects, effects) the taste of drinking water.

.... 1. Architects always recommend that a house be (adapted, adopted) to its site.

.... 2. The Open Door policy, as formulated in 1900, meant that the United States and Britain would have free (access, excess) to Chinese markets.

.... 3. The last question on the application blank reads: "What salary are you willing to (except, accept)?"

.... 4. Ottawa, a city in southeastern Ontario, is the (capital, capitol) of Canada.

.... 5. The mountains, grey-blue masses against the horizon, were (farther, further) away than we had at first supposed.

.... 6. The restaurant, which specializes in sea foods, has (adapted, adopted) as its slogan the phrase, "If it swims, I have it."

.... 7. The chairman of the board said that unless new financing could be arranged, bankruptcy of the firm was (eminent, imminent).

.... 8. Bill (affected, effected) complete innocence when his father asked about the crumpled fender.

.... 9. President Lincoln had (born, borne) the heavy responsibilities of his office with patience and firmness.

.... 10. One of the memorable characters in *Green Pastures* is the (angel, angle) Gabriel, who yearns to blow his horn.

.... 11. The boy listened (respectfully, respectively) to his grandfather's instructions on trout fishing.

.... 12. The farmers of this area often helped (each other, one another) at threshing time.

.... 13. Thieves who ransacked the apartment took clothing, jewelry, and other (personal, personnel) effects.

.... 14. The orchestra leader was a stocky, (dark-complected, dark-complexioned) man of about forty.

.... 15. Sugar is the (principal, principle) export of the island of Cuba.

.... 16. Which route do you (advice, advise) us to take?
.... 17. A Chicago woman has filed (suit, suite) against her landlord because, she charges, he shut off the gas and took out the kitchen sink.
.... 18. Because of its altitude, Mexico City has a (healthy, healthful) climate.
.... 19. In the Olympic trials for the 100-meter dash, a former Penn State star made the most (credible, creditable, credulous) showing.
.... 20. The firm was (persecuted, prosecuted) for making false and extravagant claims about its product.
.... 21. The Puritans are chiefly remembered for their intense convictions on matters of (moral, morale) conduct.
.... 22. A man does not think clearly when he (looses, loses) his temper.
.... 23. The New York State Barge Canal, which links the Hudson with Lake Erie, was (formally, formerly) known as the Erie Canal.
.... 24. I was not (all together, altogether) sure that I had returned the book to the library.
.... 25. A timid and sensitive boy, he was sometimes (persecuted, prosecuted) by his schoolmates.

To obtain score, multiply number of errors by 4 and subtract total from 100.

52. WORDS MISUSED FROM SIMILARITY OF SOUND OR MEANING—III

From the forms given in parenthesis choose the correct word for each sentence and write it in the space at the left.

EXAMPLE:

its   Put everything back in (its, it's) proper place.

1. The market reports are published in a (later, latter) edition of the newspaper.
2. In the final stages of the trial the (consul, counsel) for the defense tried to sway the emotions of the jury.
3. The waitress asked whether we wished to order a (desert, dessert).
4. A (healthful, healthy) cocker spaniel has clear, alert eyes and a glossy coat.
5. Space in the city housing development is not available to families with incomes in (access, excess) of two hundred dollars per month.
6. It does not seem (credible, creditable, credulous) that a student would ask to have his grade lowered.
7. Business leaders now (prophecy, prophesy) that the current level of activity will continue well into next spring.
8. Dr. Martin will be (formally, formerly) installed as president of the college at a ceremony to be held in April.
9. The kindly old friar hoped that the marriage of Romeo and Juliet would (affect, effect) a reconciliation between the two warring families.
10. In addition to the feature show, patrons will see a Donald Duck cartoon and the (last, latest) newsreels.
11. The manufacture of optical instruments requires an experienced, highly skilled (personal, personnel).
12. Only a most (ingenious, ingenuous) person would be deceived by a hoax like this one.
13. The (continual, continuous) roar of the giant presses had an almost hypnotic effect.
14. In the senior yearbook Arthur was listed as the student most (liable, likely) to succeed.
15. The S.P.C.A. has been active in securing legislation which will bring about (human, humane) treatment of animals.

.... 16. In the darkest hours of the war the (moral, morale) of the British people was superb.
.... 17. It was easier to take the lock apart than to put it (all together, altogether) again.
.... 18. The textile industry is conducting research to discover new methods of weaving and (dyeing, dying) cloth.
.... 19. In first and second place in the National League were Brooklyn and St. Louis (respectfully, respectively).
.... 20. There are (fewer, less) trees growing on the northern slopes of the hill.
.... 21. With a (contemptible, contemptuous) glance at my battered old car, the mechanic lifted the hood and set to work.
.... 22. Seen from the windows of a train, the trees, telephone poles, and other (stationary, stationery) objects appear to be moving at a prodigious speed.
.... 23. Grace and Harry first met (each other, one another) at a freshman "mixer" held during the opening week of college.
.... 24. Two global wars in the first half of this century have (learned, taught) us the value of military preparedness.
.... 25. The excavations show that this was once the (cite, site) of an Indian village.

To obtain score, multiply number of errors by 4 and subtract total from 100.

NAME .... DATE .... SCORE ....

53. WORDS MISUSED FROM SIMILARITY OF SOUND OR MEANING—IV

From the forms given in parenthesis choose the correct word for each sentence and write it in the space at the left.

EXAMPLE:

their   The men removed (their, there) hats during the singing of the national anthem.

1. (Their, There) were three persons on the front seat of the car.
2. Many American firms, of (coarse, course), have branch factories in Canada.
3. Mr. Jones, (disinterested, uninterested) in his wife's account of her shopping tour, dozed fitfully in his chair.
4. Next week the Emporium will celebrate (its, it's) fiftieth anniversary with a store-wide sale.
5. The post office will be closed on Thursday in (observance, observation) of Thanksgiving Day.
6. The (complement, compliment) of the ship is one hundred and fifty men.
7. The baseball park was enclosed by an (extra, unusually) high wooden fence.
8. In his talk with the newsmen, the President clearly (implied, inferred) that he would veto the measure.
9. Veterans attending the university were (accepted, excepted) from the requirements in physical education.
10. The recent rains have made the river (to, too) muddy for swimming.
11. The unending chatter of the girls (aggravated, irritated) him.
12. Indian Summer is a period of balmy weather which comes (quiet, quite) late in the fall.
13. Mr. Ellis, the (principal, principle) of the high school, coaches the track team.
14. Of the two forms of popular entertainment, the moving picture and the radio, the (later, latter) is perhaps the more significant.
15. Since his car is not here, I (expect, suppose) that he has gone to the office.
16. Recent developments in (weather, whether) forecasting have made long-distance flying safer.
17. (It's, Its) still too early in the season to plant tomatoes.

179

.... 18. The newpaper headlines told of the destructive (affect, effect) of a tornado which swept across five states.
.... 19. Bartlett pears are known for (their, there) delicious flavor.
.... 20. Henry Clay was a (famous, notorious) American statesman.
.... 21. Volunteer workers will (canvas, canvass) the city for pledges to the hospital funds.
.... 22. Almost reverently, the salesman showed us the interior of the car, with its shiny instrument panel and its (luxuriant, luxurious) upholstery.
.... 23. Charles Dickens was (born, borne) at Portsea on February 7, 1812.
.... 24. When the notes of the wedding march sounded, the procession moved toward the (altar, alter).
.... 25. Without hesitating for an (instance, instant), the rescuer leaped into the swirling waters of the creek.

To obtain score, multiply number of errors by 4 and subtract total from 100.

NAME .... DATE .... SCORE ....

54. WORDS MISUSED FROM SIMILARITY OF SOUND OR MEANING—V

From the forms given in parenthesis choose the correct word for each sentence and write it in the space at the left.

EXAMPLE:

canvas   The tent is made of waterproof (canvas, canvass).

1. The (coarse, course), wet sand soothed their aching feet.
2. The train does not leave until eleven o'clock, but you are permitted to go aboard whenever you wish (to, too).
3. A slight change of wording will sometimes (altar, alter) the meaning of a whole sentence.
4. Since he had acted with complete honesty, his (conscience, conscious) was clear.
5. With a score of ninety-nine points, he took (forth, fourth) place in the district scholarship test.
6. Freedom of speech is a basic (principal, principle) of democracy.
7. At its meeting Monday evening, the city (council, counsel) discussed the budget for the next fiscal year.
8. This bedroom (suit, suite) of Honduras mahogany is priced at two hundred and thirty-nine dollars.
9. You, (to, too), can reduce your weight by following this easy, simple method.
10. Nervous tension or anxiety can seriously (affect, effect) one's health.
11. We had intended to spend a (quiet, quite) evening at home.
12. An (instance, instant) of Lincoln's kindness is his famous letter to Mrs. Bixby.
13. The police records show that the man is a (famous, notorious) thief.
14. Do you know (weather, whether) my laundry has been delivered?
15. (Its, It's) now exactly ten minutes after twelve.
16. During the preparation of the book, he had (access, excess) to important documents in the Library of Congress.
17. The jury should weigh the evidence in the case from a thoroughly (disinterested, uninterested) point of view.

.... 18. The homesickness of the young campers was (aggravated, irritated) by the gloomy weather.
.... 19. The forecast promises good (weather, whether) for the Labor Day week end.
.... 20. We were (conscience, conscious) of the fact that the train had slackened its speed.
.... 21. The Chinese and the Japanese revere (their, there) ancestors.
.... 22. Please fill out this blank (to, too).
.... 23. His pronunciation of certain words led us to (imply, infer) that he was an Englishman.
.... 24. Clad in his great-grandfather's suit of armor, Don Quixote sets (forth, fourth) on his adventures as a knight-errant.
.... 25. The picture, which was filmed in England, had (its, it's) first American showing in Boston.

To obtain score, multiply number of errors by 4 and subtract total from 100.

SECTION III
Punctuation and Mechanics

PUNCTUATION

The purpose of punctuation is to make writing perfectly clear to the reader. The symbols are arbitrary in form but relatively absolute in use. Punctuation is a mechanical aid to clearness. After spelling, it is the most formalized element in writing. With a great deal of punctuation there is no choice: certain symbols, from long-established practice and by common consent, perform universally accepted functions in sentences.

The basic facts about punctuation marks can be stated concisely, provided refinements and exceptions are ignored. Some symbols (. ? !) close a completed unit of thought; others (; : and sometimes —) close a completed unit of thought but join this unit with a related unit or units; still others (" ", — —, ( ), [ ]) have the primary function of enclosing words, phrases, or clauses; finally, the comma (,) indicates changes or pauses in the thought, or groups words into minor units within the sentence.

I. End Punctuation

1. **The Period.** A period is used at the end of a sentence which makes a statement or gives a mild command.

> The puppy chewed up Grandfather's slipper.
> That tree was planted by my uncle.
> Take as many as you want.
> Please cut me a slice of cake.

2. **The Question Mark.** A question mark is used at the end of a sentence which asks a direct question.

> Are you coming home early?
> May I have another sheet of paper?
> When will Aunt Susan arrive?
> There will be enough beds for everybody?

That this last sentence is intended as a question is indicated only by its punctuation. The sentence has the form of a statement and, if punctuated with a period, would be a statement. However, the question mark shows that the meaning is, Will there be enough beds for everybody?

The difficulty in using the question mark arises from a confusion between direct and indirect questions. Indirect questions are noun clauses in sentences that make statements. Consequently, sentences embodying indirect questions are closed by periods.

DIRECT QUESTION: When will the train arrive?
INDIRECT QUESTION: He inquired when the train would arrive.
DIRECT QUESTION: May we pick a few apples?
INDIRECT QUESTION: The children ask whether they may pick a few apples.

3. The Exclamation Point. An exclamation point is used at the end of a sentence which expresses strong emotion or gives a forceful command.

I won't listen to such talk!
He's fallen overboard!
Get off that roof!
Watch those sharp curves!

4. The same punctuation is used after an elliptical statement, question, or word expressing strong emotion as would be used in the completed sentence.

Are you coming to our dance?
Certainly. (Certainly I am coming to your dance.)
He has sold his house.
To whom? (To whom has he sold his house?)
What is that peculiar odor?
Smoke! (That is smoke!)

II. Strong Internal Punctuation

5. The Semicolon. The semicolon is used to join independent clauses that are closely related in thought, but not joined by one of the co-ordinating conjunctions.

Lincoln was a gaunt man; his clothes hung loosely on his lean, angular frame.
Shakespeare is England's greatest dramatic poet; Milton is its greatest epic poet.

The semicolon is used with a co-ordinating conjunction if the independent clauses themselves contain commas.

This bill, if it is passed, will benefit the small merchant; but a lobby, very powerful and well organized, will oppose it.

A comma is frequently misused for a semicolon before certain words. These words do have a kind of transitional force, but they are not conjunctions. They are adverbs—sometimes even called "conjunctive" or "linking" adverbs—but adverbs do not join independent clauses. You should note the following words carefully and invariably place a semicolon before them when they introduce succeeding independent clauses: (time) now, then, still, later, finally, meantime, meanwhile, sometimes; (place) here, there; (additive) besides, also, indeed, furthermore, moreover; (adversative) however, otherwise, else, yet, nevertheless; (result) accordingly, consequently; (reason) hence, therefore, thus; (possibility) maybe, perhaps, possibly; (certainty) surely, certainly.

The semicolon is also used to separate the members of a series which contain commas within themselves.

> The ticket called for stop-overs at Columbus, Ohio; Des Moines, Iowa; and Denver, Colorado.

6. The Colon. The colon is an introductory mark of punctuation which equalizes or balances what follows it with what precedes it. It may introduce an independent clause which summarizes or particularizes the thought in the preceding clause, or it may introduce a series of words, phrases, or clauses that enumerate or specify what has been stated generally in the preceding clause.

> There is one essential qualification for a bank teller: he must be honest.
> The constitution of the club provided for these committees: finance, publicity, membership, and entertainment.
> There were three kinds of work open to beginners: in the factory, in the laboratory, or in the sales department.
> The president gave his reasons for opposing Mr. Jones's appointment: that he was too young, that he was inexperienced, that he was not potentially a good salesman.

Sometimes there is confusion as to where to place the colon. It should be placed after such expressions as "the following," "as follows"; it should precede such expressions as "for example," "namely," "specifically," and the like.

> The absent members were the following: Tompkins, Martin, and Smalley.
> Arrange the pictures on the east wall as follows: *The Horse Fair, The Blue Boy,* and *The Boy with a Rabbit.*
> There was only one solution to his financial difficulties: namely, to sell the property at a loss.
> A number of points can be truthfully stated in his favor: for example, he is unquestionably honest.

A further note of caution about the placing of the colon should be given: the first clause must be completed before the colon is used. A colon should not separate a verb from its object nor a linking verb from the subjective complement.

> WRONG: To make this cake you need: sugar, eggs, flour, milk, and baking powder.
> RIGHT: To make this cake you need sugar, eggs, flour, milk, and baking powder.
> RIGHT: To make this cake you need the following ingredients: sugar, eggs, flour, milk, and baking powder.
> WRONG: The subjects he was studying were: history, Spanish, economics, and accounting.
> RIGHT: The subjects he was studying were history, Spanish, economics, and accounting.
> RIGHT: The subjects he was studying were these: history, Spanish, economics, and accounting.

The colon is also used before long or formal quotations. In this function it replaces the more usual comma, which regularly introduces the short, informal direct quotations of conversation and even short formal quotations.

RIGHT: Mary replied, "I know you're right."
RIGHT: Heywood Broun said, "Too great a gulf has been placed between learning and laughter."
RIGHT: I shall now read the minutes of the last meeting: "At 7:30 P.M. on October 24th the meeting was called to order by the president. After the roll call the first matter of business was . . ."
RIGHT: Hamlet gave this advice to the players: "Speak the speech, I pray you, as I pronounc'd it to you, trippingly on the tongue; but if you mouth it, as many of your players do, I had as lief the town-crier had spoke my lines."

7. The Dash. The dash is used to indicate a sudden change or break in the thought of a sentence, or to introduce a summarizing or emphatic word or group of words.

I'll run upstairs and change my—there's the doorbell.
He said that he was out of work, that he was hungry, that he had been ill—the usual hard-luck excuses of the professional beggar.
All this tremendous effort has come to exactly—nothing!

You will note that the reader's attention is likely to be called emphatically to the word or words that follow the dash.

There is one thing that I admire above all others in a person—frankness.
Lincoln said that he owed whatever good there was in his life to one person—his mother.

The dash may be used instead of the colon before such expressions as *namely, that is, for example, for instance,* and the like.

He said that life had proved for him the meaning of the familiar proverb—namely, that old friends are best.
There are many things I enjoy in the country—for instance, its quietness.

The dash is, after the comma, the most misused mark of punctuation. Writers seem to feel that it can be substituted rather vaguely or loosely for other marks of punctuation, especially if they do not know precisely what punctuation should be used. The dash has its own distinct functions as a mark of punctuation. Since these functions are more subtle than the formalized uses of most other marks of punctuation, the dash should accordingly be used with discrimination and restraint.

III. Enclosing Punctuation

8. Quotation Marks. Quotation marks are used to set off the exact words of a quoted speech, or words that are to be distinguished from the rest of the context.

She said, "I am through with this book."
The word "embarrassed" is frequently misspelled.
By his own statement King Lear was a man "more sinned against than sinning."

The quotation marks indicate the beginning and the end of the speech, whether it be one sentence or many sentences. If the quoted matter extends over two or more paragraphs, quotation marks are put at the beginning of each paragraph but only at the end of the last one.

The words indicating the speaker are set off by a comma or commas unless other marks are required by the sentence. Observe the following examples closely.

> Mary replied, "My plan is very similar to yours."
> "This train doesn't go to Omaha," the conductor said.
> "Our project," Robert continued, "will require little money."
> "I have tried everything," the man complained. "I see no solution to the problem."
> "Let me try once more," he pleaded; "then I will quit."
> "Are you listening to what I say?" she asked.
> "Help! Help!" the woman screamed.

Note that the question mark comes outside the quotation marks if the sentence as a whole and not the quotation is the question.

> Did Harry say, "I am not interested in the class election"?
> Where can I find the quotation, "It is a heretic that makes the fire, Not she which burns in't"?

A quotation within a quotation is enclosed in single quotation marks.

> "Then the policeman glowered at me," Mabel continued, "and said, 'You can't go through here.'"
> "You have misspelled the word 'recommend' for the third time," the teacher said.

In formal prose, quotation marks are often used to enclose slang expressions, the jargon of a class, or highly technical terms.

> That boy is positively "goofy."
> In gangsterdom to "take one for a ride" has sinister implications.
> This method of refining petroleum is known as "heat-cracking."

9. Parentheses. Parentheses are used to enclose formal additions to a sentence or to enclose material loosely related to the thought of the sentence.

> Mr. James K. Simpson (the firm was originally Simpson and Bickford) became president of the new company.
> Willie Jones (that child has the appetite of an elephant) asked for three pieces of cake.

10. Brackets. Brackets are used to indicate the addition of editorial comment to quoted matter.

> "There are several reasons given for his [Shakespeare's] departure from Stratford."
> "James II [the author means James I] was called 'the wisest fool in Christendom.'"

11. Dashes. Dashes are used to enclose parenthetical sentence-elements that are in the nature of an abrupt addition to the thought or an explanation of it.

> That strange noise—I shudder to think of it—came from the direction of the closet.
> Two mechanically inclined American boys—I refer to the Wright brothers—invented the airplane.

Dashes are also used to enclose words in apposition, especially where attention is directed to the appositives, or where they are loosely attached to the thought of the sentence.

> Strangely enough, two men with similar names—Ben Jonson and Samuel Johnson—were both dictators in the field of English letters.
> The persons responsible for safety—the owner, the contractor, and the foreman on the job—were ordered by the police to place red flares around the excavation.
> This statement—a quotation from Washington—was wrongly used as an argument for isolation.
> This novel—a choice of the Book-of-the-Month Club, by the way—has sold over a quarter of a million copies.

Commas, dashes, and parentheses are all used to set off parenthetical and appositive elements in sentences. Their uses, however, are reasonably distinct. Commas set off closely connected, usually short, parenthetical or appositive additions to the sentence; dashes enclose loosely inserted parenthetical elements or emphatic appositives; parentheses are used when the matter added to the sentence is formally recognized as parenthetical in nature.

IV. WEAK INTERNAL PUNCTUATION

The comma is the weakest mark of punctuation; it is also the most frequently used. These two facts, no doubt, account for the frequency in its misuse.

It will be best for you to follow conservative practice in learning the many and diversified uses of the comma; if you wish later to punctuate in accordance with the modern tendency to omit certain commas once considered essential, you will at least know the established and accepted standard from which you are digressing.

Our arrangement of the rules governing the uses of the comma employs three general headings: The Main Uses of the Comma, The Conventional Uses of the Comma, and The Wrong Uses of the Comma. A careful study of the principles set forth here, together with the accompanying illustrations, should help to give you a firmer understanding of some of the most essential requirements of punctuation.

12. **The Main Uses of the Comma.** The following rules state the principal uses of the comma in formally written English.

a. A comma is used between independent clauses joined by a co-ordinating conjunction (*and, but, or, nor*).

> For years very little attention was paid to conservation, and now the soil is badly eroded.

You have just missed one bus, but another will be along in a few minutes.
There must be an adequate supply of basic products, or the cost of living will inevitably rise.

If the clauses are short or closely related in thought, the comma need not be used.

He heard that report and so did I.
He tried but he failed.
Hurry or the bus will leave.

b. A comma is used to set off an introductory adverb clause or phrase if the clause or phrase is long or loosely related in thought to the main clause.

Although he was a man of considerable wealth, he was not happy.
When all the preliminaries had been disposed of, the meeting turned to important business.
Toward the close of his eventful career as teacher and editor, he decided to write his autobiography.

If the clause or phrase is short or closely connected in thought with the main clause, the comma may be omitted.

When it rains I take the bus.
Since he did not need the car he sold it.
During the summer we spend much of our time at the lake.

c. Commas are used to set off absolute or parenthetical elements in sentences.

An absolute phrase (noun or pronoun plus a participle) has no direct grammatical relationship to the rest of the sentence.

The weather clearing, they continued on their journey.
Tom finished the game, the regular player having been injured.

Parenthetical elements include such typical sentence modifiers as *certainly, accordingly, indeed, perhaps, yes, no, in fact, on the contrary, at best, on the whole, to tell the truth, I suppose, I presume, I must admit.*

Yes, Mr. Brown is home.
We shall, accordingly, ship your goods on the date specified in your letter.
This is, in effect, a complete reversal of your previous attitude.
In general, men take more interest in politics than women do.
He could not, as a matter of principle, agree to such a proposal.
His manner, I thought, was very peculiar.

d. Commas are used to set off non-restrictive words, phrases, and clauses. A non-restrictive modifier is one that is not necessary to a basic understanding of the sentence; it gives related but not essential information.

Excited, she rushed to the telephone. (non-restrictive participle)
Penelope, waiting for years for the return of Ulysses, is often taken as an example of the faithful wife. (non-restrictive participial phrase)
The one opening the gate is my nephew. (restrictive participial phrase)

Thomas Jefferson, who was the third president, stated many of the basic principles of democracy. (non-restrictive adjective clause)
A man who is president of the United States has almost superhuman responsibilities. (restrictive adjective clause)
James was not popular at college, although he tried to be friendly with everyone. (non-restrictive adverb clause)
I shall not leave this office until I have written the letters. (restrictive adverb clause)

Note how the comma (or the lack of it) can change the meaning of sentences identical in wording.

He liked the songs, which had a Russian somberness about them.
He liked the songs which had a Russian somberness about them.
He searched all the graveyards, where old inscriptions might be found.
He searched all the graveyards where old inscriptions might be found.

e. Commas are used to set off non-restrictive appositives.

Mr. Teller, a member of council, opposed the measure.
Fra Lippo Lippi, a Florentine painter, is described in one of Browning's poems.

However, if the apposition is part of the name or restrictive in identifying the preceding word, it is not set off by commas.

Mary Queen of Scots was executed in 1587.
My brother John lives in Boston.
The poet Shelley died in Italy.
The word *disappointed* is frequently misspelled. (Either quotation marks or italics would be correct punctuation here.)

The comma should precede *such as, especially,* and *including* when these terms are used to introduce an example or enumeration.

The advertised price of the tour does not cover some personal expenses, such as laundry, entertainment, and tips.
I like fruit, especially oranges.
In our freshman composition course we studied various forms of writing, including the essay and the short story.

When *such as* is used with a restrictive application, the comma is omitted.

Magazines such as these should be consigned to the rubbish heap.

f. Commas are used to separate members of a series (words, phrases, or clauses).

This is an interesting, instructive, and inspiring book.
He was charged with misrepresentation of facts, with illegal use of the mails, and with intention to defraud.
We want a clerk who is pleasing in appearance, who is appealing in personality, and who is ambitious to advance.

The standard practice, as shown in the preceding examples, is to use a comma before the co-ordinating conjunction. Note that a misunderstanding may arise if the comma is omitted at this point.

> The catalogue listed tan, brown, blue and grey cloths.

g. Commas are used to separate two or more co-ordinate adjectives limiting the same noun.

> a clear, resonant voice
> an abandoned, desolate, eerie mansion

If the adjectives are not co-ordinate, the comma is not used.

> a large brick house
> a jolly fat man
> a battered old felt hat

To test whether the adjectives are co-ordinate, insert the word *and* between them. If a satisfactory reading is obtained, the adjectives are probably co-ordinate.

> a clear and resonant voice (co-ordinate adjectives)
> a large and brick house (adjectives not co-ordinate—*large* modifies *brick house*)

h. Commas are used to set off sentence elements which are out of their normal order.

> The cat, quiet and watchful, sat at the mouse-hole. (adjectives following the noun they modify)
> That he had done everything humanly possible, no one could doubt. (clause out of its natural order)

i. Commas are used to set off contrasted sentence elements.

> Jack, not Tom, won the prize.
> Not books, but experience, is the best teacher.

j. Commas are used whenever necessary to prevent misreading of the sentence.

> In spite of all that, man does gradually progress.
> I bought some fertilizer, for the soil of the garden had been depleted.
> By the ordinance against shooting, the birds were protected.
> The wind blew down the trees, and the houses were unroofed.
> To Mary, Jane revealed the secret of her success.
> Underneath, the car was already burning.

Commas are often necessary to prevent confusion when words are omitted from the sentence.

> To win gracefully requires a sense of consideration; to lose gracefully a sense of humor (meaning distorted)

To win gracefully requires a sense of consideration; to lose gracefully, a sense of humor. (meaning made clear)

13. **The Conventional Uses of the Comma.** Conformity to certain conventional uses of the comma is necessary to correct writing.

a. Commas are used to set off words of direct address (vocatives).

Jack, you have forgotten to sign this paper.
You have, fellow citizens, an unparalleled opportunity.

b. Commas are used to set off mild interjections.

Goodness, I am so sleepy.
Well, what do we do next?

c. Commas are used to set off words designating the speaker in a direct quotation.

"I have attended to everything," he asserted.
"This matter," she said, "will be discussed at the next meeting."

Note that in some instances, however, the speaker is designated by a complete sentence which precedes or follows the quotation.

Mr. Black's voice was reassuring. "I have attended to everything."
"I do want to tell you that I have enjoyed being with you tonight." The speaker sat down.

d. Commas are used to set off tag questions at the end of statements.

This is the house, isn't it?
You saw him last night, didn't you?

e. Commas are used to set off dates, addresses, and titles.

Every American knows that December 7, 1941, is a memorable date.
My home address is 16 North Elm Street, Waterloo, Iowa.
James Oliver, Ph.D., is the new history professor at the college.

14. **The Wrong Uses of the Comma.** The frequency of its employment in writing has resulted in a number of incorrect uses of the comma.

a. Do not use a comma before a co-ordinating conjunction that joins a pair of words, phrases, or dependent clauses.

WRONG: She was young, and pretty.
WRONG: He was a person of unusual height, and of distinguished bearing.
FAULTY: He explained how he had sifted the evidence, and how he had reached this amazing conclusion.

b. Do not use a comma before *that* introducing indirect discourse.

WRONG: He finally said, that he would sign the lease.

c. Do not use a comma to set off a restrictive prepositional phrase.

> WRONG: One cannot enter that building, without a permit.
> WRONG: At the door, stood a weeping child.

d. Do not use a comma to separate a verb from a noun clause used as its subject or as its object.

> WRONG: That he would finally come out all right, was conceded.
> WRONG: I cannot recall, what I said on that occasion.

e. Do not use a comma between paired conjunctions like *so . . . that*, or before *than* in a simple comparison.

> WRONG: So many things have happened since my childhood days, that those times seem like half-forgotten dreams.
> WRONG: When I awoke in Richmond, Virginia, I was more tired, than I had been when I went to bed the night before.

V. CONVENTIONAL PUNCTUATION

15. The Period. The period is used after abbreviations. Among the common abbreviations are Mr., Messrs., Mrs., Dr., Rev., Jr., Sr., M.D., D.D., Ph.D., A.M., P.M., A.D., and B.C.

Names of states, when more than four letters in length, are popularly abbreviated. Thus we have N.Y. for New York, Minn. for Minnesota, but not O. for Ohio.

Abbreviations for street, avenue, or boulevard should not be used in formal writing.

Three periods are used to indicate an omission, as in quoted matter. If the omission comes at the end of a sentence, four periods should be used.

16. The Colon. The colon is used in formal salutations of letters, in figures giving hours and minutes, for chapters and verses of the Bible, to separate a subtitle from a title, and in bibliographical references to separate author from title or publisher from place of publication.

> Dear Mr. Hanson: 8:27 P.M.
> Gentlemen: Luke 3:16
> H. G. Wells: *Tono-Bungay*   Methuen & Company: London

Yesterday and Today: A Comparative Anthology of Poetry

17. Quotation Marks. The titles of poems, short stories, essays, songs, tales, and subdivisions of books, such as chapter headings, are usually put in quotation marks.

> "Materialism and Idealism in American Life" is the most frequently quoted essay in George Santayana's *Character and Opinion in the United States*.
> "Annie Laurie" remains a perennial favorite with both singers and audiences.
> Possibly O. Henry's best story is "A Municipal Report."

18. Italics. Foreign words, titles of books, plays, newspapers, magazines, and the names of ships, pictures, and the like are put in italics. In writing, words to be italicized are underlined.

In the titles of newspapers, when incorporated in the text, a *The* in the title is not italicized or capitalized and the name of the city is preferably not italicized; in the title of magazines *The* is not italicized or capitalized.

the Cleveland *Plain-Dealer*   the *American Mercury*

VI. Mechanics

Closely allied to punctuation are the so-called "mechanics" of writing. The use of capitals, the apostrophe, and the hyphen come under this heading. The use of quotation marks and italics with titles and the like may be treated under mechanics or under punctuation. We have placed all the uses of these two marks under Punctuation.

19. The Use of Capitals. Many of the uses of capitals are conventional, like writing a capital for the pronoun I and interjection O or for abbreviations like A.B., M.A., Ph.D., A.D., B.C., and (often) A.M., and P.M. Likewise conventional is the capitalizing of the first word of each sentence or quoted sentence and the beginning of each line of poetry. All these uses of capitals are too familiar to you to require study.

The basis for other uses of capitals is the distinction between common nouns on one hand and proper nouns and proper adjectives on the other. Generally speaking, the following rules are based on this distinction.

a. Capitalize all proper nouns (as those of persons, places, countries, races, languages, corporations, institutions, clubs, colleges, organizations, political parties, religious denominations) and all proper adjectives derived therefrom.

George Washington   United States Rubber Company
Chicago   the Presbyterian creed
Oberlin College   the Republican platform

b. Capitalize the first word of titles of books, plays, songs, pictures, poems, themes, and the like, and all other words except articles (*a, an, the*) and short prepositions and conjunctions.

The Mill on the Floss   The Rise and Fall of Commodity Prices
The Merry Wives of Windsor   Community Spirit in My Town

c. Capitalize titles before names and titles of high officials used in place of names.

King George VI   Professor Herman McGill
President McKinley   The President saw the Secretary of State.

Usually the titles of lower state and local officers, used as names, are not capitalized.

The mayor was late to the meeting.

d. Capitalize the names of definite geographic sections but not directions nor points of the compass.

    the wheat fields of the Middle West   to drive north for three miles
    the economic problems of the South   a wind from the south-east
    the place of China in the Far East

e. Capitalize the names of months, days, holidays, historical events, and periods of history.

    April   the Thirty Years' War
    Tuesday   the American Revolution
    Easter   the Middle Ages

f. Capitalize words designating the Deity, words connected with the Deity, and pronouns referring to the Deity.

    God   the Scriptures
    the Saviour   the Bible
    the Creator   in His name we ask it

g. Capitalize names of family relationship when they designate a particular person, but not when a possessive noun or pronoun is used before them.

We visited Uncle Elmer and Aunt Millie.   My father is a lawyer.
Just then Grandfather came into the room.   Tom's uncle owns a silver mine.
Where is Father's razor?   Their sister was graduated from college.

h. Capitalize the specific part of trade names if the identity of origin is clearly felt.

    a Ford car   two tablets of Bayer's aspirin
    a bar of Swan soap   to use pasteurized milk

i. Words used in a specialized or emphatic sense are often capitalized.

I am interested in the Now, not in the Hereafter.
Must everything we cherish be sacrificed to Speed?

j. The names of specific courses are capitalized, but not the names of subjects except languages.

He is taking History 110.
He is interested in history and economics.
She found French difficult.

k. Proper nouns and proper adjectives to which prefixes are added retain their capitals.

He wrote a letter to ex-President Hoover.
He is pro-British in his sympathies.

l. Names of classes are not capitalized unless a particular class is designated.

The freshman class is usually the largest in high schools.
The Junior Class has called a meeting at four o'clock.

m. The names of streets, avenues, and other locations of addresses, and words of geographical description following proper nouns should be capitalized.

    510 Sycamore Street   the Wabash River
    on Fifth Avenue   Silver Lake

However, many newspapers use lower case letters for street, avenue, river, etc.

n. The names of the seasons (spring, summer, fall, autumn, and winter) should not be capitalized.

20. The Apostrophe. The uses of the apostrophe may be classified under three distinct headings: to denote possession, to indicate the omission of letters in contractions, and to form irregular plurals. The most frequent misuse of the apostrophe is its omission—frankly, a result of carelessness rather than a lack of knowledge. The following rules will be no cure for carelessness, but they will supply the necessary information for the correct use of the apostrophe.

a. To form the possessive singular of regular nouns add *'s* to the singular nominative case of the noun; to form the possessive plural add an apostrophe to the plural nominative. Observe the following examples carefully.

Sing. Nom.	Sing. Poss.	Pl. Nom.	Pl. Poss.
boy	boy's	boys	boys'
girl	girl's	girls	girls'
lady	lady's	ladies	ladies'
attorney	attorney's	attorneys	attorneys'
thief	thief's	thieves	thieves'
fox	fox's	foxes	foxes'
boss	boss's	bosses	bosses'

To form the possessive of irregular nouns, add *'s* to the singular and the plural forms.

Sing. Nom.	Sing. Poss.	Pl. Nom.	Pl. Poss.
man	man's	men	men's
woman	woman's	women	women's
child	child's	children	children's
goose	goose's	geese	geese's
sister-in-law	sister-in-law's	sisters-in-law	sisters-in-law's
alumnus	alumnus's	alumni	alumni's

One of the most frequent errors in the use of the apostrophe is the writing of the plural of nouns ending in *y* preceded by a consonant for the singular possessive.

WRONG: The countries welfare was in his hands.
RIGHT: The country's welfare was in his hands.

Proper nouns ending in *s* may form their possessive regularly, but often in the singular only an apostrophe is added. Hence we may write James's or James' father. Note the following singular and plural possessives carefully.

Sing. Nom.	Sing. Poss.	Pl. Nom.	Pl. Poss.
Jones	Jones's or Jones'	Joneses	Joneses'
Higgens	Higgens's or Higgens'	Higgenses	Higgenses'

Care must be taken not to use the final *s* of such names as the *'s* to show possession.

WRONG: Keat's poems, Mose's laws, Dicken's works

To insure correctness in denoting possession with proper nouns ending in *s*, write the name first. These names are Keats, Moses, Dickens. From these names form the possessive.

b. The *of*-phrase is used to denote possession by inanimate objects. Hence we have "the hinges of the door," not "the door's hinge"; "the buttons of the coat," not "the coat's buttons."

However many nouns expressing time, distance, measurement, cost, and many familiar expressions use the apostrophe to denote a possessive relation: for example, a day's pay, two months' visit, a stone's throw, a dollar's purchasing power, three cents' worth, the ocean's depth, the law's delay, the heart's desire, love's old sweet song.

c. Personal, relative, and interrogative pronouns never take an apostrophe to denote possession. Note the following correct forms: *ours, yours, hers, its, theirs, whose.*

RIGHT: All this land is ours.
RIGHT: The bird fed its young.
RIGHT: A people whose leaders are brave will prosper.

Particular attention must be paid to the personal pronoun *its*. *Its* is just as truly the possessive form of the neuter singular pronoun *it* as *his* is the possessive of *he*. No one would think of writing *his'* or *hi's*; yet these forms would be as correct as *it's* for the possessive. Every time you write *it's* you must be able to substitute *it is*. If you cannot so expand it, write *its*.

The indefinite pronouns form their possessives in the same way as nouns.

one's interests   somebody else's hat   others' rights

d. To represent joint possession, use the apostrophe with only the last name; to represent separate ownership, use the apostrophe with each name.

RIGHT: Sears and Roebuck's catalogue came yesterday.
RIGHT: Beaumont and Fletcher's dramas are primarily romantic.
RIGHT: Tom's and Jack's grades improved.
RIGHT: Clark's and Robinson's refusal to close their stores showed a selfish attitude.

e. The possessive form of the noun and pronoun should be used with the gerund.

WRONG: I dislike Mary taking my things without asking.
RIGHT: I dislike Mary's taking my things without asking.
WRONG: The teacher objected to him copying the answers.
RIGHT: The teacher objected to his copying the answers.

When the emphasis is on the noun or pronoun, the objective case is correct since the following word is then a modifying participle.

RIGHT: We saw Mary taking a walk.
RIGHT: We heard him whistling along the street.
RIGHT: She called at the company wanting a clerk.

f. An apostrophe is used in a contraction where a letter or letters are omitted.

I'm (I am) coming.　　　　They're (They are) here.
You're (You are) late.　　　They don't (do not) answer.
He'll (He will) come.　　　 It's (It is) raining.
She doesn't (does not) study.　Who's (Who is) responsible?

The apostrophe is also used to indicate omissions in such expressions as 9 o'clock (of the clock), ne'er-do-well (never-do-well), the gold rush of '49 (1849), and in writing dialects.

g. The plurals of letters, numerals, signs, and words referred to as words are formed by adding *'s*.

There are two *c's* and two *m's* in *accommodate*.
Your *7's* look like *9's*.
You must put *$'s* before these figures.
I don't want any *if's* nor *and's* about it.

21. The Hyphen. The following rules cover the principal uses of the hyphen.

a. The most frequent use of the hyphen is to indicate a break in a word at the end of a line, as illustrated by the following words: *sub-merged, mother-hood, sensa-tion*. Words of one syllable should never be broken; hence *through*, never *thro-ugh*; *friend*, never *fri-end*.

A single letter, although itself a complete syllable, should not be separated from the rest of the word by a hyphen.

about, not a-bout
ideal, not i-deal

hasty, not hast-y
wormy, not worm-y

The -ed of the past tense and the past participle of weak verbs should not be separated from the rest of the word unless it is pronounced as a separate syllable.

Right	Wrong	Right	Right
liked	lik-ed	mend-ed	blind-ed
tapped	tap-ped	molt-ed	defend-ed

The hyphen must always be inserted so that the correct syllabication of the word is not disturbed. Whenever you are in doubt about the syllabication of a word, consult a reliable dictionary. Correct hyphenization cannot be determined by the space limitations at the end of a line nor left to the writer's or typer's whim or convenience.

b. A hyphen is placed between two or more words used as an adjective before a noun.

RIGHT: a second-rate show; a tumbled-down shack; a dry-as-dust talk

If these words have more than two syllables, and especially if the first is an adverb ending in -*ly*, the hyphen is generally not used.

RIGHT: an adequately prepared lesson; a remarkably swift current

If the words follow the noun, especially as a predicate complement, the hyphen is not used unless the word itself is a compound word.

RIGHT: The show was second rate.
RIGHT: The resentment was deep-seated. (dictionary gives as compound word)
RIGHT: His ideas were old-fashioned. (dictionary gives as compound word)

No rules can determine for you whether to write words solid (baseball, starlight), or compound (star-spangled, fair-minded, Anglo-Saxon), or as separate words (fair ball, compound interest). Words not given in the dictionary as solid or compound words should be written separately.

c. The hyphen should be used with all compound numbers from **twenty-one** to **ninety-nine** and with all fractions except one half.

EXAMPLES: forty-seven, ninety-three, three-fifths, seven-ninths

d. The hyphen is used with words in which *self-* is the first part of the compound (self-inflicted wound, self-propelled rocket), with many words in which *non-* is the first part of the compound (non-interference, non-transferable), and with certain words that can have the intended meaning preserved only by using a hyphen (recreation, re-creation; prescience, pre-science; reformation, re-formation).

e. The hyphen is often used to separate vowels of the same letter which, if read together as one syllable, might render the word meaningless.

EXAMPLES: co-operate, co-owner, re-employ, re-enter

about, not a-bout
ideal, not i-deal

hasty, not hast-y
wormy, not worm-y

The -ed of the past tense and the past participle of weak verbs should not be separated from the rest of the word unless it is pronounced as a separate syllable.

Right	Wrong	Right	Right
liked	lik-ed	mend-ed	blind-ed
tapped	tap-ped	molt-ed	defend-ed

The hyphen must always be inserted so that the correct syllabication of the word is not disturbed. Whenever you are in doubt about the syllabication of a word, consult a reliable dictionary. Correct hyphenization cannot be determined by the space limitations at the end of a line nor left to the writer's or typer's whim or convenience.

b. A hyphen is placed between two or more words used as an adjective before a noun.

RIGHT: a second-rate show; a tumbled-down shack; a dry-as-dust talk

If these words have more than two syllables, and especially if the first is an adverb ending in *-ly*, the hyphen is generally not used.

RIGHT: an adequately prepared lesson; a remarkably swift current

If the words follow the noun, especially as a predicate complement, the hyphen is not used unless the word itself is a compound word.

RIGHT: The show was second rate.
RIGHT: The resentment was deep-seated. (dictionary gives as compound word)
RIGHT: His ideas were old-fashioned. (dictionary gives as compound word)

No rules can determine for you whether to write words solid (baseball, starlight), or compound (star-spangled, fair-minded, Anglo-Saxon), or as separate words (fair ball, compound interest). Words not given in the dictionary as solid or compound words should be written separately.

c. The hyphen should be used with all compound numbers from twenty-one to ninety-nine and with all fractions except one half.

EXAMPLES: forty-seven, ninety-three, three-fifths, seven-ninths

d. The hyphen is used with words in which *self-* is the first part of the compound (self-inflicted wound, self-propelled rocket), with many words in which *non-* is the first part of the compound (non-interference, non-transferable), and with certain words that can have the intended meaning preserved only by using a hyphen (recreation, re-creation; prescience, pre-science; reformation, re-formation).

e. The hyphen is often used to separate vowels of the same letter which, if read together as one syllable, might render the word meaningless.

EXAMPLES: co-operate, co-owner, re-employ, re-enter

55. END PUNCTUATION—I

Period, Question Mark, and Exclamation Point

Supply appropriate end punctuation wherever it is required in the passages below. Write the end word of each sentence or elliptical statement in the space at the left, and after the word give the correct mark of punctuation.

EXAMPLE:

away?   *least.*   How long do I expect to be away   For two or three weeks, at least

1. A thrifty housewife, anxious to obtain the best food values at the lowest possible cost, should know how to select from the cheaper cuts of meat   And, fully as important, how to prepare them for the family table

2. Who is America's most distinguished playwright   Eugene O'Neill, most critics would answer

3. Have we seen this picture before   Yes, it's the one we saw in St. Louis last month

4. What an exasperating day   Everything has gone wrong from the very start

5. We never found out where or how "Fileep" had picked up his astonishing repertoire of American swing music   Nor, for that matter, could we discover any details of his past life

6. How delicious those chocolate éclairs look   Are there enough for all of us

7. What a childish remark   He should have weighed his words more carefully

8. Put that match away   Can't you smell the odor of gasoline here

9. Bring your guest to the party, Martha   She's still with you, isn't she

10. The workman at the next machine wanted to know why I was working so fast   What a ridiculous attitude

11. Who left the telephone receiver off the hook   Was it Dorothy

.... 12. "Play ball " Those magic words heralded the opening of another season on the big-league diamonds yesterday

.... 13. What made him say he would buy the Walker place He had no such intention, I'm sure

.... 14. He walked along the street, trying to pick out familiar landmarks Wasn't that parking lot across from him the site of the old Ridley mansion

.... 15. Where did you say he had gone And have you any idea when he will return

.... 16. In the recent fight against infantile paralysis, research has been centered on two problems: Can a reliable test be developed for early diagnosis of the disease Can the newer drugs be used to combat the disease

.... 17. Somebody stop that lady She has taken the wrong suitcase

.... 18. Do you favor a municipal electric plant And will you sign this petition

.... 19. At its last session Congress passed another housing bill What its effect will be, nobody can predict

.... 20. "Watch out below " An instant later, a pile of old shingles came crashing down

.... 21. In what state were you born And what is your purpose in entering Canada

.... 22. What an overwhelming tragedy The Senior Dance was but a week away, and no one had as yet invited her

.... 23. One girl in the sightseeing party appeared hopelessly bored Why she had made the trip, no one could understand

.... 24. Don't touch that frayed wire You may cause a short-circuit

.... 25. To our left, a shaft of light swept the night sky Was it an airplane beacon

To obtain score, multiply number of errors by 2 and subtract total from 100.

56. END PUNCTUATION—II

Period, Question Mark, and Exclamation Point

Supply appropriate end punctuation wherever it is required in the passages below. Write the end word of each sentence or elliptical statement in the space at the left, and after the word give the correct mark of punctuation.

EXAMPLE:

halt!" precise. "Company, halt " The lieutenant's order was crisp and precise

1. What is the oldest town in the United States   St. Augustine, I have been told
2. He did not answer a single question correctly   Not even one question
3. Ouch   That's the second time I've bumped my head in that low doorway
4. Mrs. Briggs spent the whole evening talking about her children and their cute sayings   What a bore
5. She telephoned to the doctor's office to ask whether there is any dependable cure for hiccoughs
6. Would you like to have a set of these de luxe seat covers for your car   If so, then fill out the enclosed post card and mail it at once
7. I must find someone who will help distribute these posters   Would George   Or Dave, perhaps
8. Kindly report to the Dean's Office at 3:00 P.M. on Thursday   Or, if this is not convenient, on the following day at the same hour
9. Who is the man pictured here with the cocked hat and the military cape   Is it Napoleon
10. To which address should I send this letter   To his home or to his office
11. Where I put those automobile keys, I cannot recall   Have you seen them
12. The highest peak east of the Rockies is Clingman's Dome, isn't it   Or is it Mount Mitchell

....	13. Which of the two strong suits should I have bid Hearts, I suppose
....	14. "Fire " Following the command, there was an instant of tension as we waited for the awesome roar of the big gun
....	15. This room was papered just two years ago Or was it three years ago.
....	16. Did we recover the ball on that last fumble What a break
....	17. Has the present administration carried out its promises to the citizens Emphatically, no
....	18. "Charge " With that battle cry, the boys would race across the playground toward imaginary foes
....	19. Would you know how to set a broken arm How to treat a victim of sunstroke What to do in case of snake bite
....	20. We could barely make out what the words were on the crude, weathered sign "No Trespassing," it said with homely authority
....	21. He has promised to settle the claims of all his creditors But how and when
....	22. Did you see that photograph of a tightrope walker high above the Alpine peaks It appeared in *Life*
....	23. What nonsense How can water be located by means of this witching wand, or whatever it is called
....	24. Do physicians still adhere to the principles of the Hippocratic oath Generally speaking, yes
....	25. The judge was a portly, sedate-looking old gentleman Do you remember him

To obtain score, multiply number of errors by 2 and subtract total from 100.

NAME .... DATE .... SCORE ....

57. STRONG INTERNAL PUNCTUATION—I

Semicolon, Colon, and Dash

Supply strong internal punctuation (the semicolon, the colon, or the dash) wherever it is needed in the sentences given below. In the appropriate space at the left write the word which will precede the punctuation you are supplying, and after the word place the correct punctuation mark. If the sentence requires no change in punctuation, leave the space at the left blank.

EXAMPLE:

circumstance—   She was always taking offense as the result of some chance remark, some trivial circumstance an inexcusable habit in anyone.

hue;   1. His hair is of a reddish hue it waves and swirls as if it would defy any attempt at combing.

exploration: 2. Four names are prominently linked with polar exploration Amundsen, Scott, Peary, and Byrd.

idea;   3. The writer of "soap operas" must be haunted by one idea what new difficulties can be created for the heroine and how will she overcome them?

laughter: 4. There are five gradations of laughter the giggle, the titter, the chuckle, the cackle, and the roar.

namely—   5. With the development of unionism in this country, one principle emerged as the basis for settling disputes between labor and management namely, collective bargaining.

cars—   6. Since 1893 the American automobile industry has turned out more than one hundred million cars no small achievement.

shoes—   7. In the old-fashioned general store one could find staple groceries, meats, hardware, patent medicines, house dresses, shoes in fact, almost anything and everything needed by the average family

highway;   8. The Pennsylvania Turnpike is a much-traveled highway it reduces the driving time from Pittsburgh to Philadelphia by approximately three hours.

cheeks;   9. The old farmer had lean, leathery cheeks blue eyes, deep-set and speculative and a wide mouth which was creased in a perpetual smile.

correct   10. For his trip into the wilds he bought a poncho, a hunting knife, and a pair of boots.

11. The following persons won the top prizes in a recent quiz show a high school girl from Brooklyn, New York an insurance salesman from Baltimore, Maryland and a housewife from Des Moines, Iowa.
12. There is only one infallible cure for seasickness namely, solid earth beneath one's feet.
13. Steel makers have learned that there is an abundance of iron in the Adirondack Mountains, that the ore is of superior grade, and that mining in this region is more practicable than they once thought.
14. During the war the following items were particularly scarce automobile tires, electrical appliances, silk stockings, and white shirts.
15. To be a successful track man one must possess at least three qualifications a love of the sport, a willingness to train, and a determination to do one's best in every race.
16. I really believe that your father but here he comes up the steps. He can speak for himself.
17. No sooner had we entered the yard than the dog began to growl menacingly, causing us to retreat to the sidewalk.
18. The commencement program will be ordered as follows the academic procession, the invocation, the address to the graduating seniors, and the awarding of degrees.
19. The early Dutch settlers of America succeeded because of one excellent trait namely, thrift.
20. We had forgotten to bring a reserve supply of gasoline for the outboard motor a costly oversight.

To obtain score, allow 5 points for each sentence which has been satisfactorily corrected and for each sentence identified as correct.

208

58. STRONG INTERNAL PUNCTUATION—II

Semicolon, Colon, and Dash

Supply strong internal punctuation (the semicolon, the colon, or the dash) wherever it is needed in the sentences given below. In the appropriate space at the left write the word which will precede the punctuation you are supplying, and after the word place the correct punctuation mark. If the sentence requires no change in punctuation, leave the space at the left blank.

EXAMPLE:

distances;   The airplane has altered our sense of distances it has made our world infinitely smaller.

1. The show is booked for performances in Detroit on Monday, the twenty-seventh of September in Chicago on Friday, the first of October in Denver on Thursday, the fourteenth of October in St. Louis on Tuesday, the nineteenth of October.

2. According to Greek legend Prometheus was the god who one day gave men the gift of fire thereafter he was chained to a rock and punished for his generosity.

3. When the paper was handed to him by the lawyer, the defendant stammered: "I do not recall having seen this before, but no, I am sure I have never seen it."

4. The beginning golfer should start for the links with the following equipment a set of clubs, a generous supply of golf balls, and a sympathetic friend.

5. This region produces several varieties of apples namely the Northern Spy, the Baldwin, the Winesap, the Rome Beauty, and the Delicious.

6. Certain kinds of shale, geologists point out, hold vast quantities of petroleum the difficulty is, however, that the expense of extracting the oil is prohibitive.

7. In making his weird flight to England, Rudolf Hess evidently had the notion that the Allies would strike a bargain with Germany-a fantastic delusion.

8. On the midway you will see a merry-go-round, a Ferris wheel, a roller coaster, a house of thrills-in short all of the attractions that you would expect to find in a typical amusement park.

.... 9. In 1948 uranium ore was found north of Vancouver, British Columbia; a short time later, hundreds of prospectors were converging on the province to stake out their claims in the area of the discovery.

.... 10. Your birthday comes in the month of—I'm not quite sure. Is it July?

.... 11. Arguing that the earth's poles have shifted at various times in the past, one scientist predicts that the weight of ice in the Antarctic may cause the earth to capsize—an alarming conjecture.

.... 12. There are well-known symphony orchestras in the following places: Boston, Massachusetts; Philadelphia, Pennsylvania; and Detroit, Michigan.

.... 13. Political equality, justice, freedom of religious worship—these were the guarantees of the new democracy.

.... 14. The program for the Fourth of July celebration has been scheduled as follows: the Governor's address at three o'clock, the donkey-baseball game at four, the picnic supper at six, and the fireworks at nine.

.... 15. The first experiments in the course will require only a Bunsen burner, two test tubes, and a few simple chemicals.

.... 16. The early days on the Erie Canal, the activity along its banks, the legends that made the "big ditch" the most colorful waterway in America these are the ingredients of the new book.

.... 17. The monks of Monte Cassino have started rebuilding their ancient abbey; however the work may take more than a century and will cost thousands of dollars.

.... 18. The White House, the U.S. Capitol, the Smithsonian Institution, the Library of Congress—these places are of interest to everyone touring Washington for the first time.

.... 19. Medieval society might be divided into four large classes of people: the nobles, the clergy, the commoners, and the serfs.

.... 20. At the cabin you will find table linen, bedding, silverware, dishes, and a supply of wood for building fires.

To obtain score, allow 5 points for each sentence which has been satisfactorily corrected and for each sentence identified as correct.

NAME ....DATE ....SCORE ....

59. ENCLOSING PUNCTUATION—I

Quotation Marks

Examine carefully each passage below and write, in the space at the left, each word which should be preceded or followed by quotation marks. If the word should be followed by a comma, a period, or some other mark of punctuation, insert the appropriate mark. Finally, supply the quotation marks, making sure that they are properly placed with respect to other punctuation.

EXAMPLE:

"*Is shrinkage?*"   Is this material guaranteed against shrinkage asked Mrs. Brown.

.... 1. The girl beside her said impatiently, Well let's not stand here all day

.... 2. In the language of carnival folk, a geek is one who plays the wild man; a pinhead is a freak with an exceptionally small head.

.... 3. At the tea party Alice's interest was aroused when the Mad Hatter asked: Why is a raven like a writing desk

.... 4. George Herman Ruth was more commonly known to millions of Americans as the Babe

.... 5. Be with you in a moment, John Dr. Barton hastily closed the door of the waiting room, and again I could hear the buzzing of the drill.

.... 6. Far down the street the newsboys were shouting their familiar chant—Extra! Extra

.... 7. Mrs. Page was saying, It isn't really necessary that we keep roomers, Clara, but we're helping the housing situation, aren't we

.... 8. Heave ho! heave ho was the traditional cry of the sailors as they hoisted the anchor.

.... 9. Grinning sardonically, our Lieutenant said, Make yourselves comfortable for the night, men

.... 10. Was it President Coolidge who once said, I do not choose to run

.... 11. Some students tend to overwork the words so and very

.... 12. He looked at me sharply and asked in a suspicious tone of voice: Are you sure this bill is correct

.... 13. Does this hurt asked the doctor as he plunged a fat, stubby forefinger into my stomach.

.... 14. Words like oyster and oil are given a queer pronunciation by some New Yorkers.

.... 15. From a room down the hall came a high-pitched scream: "Girls there's a mouse here! Help, help!"

.... 16. Hit him with a broom handle suggested Cora, who was watching the mouse hunt at a safe distance.

.... 17. College slang has evolved its special labels for different types of individuals. For instance, a dull person is known as a goon

.... 18. A grinning, freckle-faced boy knocked at the door and asked, Mister can I get our football off your porch roof

.... 19. Don't chop at the ball. Take a long, easy swing said the tennis coach.

.... 20. The manager glanced at the letter of introduction and asked, Have you had any experience in hotel work

.... 21. The slogan of a New Jersey dairy farm, You can whip our cream but you can't beat our milk shows how modern advertising methods can be used to sell farm products.

.... 22. Two deceptive plays once fairly common in football are now rarely seen. In the first, known as the sleeper a player would take an inconspicuous position near the side lines to await a forward pass; in the second, known as the Statue of Liberty one player would pretend that he was about to throw a forward pass, but instead, a teammate would run with the ball.

.... 23. In the middle of the highway was a barrier with a sign which read: Road closed for repairs. Take temporary detour

.... 24. The man in the bleachers contemptuously referred to the patrons of the reserved seats as them plush-lined bums

.... 25. Was it Voltaire who said, I disapprove of what you say, but I will defend to the death your right to say it

To obtain score, multiply number of errors by 2 and subtract total from 100. (There should be fifty words in the "answer" column above.)

NAME .... DATE .... SCORE ....

60. ENCLOSING PUNCTUATION—II

Quotation Marks

Examine carefully each passage below and write, in the space at the left, each word which should be preceded or followed by quotation marks. If the word should be followed by a comma, a period, or some other mark of punctuation, insert the appropriate mark. Finally, supply the quotation marks, making sure that they are properly placed with respect to other punctuation.

EXAMPLE:
"Hold moment,"   Hold the line for a moment said the long-distance
"here's party."   operator; here's your party

1. My dear child my sister exclaimed, that place charges you ten dollars just to look at anything. You don't really intend to buy anything there, do you

2. In a book on business letter writing he found a chapter called How to Write a Letter of Application Some of its advice ran thus: When you end your letter, don't write, Hoping to hear from you soon Instead, write, May I have an interview at your convenience

3. Let's try this tan suit just for size the clerk purred softly. Do you have any particular color in mind

4. And she can't even boil water, George said Grandmother, who had now joined the argument; you'll be eating most of your meals here, same as you always have

5. I hate everything with a title—except my books wrote Jonathan Swift, and even in those the shorter the title the better

6. Harry said, Why is it that the sports writers keep referring to the football players as gridiron stars and as pigskin warriors

7. If you add water to an overheated radiator the filling-

.... station attendant warned, you should keep the motor
.... running
.... 8. Do you remember The Two Races of Men an essay in
....   which Lamb says, The human species is composed of
....   two distinct races, the men who borrow and the men
....   who lend
.... 9. After Jim Tigert had slid into home plate, a sharp dis-
....   pute arose. Waving at Jim the umpire called, You're out
....   Then, against a rising storm of protest, he repeated de-
....   fiantly, That man's out, I say—OUT
.... 10. In a scorching review the critic wrote: The descriptive
....   passages in this novel are marred by timeworn, out-
....   dated expressions like the glowing sunset and the glassy
....   waters
.... 11. Do you remember the opening line of Robert Frost's
....   poem Birches
.... 12. Anyone who is interested in trying out for the fall play,
....   the notice read, should report to the Little Theatre at
....   seven o'clock tonight

To obtain score, multiply number of errors by 2 and subtract total from 100. (There should be fifty words in the "answer" column above.)

NAME .... DATE .... SCORE ....

61. ENCLOSING PUNCTUATION—III

Parentheses, Brackets, and Dashes

Pick out, in the sentences below, passages which should be set off by parentheses, brackets, or dashes. Write, in the space at the left, the first and the last word of each passage, together with the proper enclosing marks.

EXAMPLE:

(*it   dog*)   The German shepherd dog it is popularly known as the police dog is a highly intelligent animal.

.... 1. In 1859 Asa Wells established a woolen mill on Front Street it is now Culver Road and began the manufacture of blankets.

.... 2. The statement in the book reads: "The Republicans returned to office in 1916 the author means 1920 and shaped the policies of the nation for the next decade."

.... 3. Traveling westward on the canal were men of many races Hollanders, Germans, Scandinavians taking with them their meager possessions.

.... 4. The cliff dwellings many of them can be seen in New Mexico today were not only homes but also impenetrable fortresses.

.... 5. One day Mr. Zipfel we called him "Monkey Face" told me that he had a new job for me.

.... 6. A goal-and-return glider flight of 229 miles the previous record of 212.7 miles is held by a Russian was made near Elmira recently.

.... 7. *A Handbook to Literature* was published by Doubleday, Doran & Company now Doubleday & Company in 1936.

.... 8. At that time of year it was, as I recall, about the middle of March the river was at flood stage with a swift, treacherous current.

.... 9. The object of their long, unavailing search a sad-eyed, lop-eared beagle hound named Betsy suddenly appeared at the door.

.... 10. Two Eastern industrialists their names have not been disclosed are being considered for the vacancy in the Cabinet.

.... 11. Contracts for the new bridge it is to be of steel construction have been let, and the work will begin at once.

215

.... 12. For eighty-four tense, sleepless days and nights—August 8 to October 30, 1940—Britain fought off the attacks of the German Luftwaffe.

.... 13. The newspaper item reads: "It was the Royal Air Force that bore the blunt [it should be 'bore the brunt'] of the German onslaught."

.... 14. Anger—a hot, rebellious anger—surged up within him as he reflected on the injustice of the act.

.... 15. Quoting a cynical, yet amusing epigram "An ambassador is an honest man sent abroad to tell lies for his country" the diplomat presented his credentials.

.... 16. "Our Lady's Juggler" (it is a well-known story by Anatole France) describes a miracle which took place as the result of a humble man's religious faith.

.... 17. By the tireless researches of three French scientists (Henri Becquerel, Pierre and Marie Curie) important discoveries in radioactivity were made at the turn of the century.

.... 18. The introduction sums up the importance of the *Autobiography* in this fashion: "Here is the most permanent and illuminating record of the many-sidedness of his (Franklin's genius."

.... 19. It is the "long-hair boys," (as they are called) the physicists, the geologists, and the engineers upon whom the oil companies must rely for scientific exploration of an unproved area.

.... 20. Experts in chromatics (this means the science of colors) say that intellectuals prefer blue, whereas athletes like red.

To obtain score, allow 5 points for each sentence in which the enclosing marks have been properly supplied.

NAME .... DATE .... SCORE ....

62. THE MAIN USES OF THE COMMA—I

Independent Clauses

Examine the sentences below to determine whether they need commas, stronger marks of punctuation, or no punctuation at all. To insert punctuation write, in the space at the left, the word which will precede the punctuation, and after the word place the correct mark. If no punctuation is required, leave the space at the left blank.

EXAMPLE:

Buffalo,   The vessel was loaded with a cargo of iron ore destined for Buffalo and by midnight we were ready to sail.

.... 1. Louie wiped his tar-streaked glasses on his sleeve and climbed down from his perch on the truck.

.... 2. She did not go to any of the afternoon teas, nor did she take any interest in the activities of the sewing circle.

.... 3. Nicholas and I walked along in silence for a few minutes, then he resumed his story.

.... 4. The rain began and we quickened our pace.

.... 5. The old canning factory was like a huge tinderbox, the flames spread rapidly from the main building to the adjoining sheds.

.... 6. The force of the water broke the windowpanes on the second floor, and the smoke rolled out in dense billows.

.... 7. My fear of spiders must have begun when I was quite young and it has continued to the present day.

.... 8. The town of Oldenburg is enclosed by an ancient wall, and the houses with their peaked gables contribute to the medieval effect.

.... 9. The country hotel in which we stayed had an elevator, but it was invariably out of order.

.... 10. The steaks were so charred and cindery that we could scarcely eat them; nevertheless we pretended to enjoy the meal.

.... 11. There are excellent camping facilities near the south entrance to the park, and meals may be obtained in an up-to-date cafeteria at moderate cost.

.... 12. The New England house sometimes has what is known as a "widow's walk" this is a roof platform from which one can look out to sea.

.... 13. Morris caught a pass on the five-yard line and thus put the team in scoring position.

217

.... 14. The porter called me at six o'clock in the morning and informed me that the train would be in Denver in half an hour.

.... 15. The line of cars surged forward as the light changed, and he was unable to recover the hat that had rolled into the street.

.... 16. The tests revealed that Eugene had musical ability but no aptitude for the study of engineering.

.... 17. Atomic energy may bring priceless benefits to mankind, or it may spell the doom of civilization.

.... 18. It is true that the American frontier developed the qualities of resourcefulness and individualism; nevertheless, it is equally true that frontier conditions bred lawlessness and cruelty.

.... 19. Suddenly the house lights of the theater were dimmed; the audience leaned forward in their seats and awaited the opening scene.

.... 20. Our cat "Boots" did not have the nine lives sometimes credited to her race, but she lived to the advanced age of sixteen.

.... 21. George was born in Salonika fifty-two years ago and came to America as a young man.

.... 22. During the summer Pete works as a guide for fishermen in the region, and in the winter he tramps his beloved woods as a ranger for a lumber company.

.... 23. The hired man would sometimes return after an absence of several weeks and resume his work as though nothing out of the ordinary had happened.

.... 24. The cover of the magazine depicts a Parisian street scene; in the foreground are several bicycles and horse-drawn carts.

.... 25. We followed a twisting path through the wooded ravine and came upon the ruins of an old gristmill.

To obtain score, allow 4 points for each sentence in which the punctuation has been properly inserted and for each sentence identified as correct.

63. THE MAIN USES OF THE COMMA—II

Introductory Clauses or Phrases, Absolute or Parenthetical Elements

Supply commas wherever they are needed in the sentences below. To insert such punctuation write, in the space at the left, the word which will precede the comma, and after the word place the necessary comma. If no punctuation is required in the sentence, leave the space at the left blank.

EXAMPLE:

decade, Although brilliant discoveries have advanced the science of medicine during the past decade even greater miracles of research lie ahead of us.

1. No the Allens have not lived in that house for over two years.
2. Before a student is able to take an advanced course like calculus he must have a working knowledge of algebra.
3. If they come I shall urge them to stay for the week end.
4. There has been to be sure some progress in the investigation of cancer during the last few years.
5. Flying over the Hump into China became a routine assignment for Allied airmen.
6. The view from the observation tower was I must say rather disappointing to all of us.
7. While Edwin was reading what he took to be a letter from the dean the rest of us tried to keep from smiling.
8. Before the advent of such labor-saving devices as the tractor and the combine farming was a life of unremitting toil.
9. Shortly after Anna began her work as a teacher at the Siamese court she taught her charges to sing "Home, Sweet Home."
10. A verdict having been reached the jury returned to the courtroom.
11. On the site of the original fort stands a small blockhouse of hewn logs and plaster.
12. Although the vessel was damaged beyond repair the cargo was salvaged.
13. The alterations to our store having been completed we shall reopen for business on Monday.
14. Heading the procession was a bandy-legged little Scotchman in kilts.

.... 15. In a book that told of Lincoln's virtues as well as his shortcomings William H. Herndon set down his impressions of his former partner and friend.
.... 16. After the tobacco has been gathered from the fields and has gone through the curing treatment for several days it is graded according to color and texture.
.... 17. Her aloof manner was the result I am certain of a lack of self-confidence.
.... 18. Still looking over her shoulder at the little black dress in the shop window Jane opened the glass portals of Carolyn's and hesitantly ventured in.
.... 19. The daily performance of the chimpanzees was it goes without saying one of the major attractions at the zoo.
.... 20. Yes many economists are of the opinion that increased production is the best safeguard on the whole against the danger of inflation.
.... 21. To begin with you will need a passport and certain visas before undertaking this European trip.
.... 22. On Halloween the children knock at every door in the neighborhood to beg for food or candy.
.... 23. Leading a shaggy little donkey was a Mexican peasant in gay costume.
.... 24. No report was filed with the police however regarding a holdup in that locality.
.... 25. The plan outlined at the last meeting has some merit to be sure.

To obtain score, allow 4 points for each sentence in which the punctuation has been properly inserted and for each sentence identified as correct.

NAME .... DATE .... SCORE ....

64. THE MAIN USES OF THE COMMA—III

Non-restrictive Modifiers and Appositives

Analyze the sentences below to determine where commas are needed to set off non-restrictive modifiers or non-restrictive appositives. To insert such punctuation write, in the space at the left, the word which will precede the comma, and after the word place the necessary comma. If no punctuation is required in the sentence, leave the space at the left blank.

EXAMPLE:

Wilcox, engineer,   Mr. Wilcox the city engineer will make a report on the project.

1. Medieval plays most of which were religious in character were presented by the various guilds.
2. Midsummer Eve which was the night of June the twenty-third was regarded as a time of magic and sorcery.
3. The nickname "Black Jack" had clung to John J. Pershing since his early days as an instructor at West Point.
4. On the stepladder was Father who was fastening a clothesline to the garage wall.
5. In ports like Buffalo and Duluth where lake freighters discharge their cargoes there are huge grain elevators along the waterfront.
6. Ice hockey is a sport which calls for nerve and skill.
7. A book such as that can have a tremendous effect upon popular opinion.
8. Charles Evans Hughes a famous American jurist was Secretary of State during the Harding administration.
9. His sister Julie is an art student in Chicago.
10. The term "scab" was hurled at every worker who tried to cross the picket line.
11. John Rolfe the first English colonist to grow American tobacco found the business a profitable one.
12. He had mastery of several languages including Russian.
13. Tom the handy man of the camp built a fireplace for the recreation hall.
14. Bored and irritated he listened to the talk with growing impatience.
15. Is that the type of musket which was used by the early colonists?

.... 16. New Bedford which was once a famous whaling port lies on the southeastern coast of Massachusetts.
.... 17. All the students who saw the play said that it was brisk and entertaining from start to finish.
.... 18. After walking for several blocks in the sticky July heat I found the store to which I had been directed.
.... 19. He was stationed in Hawaii when this picture was taken.
.... 20. Finding ourselves without a key we took a flashlight from the car and tried to find an unlocked window.
.... 21. It is often difficult to start the car when the weather is cold.
.... 22. Yawning he glanced at the watch on the table beside him.
.... 23. Is he the mason whom you hired to repair the chimney?
.... 24. I intend to see him before he leaves for his summer vacation.
.... 25. Mr. Archer who was absent-minded tried to remember what it was that he was supposed to get at the store.

To obtain score, allow 4 points for each sentence in which the punctuation has been properly inserted and for each sentence identified as correct.

65. THE MAIN USES OF THE COMMA—IV

Non-restrictive Modifiers and Appositives

Analyze the sentences below to determine where commas are needed to set off non-restrictive modifiers or non-restrictive appositives. To insert such punctuation write, in the space at the left, the word which will precede the comma, and after the word place the necessary comma. If no punctuation is required in the sentence, leave the space at the left blank.

EXAMPLE:

Texas, Union,   Texas which has more land than any other state in the Union was annexed in 1845.

.... 1. The Cologne Cathedral which is richly ornamented on its façade and towers is a perfect example of Gothic architecture.

.... 2. A man who fails to vote neglects his responsibilities as a citizen.

.... 3. He starts the day with a brisk walk to his office which is on the fourth floor of the Mason Building.

.... 4. The plane will take off on schedule if the weather is favorable.

.... 5. In Shakespeare's time it was generally thought that the night air was poisonous an erroneous belief which persisted for many years.

.... 6. La Guardia writes that at Fiume where he served as a consular agent from 1903 until 1906 he came to understand the political turmoil of southeastern Europe.

.... 7. The sign "Rooms for Rent" was tacked to the door of the neat frame house.

.... 8. The peace settlement after World War I created some new states including Czechoslovakia and Yugoslavia.

.... 9. The Chaillot Palace which furnished the background for one of the meetings of the United Nations Assembly was built for the World's Fair of 1937.

.... 10. He had enjoyed reading Conrad's stories particularly *Lord Jim*.

.... 11. Thousands of workers who are looking toward the future and its opportunities are taking advantage of the night school courses offered in various cities.

.... 12. Tom shook his head when the waitress asked him whether he would like to have another cup of coffee.

.... 13. Many American pilots are familiar with Gander Bay the point of departure for trans-Atlantic flights.
.... 14. The novel *Candide* ends with the idea that the person who cultivates his own garden is better off than the person who roams the world in search of idle pleasure.
.... 15. Glued to the mirror was a half dollar the first money the barber had earned in that shop.
.... 16. The motto "They Shall Not Pass" was adopted by the French at the Battle of the Marne.
.... 17. Puzzled he started investigating and retraced his steps hoping to find the missing wallet.
.... 18. Captain Johnson who had spent thirty years at sea told us that he would buy a farm in New Jersey when he retired from his command.
.... 19. Fruit which is allowed to ripen on the tree has a superior flavor.
.... 20. Along the wide concrete highway leading out of town are shabby little houses their porches sagging and their yards overgrown with weeds.
.... 21. The poet Whitman was regarded in many quarters as a dangerous radical.
.... 22. Stravinsky's *The Rite of Spring* performed as a ballet score in Paris in 1913 had a sensational effect on the audience.
.... 23. Everyone who has been out in a small fishing boat when a sudden squall has come up realizes how dangerous the situation can be.
.... 24. Scientists have discovered a metal which may prove more useful than aluminum or stainless steel.
.... 25. Several writers that were active in the Twenties such as Anderson and Masters were experimenting with a new kind of realism.

To obtain score, allow 4 points for each sentence in which the punctuation has been properly inserted and for each sentence identified as correct.

NAME .... DATE .... SCORE ....

66. THE MAIN USES OF THE COMMA—V

Members of a Series, Co-ordinate Adjectives

Supply additional commas wherever they are needed and take out unnecessary commas in the sentences below. To add a comma write, in the space at the left, the word which will precede the comma, and after the word place the comma. To take out an unnecessary comma write, in the space at the left, the word which precedes it, and after the word place an encircled comma. If the sentence is correctly punctuated, leave the space at the left blank.

EXAMPLES:

weird,   The lecturer described the weird mysterious rites of the voodoo cults.

large(,)   Mr. Vance lives in a large, stone house.

1. A dignified young man greeted me with a nod and asked me what books I wanted to examine.
2. Her costume for the party was a faded, old gingham dress and a shapeless straw hat trimmed with daisies.
3. He answered my question with a vague indecisive shrug of the shoulders.
4. A group of tight-lipped grim-faced coal miners stood near the entrance to the shaft.
5. Railroad facilities a supply of skilled labor and good factory sites are the inducements offered to any firm willing to set up business in this community.
6. The men's clothing department now offers a fine selection of fall suits in worsteds tweeds and gabardines.
7. Man lives in the physical world of the five senses—sight, hearing, touch, smell and taste.
8. On the stand were some brightly colored, ash trays, a pair of bronze book ends, and a chromium-plated flower vase.
9. Wars against the Spaniard, malnutrition, and smallpox, carried off most of the Indian population on the islands discovered by Columbus.
10. A gaunt, forlorn chimney was all that remained of the historically famous mansion.
11. The governor recommended that appropriations be made for a large experiment station a well-equipped laboratory and a trained research staff.

.... 12. Gulliver is represented as a stodgy unimaginative ship's surgeon who embarks on a voyage to the South Pacific gets shipwrecked and discovers an island inhabited by a race of tiny people.
.... 13. The old man walked across the lawn with a firm springy step.
.... 14. For Sale: a waterproof shock-resistant wrist watch.
.... 15. At some distance from the road stood an old, cobblestone house and a large barn.
.... 16. A small slender brunette had the rôle of Carmen in the summer opera performance.
.... 17. He followed the line of least resistance in everything he encountered—work, play, or social life.
.... 18. An excellent golf course hunting and fishing privileges and horseback trips are available to guests registered at the inn.
.... 19. The harsh inflexible discipline of the old-fashioned school has yielded to new ideals—self-expression, individualism and freedom from restraint.
.... 20. The Strauss waltzes recall the romance the gaiety the courtly dances that were once a part of old Viennese life.
.... 21. At the center of this barren, desolate, region is an abandoned mining town.
.... 22. The motors had been checked the gas tanks had been refueled and the plane was ready for the take-off.
.... 23. The comedian was a ludicrous little man, his expression varying from wide-eyed surprise to shocked horrified dismay.
.... 24. The West Side Realtors have listings of several moderately priced houses in the most desirable residential areas.
.... 25. The furnishings of the tent consisted of two iron cots an orange crate or two and a smoke-stained oil lamp dangling from the ridgepole.

To obtain score, allow 4 points for each sentence in which the punctuation has been correctly inserted and for each sentence identified as correct.

NAME .... DATE .... SCORE ....

67. THE MAIN USES OF THE COMMA—VI

Inverted Order, Contrasted Elements, Prevention of Misreading

Supply commas wherever they are needed in the sentences below. To add a comma write, in the space at the left, the word which will precede the comma, and after the word place the required comma.

EXAMPLE:
summer,   In the summer hotels near the lake are likely to be crowded.

....   1. On the northern boundary of the farm was a winding ravine narrow and densely wooded.
....   2. As one town is left behind the advance units of the pipe-laying crew move "up line" to another town on the right of way.
....   3. Effective speech requires that words be clearly pronounced not mumbled or slurred.
....   4. While she was unpacking her roommate dusted the furniture and helped to put things in order.
....   5. With the development of the atomic bomb warfare took on new and incredible dimensions.
....   6. The action of the play is rapid building up to a strong climax in the third act.
....   7. The highest temperatures of the season were recorded in August not in July.
....   8. Down the street cars were lining up before the church where the wedding was to take place.
....   9. That he had said the wrong thing he could tell immediately.
....   10. As we peered inside a dog rushed to the window and began barking frantically.
....   11. That the old-fashioned coaches hot and dusty made travel irksome no one would deny.
....   12. Not genius but a constant attention to duty is the key to success.
....   13. The game over the stadium was soon empty except for a few vendors packing up their wares.
....   14. With his electric shaver turned on the radio makes a buzzing noise.
....   15. That the love letter was a practical joke engineered by his friends he never suspected.
....   16. To many children reading means devouring the comics or looking over the pictorial magazines.

.... 17. The Ruhr valley not the Berlin area was the heart of industrial Germany.
.... 18. To think straight takes logic; to write clearly logic and a command of words.
.... 19. With the advent of autumn vacationists start homeward, and the little town empty and desolate settles down to await the long Maine winter.
.... 20. When wages go up the standard of living improves for a time; but higher wages often mean higher prices not increased buying power.
.... 21. Why he chose to be so secretive about his affairs no one could understand.
.... 22. The citizens themselves not the politicians are responsible for the laxity in city government.
.... 23. For dancing a portion of the street had been roped off near the bandstand.
.... 24. A day or so before he had rented a deck chair from the steward; now it was occupied by an old lady prim and sedate who was busily knitting a muffler.
.... 25. The municipal waterworks windowless and gloomy resembled a medieval fortress.

To obtain score, allow 4 points for each sentence in which the punctuation has been properly inserted.

68. THE CONVENTIONAL USES OF THE COMMA—I

Supply commas wherever they are needed in the sentences below. To add a comma write, in the space at the left, the word which will precede the comma, and after the word place the required comma. Follow the same procedure for punctuating numbers or abbreviations.

EXAMPLE:
painted,   Your house has recently been painted hasn't it?

1. My isn't that a magnificent view?
2. On May 7 1945 the surrender of the German forces took place.
3. "Ask your mother for some money" he said "and then run up to the hardware store for two dry cells."
4. "I am quite willing" he continued "that all the facts in the case be made public."
5. Mrs. Hoskins said acidly "That is a unique hat you are wearing Adele."
6. Why you must be mistaken.
7. Be sure Henry that you have closed all the windows before you leave the house.
8. Please answer the doorbell Frank.
9. Ah this is solid comfort.
10. Your coat Dora is the black one isn't it?
11. You have a fishing license have you not?
12. "Frankly sir" the clerk said "I think the brown suit looks better on you."
13. "I can give you an appointment" the dentist said "on Monday or Tuesday."
14. The convention was held at Philadelphia Pennsylvania in the month of July.
15. "I won't sign this contract" he said brusquely.
16. You live in Brooklyn don't you?
17. Send in the wrappers boys and girls together with your contest entries.
18. I forgot to say Mrs. Hibbs that this sewing machine is guaranteed for one year from the date of purchase.

.... 19. According to the catalogue, Robert T. Kane A.M. is the registrar of the school.
.... 20. Harvey E. Willis M.D. is in charge of the clinic.
.... 21. You are urged fellow alumni to attend a celebration which marks the hundredth anniversary of the founding of the college.
.... 22. "I had rather hoped" Father said "that you would want to go into business with me."
.... 23. James Whitcomb Riley lived in a house on Lockerbie Street, Indianapolis, Indiana for many years.
.... 24. You remember this tune don't you?
.... 25. In the first week of November 1948 the play opened on Broadway.

To obtain score, allow 4 points for each sentence in which the punctuation has been properly inserted.

69. THE CONVENTIONAL USES OF THE COMMA—II

Supply commas wherever they are needed in the sentences below. To add a comma write, in the space at the left, the word which will precede the comma, and after the word place the required comma. Follow the same procedure for punctuating numbers or abbreviations.

EXAMPLE:

1918,   The World War ended in 1918 didn't it?

1. Rail lines from the East and the West met at Promontory Point Utah on April 10 1869.
2. "Did you turn off the stove dear?" Mrs. Black called to her husband.
3. The elderly gentleman looked up from his desk and said "What can I do for you young man?"
4. I move Mr. Chairman that the meeting be adjourned.
5. "Well that settles it" he said resignedly.
6. "Goodness this is a slow train isn't it?" she remarked.
7. Oh here's the page I've been looking for.
8. You can obtain the information you want by writing to the French National Tourist Office 610 Fifth Avenue New York City.
9. On Saturday September 11 1948 Queen Wilhelmina abdicated the throne after fifty years as Queen of the Netherlands.
10. "Well at all events" he said "we know the motives for the crime."
11. Richard you stopped at the cleaning shop for your suit didn't you?
12. "Our age thank goodness is not as hopeless as it is sometimes pictured" the historian said drily.
13. Britain and France declared war on Germany after the invasion of Poland September 1939.
14. The conductor looked at my ticket and said "You're on the wrong train brother."

....	15.	Samuel Small Ph.D. is the superintendent of schools at Westport.
....	16.	Heidelberg Germany is an old university town.
....	17.	"You'll need some money won't you son?" Father said.
....	18.	"Put on another record Ann" said Martha.
....	19.	This train goes to Providence Rhode Island doesn't it?
....	20.	Horace Long Litt.D. has been appointed editor-in-chief of the new magazine.
....	21.	Our address after August 15 will be the Northway Lodge Watertown New York.
....	22.	The editorial offices will be moved on September 1 to Chicago Illinois.
....	23.	The residence of the British prime minister is at 10 Downing Street London.
....	24.	You can repair this radio can't you Mark?
....	25.	"Let's go to the movies Mother" Grace suggested.

To obtain score, allow 4 points for each sentence in which the punctuation has been properly inserted.

70. THE WRONG USES OF THE COMMA—I

Remove all unnecessary commas which appear in the sentences below. To take out a comma write, in the space at the left, the word which precedes the error, and after the word place an encircled comma. If the sentence is correctly punctuated, leave the space at the left blank.

EXAMPLE:

old (,)   The dog had grown old, and ill-tempered.

1. The Senator told the reporter, that what he had said about the bill, was an off-the-record opinion.
2. It is an experience, such as the one I have just described, that teaches a man the value of human loyalty and courage.
3. People are not, on the whole, as hopeful about world security, as they were at the close of the war.
4. Upon the mantelpiece, was a varied assortment of odds and ends.
5. That she had set out to be the life of the party, was immediately apparent from her actions.
6. What you will see in the planetarium, of course, is a small-scale replica of the heavens.
7. Above the main roof, rose a glassed-in cupola from which we could survey the neighboring roof tops, and the more distant church spires of the city.
8. That he already knew the secret of the trick, I was reasonably sure.
9. In the fall, comes the harvest season, a period of jubilation or of grim despair.
10. Kay was so well liked by everyone in the group, that anything she did or said seemed perfectly all right.
11. Yes, I have absolute confidence in his ability and in his judgment.
12. We were notified that the moving van would be at our house, by eight o'clock.
13. In the picture were a shabby tenement building, and some sagging telephone poles.
14. That the city is in desperate need of a modern rail terminal, no one will deny.
15. We cannot reconstruct, what Thoreau envisioned as the ideal world, nor can we project ourselves into the imaginary utopias of H. G. Wells' novels.

_____ 16. Don't alter, what you have written, or you may spoil the effect.
_____ 17. As police records show, many persons, that are ordinarily law-abiding citizens, will carelessly violate the traffic regulations.
_____ 18. I asked the child, what she wanted, as a birthday present.
_____ 19. We are unable, of course, to say just how soon a vacancy may occur.
_____ 20. The judge was, everyone agreed, a person of sharp wit, and of abundant wisdom.
_____ 21. The cashier at the restaurant, a nervous, and flustered young woman, could neither add a column of figures, nor give the correct change.
_____ 22. The autobiography tells how he arrived in Philadelphia penniless, and how he gradually rose to wealth and fame.
_____ 23. The house was middle-class, middle-aged, and comfortable as an old shoe.
_____ 24. "Boot camp," a six weeks' training period, was both lively and harrowing.
_____ 25. The doctor, sharp-tongued and candid, said that he had no time for persons, with imaginary ailments.

To obtain score, allow 4 points for each sentence in which the punctuation has been correctly revised and for each sentence identified as correct.

NAME ....DATE ....SCORE ....

71. THE WRONG USES OF THE COMMA—II

Remove all unnecessary commas which appear in the sentences below. To take out a comma write, in the space at the left, the word which precedes the error, and after the word place an encircled comma. If the sentence is correctly punctuated, leave the space at the left blank.

EXAMPLE:

right ⊙ *trees* ⊙   On our right, was a clump of trees, and an abandoned farmhouse.

.... 1. After he had returned from lunch, a tall, stoop-shouldered man entered the store, and asked him, whether he had advertised for a bookkeeper.

.... 2. Robert is revealed in the play as a weak, spineless, young man completely dominated by his selfish mother.

.... 3. Mahatma Gandhi was a Hindu leader, and a famous social reformer.

.... 4. We have borrowed the words, *goulash* and *coach*, from the Hungarian language.

.... 5. Exactly what happened to Mallory in his ill-fated attempt to climb Mount Everest, no one ever knew.

.... 6. The article relates, how a young Canadian soldier found a set of plans for the pending Normandy invasion, how he delivered the papers to his superiors, and how he won the British Empire Medal as a reward.

.... 7. We have traveled over this route so often, that it is very monotonous to us.

.... 8. His chief criticism is, that modern poetry is too often concerned with style, not with ideas.

.... 9. Color blindness, of course, is much more common among men than it is among women.

.... 10. The six weeks' tour of Europe was once popular with college students, with teachers, and with people, of various professions.

.... 11. I never knew, that Independence Hall once housed a small zoo, and a science museum.

.... 12. *The Gardener's Guide* explains, how to prepare the soil, when to set out various plants, and how to care for your flower or vegetable garden.

.... 13. When we think about traveling in Italy, we think of such places as, Capri, Amalfi, and Sorrento.

.... 14. His acting for the screen was as good as, if not better than, his performance on the regular stage.

.... 15. When an expert was asked to give his opinion, he said that it was either a genuine Rembrandt, or a very clever forgery.

.... 16. A store which has a modern, up-to-date appearance, and neat, courteous salesclerks, will always attract customers.

.... 17. To show the differences between the American code of sportsmanship and the British code, he cited some of the comments, which were made by British spectators at a cricket match.

.... 18. Solving crossword puzzles, and making up limericks about his friends, were his principal diversions during his convalescence.

.... 19. Pictured on the cover is a brown-haired, blue-eyed young woman, her attention centered on a gray kitten she is holding near her face.

.... 20. I wanted to take Advanced Psychology this year, but the course is open, to juniors and seniors only.

.... 21. Tell us, what you remember about the accident, won't you?

.... 22. An announcer who speaks too rapidly, is sometimes irritating to listeners.

.... 23. A Red Cross representative will demonstrate how to rescue a drowning person, and how to apply artificial respiration.

.... 24. Certain of the medieval universities, such as those at Padua, Rome, and Bologna, were governed by the students, not by the professors.

.... 25. To be sure, there has been a stronger, postwar demand for automobiles and building materials than for other types of manufactured goods.

To obtain score, allow 4 points for each sentence in which the punctuation has been correctly revised and for each sentence identified as correct.

NAME .... DATE .... SCORE ....

72. THE USES OF THE COMMA

General Review

Supply commas wherever they are needed in the sentences below, and take out unnecessary commas. To add a comma write, in the space at the left, the word which will precede it, and after the word place the comma. To take out an unnecessary comma write, in the space at the left, the word which precedes the error, and after the word place an encircled comma. If the sentence is correctly punctuated, leave the space at the left blank.

EXAMPLE:

house, rambling, The house low and rambling had a fresh coat of
gleaming ⊙ gleaming, white paint.

.... 1. Every person who has kissed the Blarney Stone is supposed to be an expert in flattery.
.... 2. In the summer canning factories in this area employ hundreds of women to peel tomatoes.
.... 3. On August 10 1946 Italian leaders were present at a peace conference held in Paris.
.... 4. What does the word *eleemosynary* mean?
.... 5. The sycamore tree straight and well-proportioned is often seen along the banks of creeks and rivers.
.... 6. Oh you must look at this; it is an old-fashioned, writing desk.
.... 7. He intends to go to law school doesn't he?
.... 8. Some ten minutes before I had called the porter, and told him to make up the berth.
.... 9. Horatio Alger an American novelist of the nineteenth century wrote countless stories employing the popular, rags-to-riches theme.
.... 10. Obviously embarrassed he hastily changed the subject.
.... 11. A special exhibit of Reynolds' paintings will be shown at the Albright Art Gallery Buffalo New York next month.
.... 12. A popular superstition holds that anyone who breaks a mirror will have seven years of bad luck.
.... 13. Mrs. Baker who was a trusting, old soul never doubted what we told her.
.... 14. "You may fire when you are ready Gridley" said Admiral Dewey at the battle of Manila Bay.

.... 15. After we had racked our brains trying to identify an ancient king whose name begins with the letter X we asked the teacher what the next question was.
.... 16. "That car of yours" my father said "is a public menace."
.... 17. *The White Tower* is a novel about a group of persons who set out to climb an Alpine peak who encounter numerous hazards along the way and who reveal their diverse characters in this grueling perilous adventure.
.... 18. Everyone who calls himself a Texan remembers with pride the story of the Alamo.
.... 19. I think Mary that the house cleaning is almost over thank goodness.
.... 20. We had spent a fairly comfortable night in our tent but some of our companions we later discovered had not fared so well.
.... 21. He could recall the softly etched shadows of a summer afternoon the graceful sweep of fine old elms the rhythmic clatter of a passing carriage.
.... 22. That the Plains of Abraham lofty and heavily fortified could be reached by the British soldiers no one would have believed.
.... 23. "Supper will be served at six not a minute before" said my mother.
.... 24. I do not remember the name of the hotel at which we stayed but I believe that it is listed in the Duncan Hines guide.
.... 25. Barry Fitzgerald's rôle in *Going My Way* was that of a lovable old priest with a conservative outlook a caustic wit and an unreasoning unrelenting distrust of his new assistant.

To obtain score, allow 4 points for each sentence in which the punctuation has been correctly revised and for each sentence identified as correct.

NAME .... DATE .... SCORE ....

73. CONVENTIONAL PUNCTUATION—I

Periods, Colons, Quotation Marks, and Italics

Write, in the space at the left, each of the underscored passages in the sentences below, and add periods, colons, quotation marks, or italics wherever they are needed. Italics should be indicated by underlining.

EXAMPLE:

S. S. Gripsholm   Many Americans who had been interned in the Orient came back on the SS Gripsholm.

.... 1. John Gunther's Inside USA, a spacious commentary on the American scene, was widely read.

.... 2. A condensed version of the story appears in the June issue of the Reader's Digest.

.... 3. A turntable which operates at a speed of 33⅓ rpm has been designed for the new long-playing records.

.... 4. The battle of Agincourt, which took place in 1415 AD, made King Henry V a national hero.

.... 5. His summer address will be RFD 1, Ovid, New York.

.... 6. The program will be broadcast at 10 15 PM over the Columbia network.

.... 7. Physicists measure heat in terms of the BTU standard.

.... 8. Is he the new secretary of the local YMCA?

.... 9. Dear Mr Hammond (salutation of a business letter)

.... 10. Kindly report to this office for an interview at 9 30 AM, Wednesday, September 3.

.... 11. The apostle Paul was originally named Saul (see Acts 9 1–30).

.... 12. The store will accept mail and telephone orders within the New York delivery area. No COD orders, please.

.... 13. The Chicago Sun, launched in 1941, soon achieved a wide circulation throughout the Middle West.

....	14. With great fervor and volume, the radio crooner was singing Nature Boy.
....	15. The baccalaureate sermon will be given by the Rev John Kroll.
....	16. The DAR organization is holding a convention in Washington next month.
....	17. The author tells in his journals of his meeting with Mme Chiang Kai-shek.
....	18. This product is available in Canada through the Regency Paper Co, Ltd, Montreal.
....	19. Baskets, woolen goods, Indian pottery, etc, may be purchased in the novelty shop just off the lobby of the hotel.
....	20. The Silver Bracelet is a short story describing an American pilot's experience in a Japanese prison camp.
....	21. The party will make the voyage to Hawaii on the SS Lurline, a cruise ship of the Matson Lines.
....	22. The Atlantic Monthly, founded nearly a century ago, continues its tradition as a literary periodical.
....	23. In the June issue of the magazine is a poem called Death's Jester, by Alastair W. R. Miller.
....	24. To be eligible for the MA degree, a student must have completed at least one year of graduate study.
....	25. Herbert S. Allan's John Hancock Patriot in Purple is a biography of the well-known revolutionary aristocrat.

To obtain score, multiply number of errors by 4 and subtract total from 100.

NAME .... DATE .... SCORE ....

74. CONVENTIONAL PUNCTUATION—II

Literary Titles

Insert colons, quotation marks, italics, and such other marks of punctuation as may be required in the sentences below. Italics should be indicated by underlining.

EXAMPLE:
Edith Wharton's <u>The Age of Innocence</u> is a novel which satirizes New York social life in the Victorian era.

1. David Karsner's Silver Dollar The Story of the Tabors is a book which records the history of a family prominent in the early annals of Denver.

2. Magazines like House Beautiful and Better Homes and Gardens contain articles on gardening landscaping interior decorating and other topics of interest to the home owner.

3. Dr. William C. Menninger a leading specialist in his field outlines the background and the scope of an important branch of medical science in his volume called Psychiatry Its Evolution and Present Status (Cornell University Press Ithaca New York).

4. College Life an entertaining chapter in Henry S. Canby's American Memoir tells of the author's experience as a Yale undergraduate at the turn of the century.

5. Edna Ferber's story Mother Knows Best is included in a volume of short stories titled One Basket (Simon and Schuster New York).

6. We Called It Culture a book describing the growth of the Chautauqua movement in America states that the song The End of a Perfect Day was a perennial favorite with Chautauqua audiences.

7. Two versions of Casey Jones the classic ballad of American railroading

are given in The American Songbag a collection of folksongs edited by Carl Sandburg.

8. Adventure on the high seas awaits the reader of Edmund Gilligan's Voyage of the Golden Hind a novel about a sailing trawler of the Gloucester fleet.

9. Falstaff's reference (in the play Henry the Fourth) to "Dives that lived in purple" is explained in Luke 16 19–31.

10. Robert Wood Johnson's The Maginot Line of America an article appearing in Harper's discloses certain weaknesses in our present military system and offers suggestions about the training of future officers.

11 Mr. Reginald Peacock's Day a short story by Katherine Mansfield is a satirical portrait of a vain and self-centered music teacher.

12 In the poem We Are Seven Wordsworth reveals the attitude of an eight-year-old girl toward death.

To obtain score, allow 8½ points for each sentence in which the punctuation has been correctly supplied.

75. THE USE OF CAPITALS—I

Examine carefully each passage below to determine which words, aside from the first word of the sentence, should be capitalized. Enter such words in capitalized form in the spaces at the left. If the sentence requires no further capitalization, leave the spaces at the left blank.

EXAMPLE:
West
Grand Canyon
During our trip through the west we saw many things of interest, including the grand canyon.

Michigan
Lake Huron
1. On the eastern side of michigan are the blue waters of lake huron.

India
2. Because of its special properties, india ink is widely used by artists and engravers.

3. The songs of the bob-white and the whippoorwill are familiar to every country boy.

Spanish
4. When the waiter came to take our orders, I asked for a spanish omelet.

White Mountains
New Hampshire
5. Last summer we drove through the white mountains, which are in northern new hampshire.

Deep Are the Roots
Broadway
6. We had tickets for the play *deep are the roots*, which was being presented by the original broadway cast.

Freudian
7. The freudian doctrines, it is generally conceded, have influenced the literature of our times.

Kleenex
Ivory
8. On the dressing table were a box of kleenex, some bobby pins, and a cake of ivory soap.

English
9. In his freshman year at college he took four courses: history, english, physics, and mathematics.

Coca-Cola
10. The principal items on the menu for the picnic were frankfurters and coca-cola.

May
11. This plant, which has white flowers and bears yellow fruit, is known as the may apple.

Davis Cup / *Forest Hills*   12. The davis cup matches, which will be played at forest hills next month, may produce new tennis champions.

.... 13. In the display window she noticed a dark-blue chesterfield coat priced at $39.95.

Civil War / *South*   14. At the close of the civil war, the south faced a difficult period of economic readjustment.

Good Friday   15. On good friday, special services will be held in most of the churches of the city.

.... 16. Sam was a jack-of-all-trades, but he took a special pleasure in mending old clocks.

West / *Fifty-seventh Street*   17. I ordered the records by mail from a shop at 33 west fifty-seventh street.

"Jeanie with the Light Brown Hair"   18. Foster's lyrics are numerous; one of the best-known is "jeannie with the light brown hair."

Father's   19. Mother told the laundress to take special pains in ironing father's white shirts.

July / *Democrats*   20. In mid-july the democrats met to draft their political platform and to name their candidates.

.... 21. If you walk two blocks north on this street, you will find an entrance to the subway.

Arctic Circle   22. A scientific expedition will soon leave for a year of biological research within the arctic circle.

Old Testament / *Ruth*   23. One of the most poignant narratives of the old testament is the account of ruth.

.... 24. Within a week's time my mother and two of us children had picked thirty quarts of strawberries.

New Deal / *American*   25. Roosevelt's opponents contended that his new deal reforms violated the traditions of american democracy.

To obtain score, allow 4 points for each sentence in which the capitalization has been correctly supplied and for each sentence identified as correct.

244

76. THE USE OF CAPITALS—II

Examine carefully each passage below to determine which words, aside from the first word of the sentence, should be capitalized. Enter such words in capitalized form in the spaces at the left. If the sentence requires no further capitalization, leave the spaces at the left blank.

EXAMPLE:
Thanksgiving Day   Traditionally, thanksgiving day has been the
Thursday   November   last thursday in november.

_____   1. With his bushy hair and his squat, powerful frame, he
Stone Age   looked like a character out of the stone age.

_____   2. The high collar and the perky bow tie could not hide his
Adam's   prominent adam's apple.

Gen. Elec. Co.   3. The general electric company has conducted extensive
_____   research in the field of plastics.

Pearl Harbor   4. In the surprise attack at pearl harbor, heavy losses were
Navy   sustained by our navy.

Indian   5. For dessert we had indian pudding, made from a recipe
New England   which my grandmother used in new england.

_____   6. Health authorities have repeatedly warned that house-
Pasteurized   wives should buy only pasteurized milk.

_____   7. Hardy's best-known novel, and one which reflects his
The Return of the Native characteristic philosophy, is *the return of the native*.

Madras   8. A group of unusually fine madras shirts will be included
_____   in a clearance sale which starts tomorrow.

Atlantic   9. The vessel lost her rudder in mid-atlantic, and her skip-
S.O.S.   per ordered an sos call for help.

Government   10. According to this schedule, the examination in govern-
Friday   ment 200 will be given on friday afternoon.

Italian   11. Michelangelo, an italian painter and sculptor, is remem-
Sistine Chapel   bered for his work in the sistine chapel.

245

Uncle Tom 12. Henson, a negro preacher active in the fight against slavery, may have been the original uncle tom.

Oriental 13. In the living room were several oriental rugs, their warm
.... tones blending with the brightly colored drapes.

Cheerios 14. An advertisement for cheerios bears this caption: "a bet-
"A better..." ter breakfast makes housework fly."

.... 15. After studying his face in the mirror, he cautiously
.... picked up his father's razor.

Job 16. His patience was like that of job, whose sufferings are
Bible chronicled in the bible.

Cape Cod 17. The cape cod house, with its compact floor plan and
American pleasant exterior, is a favorite with american builders.

Pekinese 18. After mother had gone upstairs, she heard our pekinese
Mother dog barking excitedly.

Pres. Roosevelt 19. In the election of 1912, ex-president roosevelt broke
Republicans with the republicans and headed an independent ticket.

.... 20. In the fall, the colleges and universities across the land
Freshmen welcome the entering freshmen.

.... 21. After looking at the menu, he ordered a steak and
.... french-fried potatoes.

.... 22. Our history teacher, a tall, sandy-haired man of fifty,
Baptist was a baptist minister.

Alice in Wonderland 23. This edition of _alice in wonderland_ contains the famous
Tenniel illustrations by the artist tenniel.

.... 24. In the store window he saw the very shoes he wanted:
Cordovan Blucher of cordovan leather cut in the blucher style.

Ford 25. Parked in the driveway was a green ford convertible
Iowa with iowa license plates.

To obtain score, allow 4 points for each sentence in which the capitalization has been correctly supplied and for each sentence identified as correct.

NAME ....DATE ....SCORE ....

77. THE USES OF THE APOSTROPHE—I

To Form Possessives

Supply, in the space at the left, the correct possessive form of each term enclosed in parenthesis in the sentences below.

EXAMPLE:

months' — The judge gave him a six (months) sentence.

Doris' — 1. "Swell" is (Doris) usual comment.
week's — 2. Send two dollars for a ten (weeks) subscription.
cockney's — 3. Is he trying to imitate a (cockney) pronunciation?
hers — 4. Have you seen that diamond ring of (she)?
men's — 5. (Men) colleges are more numerous in the East.
Holmes' — 6. Dr. Watson was Sherlock (Holmes) closest friend.
ladies' — 7. There are several bargains in (ladies) wrist watches.
Neilson and Hill's — 8. He wanted (Neilson and Hill) edition of Shakespeare.
anyone else's — 9. Your golf score is lower than (anyone else).
Harrises' — 10. Is that the (Harrises) dog?
dollars' — 11. We used two (dollars) worth of gasoline on the trip.
Flint and Horner's — 12. She bought the sofa at (Flint and Horner) sale.
actress' — 13. Do you recall the (actress) name?
year's — 14. He was granted a (year) leave of absence.
city's — 15. The (city) rapid growth has created certain problems.
secretaries' — 16. Are you going to the (secretaries) luncheon?
Evans' — 17. George Eliot was Mary Ann (Evans) pen name.
brothers-in-law's — 18. With his (brothers-in-law) help, Sam found a job.
children's — 19. On the lower shelves is a display of (children) books.
yours — 20. "What concern is it of (you)?" he snapped.
sister-in-law's — 21. She wore her (sister-in-law) evening wrap.
country's — 22. The Navy is the (country) first line of defense.
girls' — 23. She is attending a (girls) boarding school.

nobody's 24. It was actually (nobody) fault.
its 25. The skiing was at (it) best in February.
Lincoln and Douglas' 26. (Lincoln and Douglas) debates touched vital issues
Wives' 27. Bennett wrote *The Old (Wives) Tale*.
theirs 28. The car behind us must be (their).
landlady's 29. The (landlady) son handed the package to me.
doctor's 30. I cannot understand the (doctor) prescribing this.
whose 31. During (who) administration was Alaska purchased?
Jones' 32. Fires have sent many ships to Davy (Jones) locker.
Women's 33. Susan B. Anthony was a crusader for (women) rights.
money's 34. We had our (money) worth with that double feature.
James' 35. Have you read any of Henry (James) novels?
hero's 36. He played the (hero) rôle in a recent melodrama.
William and Mary's 37. (William and Mary) reign began in 1689.
Stern Brothers' 38. She is employed as a buyer at (Stern Brothers) store.
Journey's 39. (Journey) End is an English play by R. C. Sherriff.
Walter's 40. He did not approve of (Walter) buying a motorcycle

To obtain score, multiply number of errors by 2½ and subtract total from 100.

78. THE USES OF THE APOSTROPHE—II

To Indicate Omissions and to Form Irregular Plurals

Examine carefully the sentences below and pick out the expressions which require apostrophes. Enter such terms in the spaces at the left and insert the necessary apostrophes.

EXAMPLE:

c's r's   There are two *cs* and two *rs* in *occurred*.

_____ 1. There are too many *ifs* and *buts* in this proposition.
_____ 2. The panic of 93 had serious effects.
_____ 3. He always pronounced *ls* as if they were *ws*.
_____ 4. The Model Ts were the joy of amateur mechanics.
_____ 5. "Whos the pretty girl milkin the cow?" he sang.
_____ 6. Youll go to the bank, wont you?
_____ 7. The B-29s were flying in close formation.
_____ 8. The lettering on the door read: "John Sims, Secy."
_____ 9. This windows stuck fast; lets open the other.
_____ 10. Isnt the term *cellar door* melodious?
_____ 11. The *ls* and *rs* give a pleasing sound effect.
_____ 12. "Shine em up, Mister?" called the bootblack.
_____ 13. He was driving a 48 Chevrolet sedan.
_____ 14. Theyre going to Maine, arent they?
_____ 15. Use *Rs* and *Ws* to mark right and wrong answers.
_____ 16. There are some size 39s here, Im sure.
_____ 17. I didnt order that, and I cant use it.
_____ 18. "The librarys closing at nine oclock," Bob said.
_____ 19. In the 1920s American prose took on new vigor.
_____ 20. The Johnsons were there, werent they?
_____ 21. The boy answered our questions with *Nopes* and *Yeps*
_____ 22. His grades were poor: one C and four Ds.

....	23.	"Soups on," shouted the camp cook.
....	24.	The alma mater song was written by Dan Foss, 03.
....	25.	Id like to speak to your father.
....	26.	He has a local reputation as a neer-do-well.
....	27.	The lines across the *ts* look like pump handles.
....	28.	Men with high IQs were given special opportunities.
....	29.	Theres a note on your desk; its from Ed, I think.
....	30.	A neon sign pointed to the Spic n Span Cabins.
....	31.	Its getting late; I must be going.
....	32.	Dont leave until weve had supper.
....	33.	Notice the number of *verys* in this paragraph.
....	34.	The cat-o-nine-tails was used in floggings.
....	35.	Whats the most romantic of all melodies?
....	36.	I often mistake your *2s* for *3s*.
....	37.	Do not capitalize *thes* and *ofs* within titles.
....	38.	The "Ship o Dreams" program is at half-past eleven.
....	39.	One line of type was cancelled by a row of *xs*.
....	40.	Havent you seen the Clarks recently?

To obtain score, allow 2½ points for each sentence in which the apostrophes have been properly supplied.

79. THE USES OF THE HYPHEN—I

To Divide Words at Line Endings

Each of the phrases below, you are to assume, involves the breaking of a word at the end of a line. Determine, with the help of your dictionary, whether the word has been properly divided for a line ending. If the division is incorrect, write the word in the space at the left, indicating the syllables on which it may be divided. If the word should not be divided, write it solid. At least one word in each group is correctly divided. Make no entry in the space at the left for such a word.

EXAMPLE:

ide-al-is-tic   This thoroughly i-   to fly ver-   the bas-
                   dealistic concept   y high   ic plan

very

....   1. having happen-   the old Rom-   the ineligi-
                      ed quickly   an coin   ble player

....

....   2. after call-   having drop-   then start-
                      ing my name   ped the pen   ed the car

....

....   3. a prescrip-   an exceedingly i- journeying thr-
                      tion to fill   rate landlady   ough France

....

....   4. a new symphon-   on the base-   waving a handkerch-
                      y   ball field   ief

....

....   5. on the prev-   a long col-   with an e-
                      ious page   umn   lectric needle

....

....   6. a tense situat-   a velvet cur-   a novel expe-
                      ion   tain   rience

....

....   7. on the thirt-   a thrilling West- reading my for-
                      ieth of July   ern movie   tune

....

....   8. this negotia-   having tou-   a horizont-
                      ble security   gh fibers   al line

....

....	9. a feline creature	in her possession	a gold thimble
..-...................	10. with my father's permission	feeling rather weary	without bothering anyone
....	11. for road maintenance	the medical profession	hardly a ripple
....	12. rooms for patients	a full measure	a drinking fountain
....	13. within the borough limits	having fatty tissue	a resourceful man
....	14. having played golf	while stirring the soup	with a condescending air
....	15. with much enterprise	on his disappearance	an older college
....	16. stating our intentions	after talking about him	made of wrought iron
....	17. a coughing spasm	the antarctic explorer	turning the tables
....	18. a point of reference	by a Russian official	the matter referred to
....	19. for some length of time	being startled by a noise	a rare opportunity
....	20. a vote of affirmation	the late evening	a good product
....			

To obtain score, allow 5 points for each group of phrases in which the answers have been correctly indicated.

NAME .... DATE .... SCORE ....

80. THE USES OF THE HYPHEN—II

To Divide Compound Words

Determine, with the help of your dictionary, whether the italicized expressions in the sentences below should be written as separate words, as hyphenated compounds, or as solid words. If the words should be written separately, or as hyphenated compounds, write them in their correct form in the spaces at the left. If the words are correct as given, leave the spaces at the left blank.

EXAMPLE:
first-class   It was a *firstclass* picture.

.... 1. The *diningroom* has oak paneling.

.... 2. He is campaigning for *reelection* to Congress.

.... 3. Let's settle this dispute on a *giveandtake* basis.

.... 4. On the *titlepage* you will see the publisher's name.

.... 5. The *streetcar* lurched around a curve.

.... 6. On his birthday he received a *selfwinding* watch.

.... 7. The *postoffice* closes at noon on Saturdays.

.... 8. A brisk, *wellgroomed* salesman met me at the door.

.... 9. In the gallery is a *lifesize* portrait of Lincoln.

.... 10. The *railroads* are seeking an increase in rates.

.... 11. Rupert Brooke died at the age of *twentyseven*.

.... 12. He uses *onehalf* of his income for food and rent.

.... 13. It will take two yards to *recover* this chair.

.... 14. Beowulf is the hero of the *AngloSaxon* epic.

.... 15. The *airport* is five miles from the city.

.... 16. We made an *overnight* stop in Utica.

.... 17. She is a *coauthor* of a book about old china.

.... 18. The rain beat savagely against the *windshield*.

.... 19. He took a *threeyear* contract as football coach.

.... 20. The doctor clung to his *oldfashioned* ideas.

.... 21. Ring Lardner was a *wellknown* story writer.
.... 22. The smoke is caused by the university *powerplant*.
.... 23. The delegates applauded *exPresident* Hoover's speech.
.... 24. Nine *wouldbe* actors were on hand for the rehearsal.
.... 25. Steel rods are used to *reenforce* the concrete.
.... 26. The Middle West sweltered under a *heatwave*.
.... 27. A cascade of noise poured from the *loudspeaker*.
.... 28. The *highschool* orchestra was giving a broadcast.
.... 29. An *eightyearold* boy was the team's mascot.
.... 30. He had only a *lukewarm* interest in poetry.
.... 31. The officer told him that it was a *oneway* street.
.... 32. Use blue or green *wallpaper* in that south room.
.... 33. There is a *fillingstation* two miles up the road.
.... 34. On the shelf was a *dogeared* telephone directory.
.... 35. The *sodafountain* is at the back of the store.
.... 36. Television is no longer just a *newfangled* toy.
.... 37. *Stockholders* will receive an extra dividend.
.... 38. O. Henry's stories were once *widelyknown*.
.... 39. There may be some *lastminute* changes in the script
.... 40. By *midApril* the trees are in leaf.

To obtain score, multiply number of errors by 2½ and subtract total from 100.

81. REVIEW OF MECHANICS

Capitals, Apostrophes, and Hyphens

Pick out errors in the use of capitals, apostrophes, or hyphens in the sentences below. Draw a circle around each error and write the correct form in the space at the left. If the sentence is free from errors, leave the space at the left blank.

EXAMPLE:

men's   On what floor are (mens') suits?

1. He dotted the *i*s and crossed the *t*s with meticulous care.
2. If our's is the winning ticket, we'll drive home a new ford car tomorrow evening.
3. Lewis and Clark's expedition opened the lands west of the Mississippi to American traders.
4. Cyprus, a tiny island in the Mediterranean, guards Britain's life line to the middle east.
5. Episodes from Moses' life are given in the early books of the bible.
6. To photograph wildlife in the hudson bay region, the party carried two thousand dollars worth of camera equipment.
7. Have you heard who's moving into the Smiths' old house on South Liberty Street?
8. After a glance at the morning paper, he reentered the house to get his suitcase and a raincoat.
9. Hitler, obsessed by a napoleonic complex, promised to build an empire that would stand for a thousand years.
10. The second line of gray's poem reads: "the lowing herd wind slowly oer the lea."
11. From 1921 until 1930, the year of his death, ex-President Taft served on the U.S. Supreme Court.
12. Eking out a bare existence in war-ravaged Berlin are countless persons who's homes were destroyed in the bombings.
13. Doctors know that children's diseases, such as whooping cough and measles, may have serious aftereffects.
14. In his autobiography, Logan Pearsall Smith describes his quaker upbringing in Germantown, a suburb of Philadelphia.
15. The city's newest hotel is an up to date structure that makes its competitors look dowdy and old-fashioned.

.... 16. A farm hand walked over to the car and said: "If your lookin for the boss, he's not here today."
.... 17. The spanishamerican conflict, which lasted only a few months, marked the emergence of the United States as a world power.
.... 18. George is now a sophomore at Amherst college, isnt he?
.... 19. A blue-eyed, white-bearded giant of a man, he made me think of an ancient Norseman.
.... 20. Carl Carmer's *listen for a lonesome drum* is a book which reveals some of the indian legends of western New York.
.... 21. Palestine, long regarded as a primitive and backward country, has been transformed by its' recent settlers into a modern, forward-looking republic.
.... 22. Tolstoy drew upon his young sister's in law character for his portrayal of Natasha, the heroine of the novel.
.... 23. On a survey made recently, seventy seven per cent of the womens replies were in favor of a self-service counter for meats and poultry.
.... 24. We rose at five oclock, ready to make an early start on our days journey into the Grand Canyon.
.... 25. During his high school course, french and algebra were his favorite subjects.

To obtain score, allow 4 points for each sentence which has been properly corrected and for each sentence which has been identified as correct.

SECTION IV
Spelling

SPELLING

Spelling is primarily a matter of observation and concentration. To a lesser extent, it is a matter of association and of clear, correct pronunciation.

First, to spell a word one must actually *see* it—not merely glance at it and have an impression of a number of letters placed together. He must see these letters distinctly, in their order, and related to each other in creating certain sounds and syllables.

But seeing these letters is not enough. If the word is difficult to spell or if it is long, one must concentrate his attention on the letters and their order until he is as certain of spelling the word as he is of spelling his own name. This is not an exaggeration. Spelling is the only part of English that is absolute; it should appeal, therefore, to all persons who have, or think they have, scientific or mathematical minds. There is little difference between learning how to spell correctly and learning the multiplication tables: they both require strenuous mental exercise.

Although there is no substitute for concentration and repetition in learning how to spell, there are several effective aids in mastering spelling. Association is one of the natural processes of the mind, and this process should be used constantly by the student in relating and grouping words. For instance, with se*para*te one naturally thinks of *parts*, and by associating se*para*te and *parts* the frequently misspelled syllable is corrected. We *labor* in a *labor*atory; *there* is *here* moved farther away; a *villa*in was once associated with a *villa*; de*fini*te and inde*fini*te and in*fini*te have the same vowels before and after *n* as *fini*sh.

Let us take one of the most difficult word groups in the English language—words having the "seed" sound. You can master the entire group by learning only four words.

supersede. This is the only one in the group that has *s*, and the *s* is in the origin of the word. The word is derived from *super,* "above" and *sedeo,* "to sit." To *supersede* a person is "to sit above him."

exceed, proceed (with its derivatives *proceeding* and *proceedings*) and *succeed* have *ceed.* Remember: to *succeed* one must *proceed* to *exceed* others.

You need to learn only the four words given above, for all the other words in this sound-group have *ced.* Among them are *accede, concede, intercede, precede, procedure, recede, secede,* but you need not learn them. By memorizing four words you can spell correctly every word in this vexatious group.

Finally, distinct pronunciation is helpful in learning correct spelling, for it brings in the additional aid of hearing. In careless pronunciation letters are inverted, omitted, or even added. Consequently many persons say *chimbley* for *chimney, prespiration* for *perspiration, accidently* for *accidentally, boundry* for *boundary, goverment* for *government, discription* for *description, humerous* for *humorous, lightening* for *lightning, temperment* for *temperament, athelete* for *athlete, disasterous* for *disastrous*, and *grevious* for *grievous*. The list could be prolonged indefinitely. Clear pronunciation of words is the corrective of this spelling fault.

There are, fortunately, a few rules of such general application to spelling that they repay many fold the effort required to learn them.

1. Doubling the final consonant. Words of one syllable or words accented on the last syllable, ending in a single consonant preceded by a single vowel, double that consonant before a suffix beginning with a vowel.

Words of one syllable ending in a single consonant preceded by a single vowel:

cram	crammed	red	reddish
grip	gripped	sad	sadder
bud	budding	thin	thinnest
stir	stirring	fog	foggy
run	runner	god	goddess

Words of more than one syllable accented on the last syllable and ending in a single consonant preceded by a single vowel:

recur	recurring	recurred	recurrence
remit	remitting	remitted	remittance
commit	committing	committed	committee
control	controlling	controlled	controller

Note, in the following list, that the words in the last column do not have the accent on the last syllable and therefore do not double the consonant.

confer	conferring	conferred	conference
infer	inferring	inferred	inference
equip	equipping	equipped	equipage

The one important exception to the preceding rule is *excellence*.

| excel | excelling | excelled | excellence |

Note the effect of the accent in the following words:

benefit	benefiting	benefited	benefiter
sever	severing	severed	severance
inherit	inheriting	inherited	inheritance
listen	listening	listened	listener

Note the effect of two consonants at the close of the following words.

| pick | picking | picked | picker |
| garnish | garnishing | garnished | garnisher |

The importance of this rule can be seen from the following: *hopping* along on one foot, *hoping* to hear from you; a flower *pinned* on his coat, the maiden *pined* away and died; *scarred* with battle wounds, *scared* to death; *barring* accidents, a dog *baring* his teeth; arguments *dinned* into my ears, I *dined* at the Waldorf; he *shammed* illness, he was *shamed* into confessing; *starring* in a picture, *staring* at a movie actress; he *planned* to retire, he *planed* the board smooth; a man *robbed* of his money, a priest *robed* in black.

2. Final silent e. Silent *e* at the end of a word is dropped before a suffix beginning with a vowel but retained when the suffix begins with a consonant.

Silent *e* is dropped before a suffix beginning with a vowel.

rise	rising	like	likable
make	making	adore	adoration
arrange	arranging	fame	famous

Words ending in *ce* or *ge* retain the *e* before suffixes beginning with *a* or *o* when the soft sounds of *c* and *g* are desired.

| trace | traceable | manage | manageable |
| service | serviceable | advantage | advantageous |

The silent *e* is sometimes retained to preserve the identity of the original word or to prevent confusing with some similar word.

mileage	hoeing	eyeing
acreage	shoeing	dyeing
canoeing	toeing	singeing

Silent *e* is retained before suffixes beginning with a consonant.

care	careful	hope	hopeless
like	likely	white	whiteness
state	statement	nine	nineteen
entire	entirely	nine	ninety

The following exceptions to the preceding rule should be noted.

abridgment	argument	truly
acknowledgment	awful	wholly
judgment	duly	ninth

3. Final y. Final *y* preceded by a consonant changes *y* to *ie* before adding *d* or *s*, and to *i* before adding any other ending except one beginning with *i*. Final *y* is not changed when preceded by a vowel.

Preceded by a consonant and adding *s* and *d* and *ing* of verbs. Other suffixes are illustrated in the last column.

verb	add *s*	add *d*	retain *y* before *i*	other suffixes
deny	denies	denied	denying	deniable
defy	defies	defied	defying	defiance
apply	applies	applied	applying	applicant
try	tries	tried	trying	trier
study	studies	studied	studying	studious
busy	busies	busied	busying	business
marry	marries	married	marrying	marriage
rely	relies	relied	relying	reliance

Preceded by a consonant and adding *s* to form plurals of nouns.

| lady | ladies | enemy | enemies |
| sky | skies | ally | allies |

Preceded by a consonant and adding the suffixes of the comparative and the superlative degrees and of noun formations.

heavy	heavier	heaviest	heaviness
happy	happier	happiest	happiness
merry	merrier	merriest	merriment
wealthy	wealthier	wealthiest	wealthiness

Preceded by a vowel.

stay	stays	boy	boys
annoy	annoyed	monkey	monkeys
pray	prayer	attorney	attorneys
coy	coyly	coy	coyness

The following are exceptions to the preceding rule.

| day | daily | pay | paid |
| lay | laid | say | said |

4. The digraphs ie and ei. When *ie* and *ei* are sounded as long *e* (as in *see*), write *i* before *e* except after *c*.

Words with *i* before *e*.

chief	grieve	reprieve	believe
thief	field	relieve	belief
yield	priest	fiendish	besiege
piece	shield	achieve	fierce
brief	wield	retrieve	pierce
shriek	mien	mischief	niece

Words with *e* before *i* after *c*.

| receive | perceive | conceive | deceit |
| receipt | deceive | conceit | ceiling |

The following are exceptions to these two rules.

| either | leisure | seize | financier |
| neither | weird | seizure | species |

NAME .... DATE .... SCORE ....

82. SPELLING—I

Divide each of the following words into syllables and place the primary accent on the correct syllable. Use the dictionary for any word about which you are not absolutely certain.

EXAMPLES:
temperament   tem'per-a-ment
monstrous   mon'strous

1. restaurant ....
2. occasionally ....
3. medicinal ....
4. sacrilegious ....
5. library ....
6. curiosity ....
7. primitive ....
8. original ....
9. prejudice ....
10. hungry ....
11. valuable ....
12. momentous ....
13. applicable ....
14. statistics ....
15. thorough ....
16. despicable ....
17. villain ....
18. athletic ....
19. exquisite ....
20. adult ....
21. liable ....
22. generally ....

23. perseverance ....
24. business ....
25. dormitory ....
26. quantity ....
27. conscientious ....
28. candidate ....
29. prevalent ....
30. unanimous ....
31. efficient ....
32. grievous ....
33. comparable ....
34. entrance ....
35. exceptionally ....
36. cavalry ....
37. considerable ....
38. recognize ....
39. children ....
40. chocolate ....
41. preferable ....
42. suppress ....
43. hospitable ....
44. similar ....

263

45. accumulate .... 48. alternate ....
46. profession .... 49. permanent ....
47. address .... 50. admirable ....

To obtain score, multiply number of errors by 2 and subtract total from 100.

83. SPELLING—II

In the space to the left, supply the missing letter in each of the following words.

1. .... p rsue
2. .... signifi ant
3. .... ecsta y
4. .... confection ry
5. .... tim rous
6. .... intell gent
7. .... prophe y (noun)
8. .... admiss ble
9. .... spa ious
10. .... insist nce
11. .... invis ble
12. .... friv lous
13. .... underpriv leged
14. .... super eding
15. .... obst cle
16. .... bachel r
17. .... advi e (noun)
18. .... inten ion
19. .... diction ry
20. .... sens tive
21. .... prep ration
22. .... d scribe
23. .... practic ble
24. .... le sure
25. .... sle ve
26. .... substan ial
27. .... hum rist
28. .... sembl nce
29. .... s mphony
30. .... chall nge
31. .... aristocra y
32. .... resist nce
33. .... wom n (plural)
34. .... contemp rary
35. .... desp ration
36. .... guid nce
37. .... spe ch
38. .... ineff cient
39. .... par nership
40. .... subsist nce
41. .... sup rb
42. .... sacr fice
43. .... manu l
44. .... ficti ious

45. .... r   diculous
46. .... expen   ive
47. .... furn   ture
48. .... consist   nt
49. .... prim   tive
50. .... appear   nce

To obtain score, multiply number of errors by 2 and subtract total from 100.

NAME ....DATE ....SCORE ....

84. SPELLING—III

In the italicized words which appear in the phrases below, parentheses are placed where errors in spelling usually occur. The parenthesis marks do not necessarily indicate that a letter has been omitted from the word. Write the correct spelling of each word in the space at the left.

.... 1. a confirmed *opt( )mist*
.... 2. an *invalu( )ble* discovery
.... 3. a brilliant *achiev( )ment*
.... 4. not *af( )raid* to speak
.... 5. an unusual *coin( )id( )nce*
.... 6. at the age of *nin( )ty*
.... 7. "The better part of valor is *discre( )ion.*"
.... 8. according to the *princip( )s* of economics
.... 9. strict military *di( )ipline*
.... 10. an *ath( )letic* young man
.... 11. *ped( )ling* newspapers for a living
.... 12. *ac( )ross* the street
.... 13. the legal *prof( )ession*
.... 14. a *je( )lous* wife
.... 15. a statesman having *for( )sight*
.... 16. tickets for the evening *p( )formance*
.... 17. a suit of *cloth( )s*
.... 18. without *pre( )judice*
.... 19. debating *whe( )ther* to go
.... 20. a rambling and *rep( )titious* talk
.... 21. a woman of *perse( )verance*
.... 22. the voting *priv( )lege*
.... 23. an employer *intens( )ly* disliked
.... 24. *dis( )ap( )earing* from view

267

....	25. food *pois*( )*ning*
....	26. a *shep*( )*rd* watching his flock
....	27. *shin*( )*y* nose
....	28. saying what he *me*( )*nt*
....	29. faulty *pron*( )*nciation*
....	30. of the *prec*( )*ding events*
....	31. a *pl*( )*sant* afternoon
....	32. her *misch*( )*v*( )*ous* smile
....	33. a *veg*( )*table* dinner
....	34. not *altoge*( )*ther* true
....	35. under *simil*( )*r* circumstances
....	36. his *tra*( )*gic* mistake
....	37. at the *maint*( )*nance* building
....	38. a *suc*( )*essful* party
....	39. unable to *breath*( )
....	40. car *proc*( )*ding* slowly
....	41. willing to *rec*( )*o*( )*mend* him
....	42. at a dress *reh*( )*rsal* of the play
....	43. a flash of *light*( )*ning*
....	44. the debt having been *p*( )*d*
....	45. with *compar*( )*tive* safety
....	46. *accident*( )*ly* hearing the remark
....	47. this strange *occur*( )*nce*
....	48. whatever you *dec*( )*de* to do
....	49. a *tempe*( )*mental* actress
....	50. to my complete *su*( )*prise*

To obtain score, multiply number of errors by 2 and subtract total from 100.

NAME .... DATE .... SCORE ....

85. SPELLING—IV

The first part of the following list (1-25) contains words from which the letters a, ai, or ia have been omitted. Supply the missing letters by writing the complete words in the spaces at the left.

....	1. fount—n	....	14. carr—ge
....	2. spec—lty	....	15. custod—n
....	3. prep—ration	....	16. procl—mation
....	4. invar—bly	....	17. plant—n
....	5. cl—rify	....	18. enunc—tion
....	6. spont—neous	....	19. cert—nty
....	7. physic—n	....	20. Paris—n
....	8. Victor—n	....	21. famil—rity
....	9. terr—n	....	22. chapl—n
....	10. simil—rity	....	23. vill—nous
....	11. commerc—l	....	24. resident—l
....	12. excl—mation	....	25. pictor—l
....	13. Ren—ssance		

The remaining words in this list end with -ent, or -ant. Supply the appropriate endings by writing the complete words in the spaces at the right.

ingredi—	26.	irrelev—	35. ....
domin—	27.	corpul—	36. ....
incid—	28.	immigr—	37. ....
attend—	29.	incess—	38. ....
lieuten—	30.	compet—	39. ....
parliam—	31.	defend—	40. ....
insist—	32.	correspond—	41. ....
constitu—	33.	const—	42. ....
reluct—	34.	resist—	43. ....

preced— 44. .... inhabit— 48. ....
instrum— 45. .... appar— 49. ....
radi— 46. .... vali— 50. ....
conveni— 47. ....

To obtain score, multiply number of errors by 2 and subtract total from 100.

NAME .... DATE .... SCORE ....

86. SPELLING—V

The first part of the following list (1–25) contains words from which the letters ei or ie have been omitted. Supply the missing letters by writing the complete words in the spaces at the right.

1. rel—ve ....
2. conc—t ....
3. f—ld ....
4. hurr—dly ....
5. for—gn ....
6. ch—fly ....
7. hyg—ne ....
8. rev—w ....
9. n—ther ....
10. gr—f ....
11. financ—r ....
12. d—ty ....
13. re—gn ....
14. cash—r ....
15. n—ghbor ....
16. rec—pt ....
17. pr—st ....
18. forf—t ....
19. w—ght ....
20. bel—f ....
21. repr—ve ....
22. bes—ge ....
23. th—r ....
24. s—zure ....
25. sh—ld ....

The remaining words of this list (26–50) have the letters s, c, or sc omitted. Supply the missing letters by writing the complete words in the spaces at the right.

26. absen—e ....
27. inter—ede ....
28. hypocri—y ....
29. de—end ....
30. spe—imen ....
31. mu—le ....
32. vi—ious ....
33. fa—ist ....
34. resu—itate ....
35. prophe—y (verb) ....
36. tran—end ....
37. choi—e ....
38. ex—essive ....
39. con—ise ....
40. di—iple ....
41. existen—e ....
42. here—y ....
43. remini—ent ....

44. nonsen—e ....
45. nuisan—e ....
46. scar—ity ....
47. mi—ellaneous ....

48. merchandi—e ....
49. resour—es ....
50. omni—ient ....

To obtain score, multiply number of errors by 2 and subtract total from 100.

NAME .... DATE .... SCORE ....

87. SPELLING—VI

*In the space at the right, give the spelling of the present participle of **each** verb listed below.*

EXAMPLE: raise *raising*

1. defer ....
2. write ....
3. mimic ....
4. waver ....
5. arise ....
6. skid ....
7. submit ....
8. deny ....
9. plunge ....
10. apply ....
11. inhabit ....
12. tie ....
13. resume ....
14. try ....
15. face ....
16. tap ....
17. tape ....
18. secure ....
19. admit ....
20. perceive ....
21. merge ....

22. echo ....
23. shoe ....
24. accrue ....
25. interfere ....
26. concur ....
27. cure ....
28. soothe ....
29. traffic ....
30. annoy ....
31. pledge ....
32. slue ....
33. impel ....
34. construe ....
35. deliver ....
36. copy ....
37. run ....
38. murmur ....
39. demur ....
40. breathe ....
41. die ....
42. dye ....

43. glue .... 47. space ....
44. dredge .... 48. occur ....
45. praise .... 49. polish ....
46. enter .... 50. tinge ....

To obtain score, multiply number of errors by 2 and subtract total from 100.

NAME .... DATE .... SCORE ....

88. SPELLING—VII

In the spaces at the right, give the plural form of each of the following words.

1. supply ....
2. wife ....
3. alumna ....
4. entry ....
5. watch ....
6. self ....
7. tomato ....
8. alloy ....
9. cargo ....
10. loaf ....
11. tax ....
12. synthesis ....
13. penny ....
14. taxi ....
15. torpedo ....
16. handkerchief ....
17. Jones ....
18. stadium ....
19. child ....
20. sheaf ....
21. freshman ....

22. abbey ....
23. life ....
24. turkey ....
25. company ....
26. axis ....
27. piano ....
28. memoir ....
29. winch ....
30. copy ....
31. donkey ....
32. echo ....
33. half ....
34. folly ....
35. stitch ....
36. chateau ....
37. passer-by ....
38. berry ....
39. circus ....
40. tally ....
41. dynamo ....
42. brother-in-law ....

43. ottoman ....
44. bench ....
45. innuendo ....
46. plateau ....
47. six ....
48. pulley ....
49. belief ....
50. focus ....

To obtain score, multiply number of errors by 2 and subtract total from 100.

Appendix

Appendix

SYNOPSIS OF THE CONJUGATION OF A WEAK VERB

Indicative Mood

ACTIVE VOICE   **PASSIVE VOICE**

Present Tense

I ask	we ask	I am asked	we are asked
you ask	you ask	you are asked	you are asked
he asks	they ask	he is asked	they are asked

Past Tense

I asked	we asked	I was asked	we were asked
you asked	you asked	you were asked	you were asked
he asked	they asked	he was asked	they were asked

Future Tense

I shall ask	we shall ask	I shall be asked	we shall be asked
you will ask	you will ask	you will be asked	you will be asked
he will ask	they will ask	he will be asked	they will be asked

Present Perfect Tense

I have asked, etc.   I have been asked, etc.

Past Perfect Tense

I had asked, etc.   I had been asked, etc.

Future Perfect Tense

I shall have asked, etc.   I shall have been asked, etc.

Subjunctive Mood

Present Tense

If I ask	If we ask	If I be asked	If we be asked
If you ask	If you ask	If you be asked	If you be asked
If he ask	If they ask	If he be asked	If they be asked

Past Tense

If I asked, etc.   If I were asked, etc.

ACTIVE VOICE	PASSIVE VOICE

Present Perfect Tense

If I have asked, etc.	If I have been asked, etc.

Past Perfect Tense

If I had asked, etc.	If I had been asked, etc.

IMPERATIVE MOOD

ask	ask	be asked	be asked

VERBALS

INFINITIVES

Present: to ask	to be asked
Perfect: to have asked	to have been asked

PARTICIPLES

Present: asking	being asked
Past:	asked
Perfect: having asked	having been asked

GERUNDS

Present: asking	being asked
Perfect: having asked	having been asked

PROGRESSIVE CONJUGATIONS

Present: I am asking, etc.
Past: I was asking, etc.

EMPHATIC CONJUGATIONS

Present: I do ask, etc.
Past: I did ask, etc.

SYNOPSIS OF THE CONJUGATION OF A STRONG VERB

INDICATIVE MOOD

ACTIVE VOICE	PASSIVE VOICE
Present tense: I see, etc.	I am seen, etc.
Past tense: I saw, etc.	I was seen, etc.
Future tense: I shall see, etc.	I shall be seen, etc.
Present perfect tense: I have seen, etc.	I have been seen, etc.
Past perfect tense: I had seen, etc.	I had been seen, etc.
Future perfect tense: I shall have seen, etc.	I shall have been seen, etc.

ACTIVE VOICE   PASSIVE VOICE

Subjunctive Mood

Present tense: It I see, etc.   If I be seen, etc.
Past tense: If I saw, etc.   If I were seen, etc.
Present perfect tense: If I have seen, etc.   If I had been seen, etc.
Past perfect tense: If I had seen, etc.   If I had been seen, etc.

Imperative Mood

see   be seen

Verbals

Infinitives

Present: to see   to be seen
Perfect: to have seen   to have been seen

Participles

Present: seeing   being seen
Past: seen
Perfect: having seen   having been seen

Gerunds

Present: seeing   being seen
Perfect: having seen   having been seen

Progressive Conjugations

Present: I am seeing, etc.
Past: I was seeing, etc.

Emphatic Conjugations

Present: I do see, etc.
Past: I did see, etc.

CONJUGATION OF *TO BE*

Indicative Mood

SINGULAR	PLURAL	SINGULAR	PLURAL
Present Tense		*Past Tense*	
I am	we are	I was	we were
you are	you are	you were	you were
he is	they are	he was	they were

SINGULAR	PLURAL	SINGULAR	PLURAL

Future Tense

I shall be	we shall be
you will be	you will be
he will be	they will be

Past Perfect Tense

I had been	we had been
you had been	you had been
he had been	they had been

Present Perfect Tense

I have been	we have been
you have been	you have been
he has been	they have been

Future Perfect Tense

I shall have been	we shall have been
you will have been	you will have been
he will have been	they will have been

SUBJUNCTIVE MOOD

Present Tense

If I be	If we be
If you be	If you be
If he be	If they be

Present Perfect Tense

If I have been	If we have been
If you have been	If you have been
If he have been	If they have been

Past Tense

If I were	If we were
If you were	If you were
If he were	If they were

Past Perfect Tense

If I had been	If we had been
If you had been	If you had been
If he had been	If they had been

IMPERATIVE MOOD

be

	INFINITIVES	PARTICIPLES	GERUNDS
Present:	to be	being	being
Past:	to have been	been	having been

LIST OF STRONG AND IRREGULAR VERBS

PRESENT	PAST	PAST PARTICIPLE	PRESENT	PAST	PAST PARTICIPLE
arise	arose	arisen	bring	brought	brought
beat	beat	beaten	burst	burst	burst
become	became	become	buy	bought	bought
begin	began	begun	catch	caught	caught
bend	bent	bent	choose	chose	chosen
bet	bet	bet	cling	clung	clung
bid	bid	bid	come	came	come
bid	bade	bidden	cost	cost	cost
bind	bound	bound	deal	dealt	dealt
bite	bit	bitten, bit	dig	dug	dug
blow	blew	blown	do	did	done
break	broke	broken	draw	drew	drawn

PRESENT	PAST	PAST PARTICIPLE	PRESENT	PAST	PAST PARTICIPLE
drink	drank	drunk	ride	rode	ridden
drive	drove	driven	rise	rose	risen
eat	ate	eaten	run	ran	run
fall	fell	fallen	say	said	said
feed	fed	fed	see	saw	seen
fight	fought	fought	seek	sought	sought
find	found	found	sell	sold	sold
flee	fled	fled	send	sent	sent
fling	flung	flung	set	set	set
fly	flew	flown	shake	shook	shaken
forget	forgot	forgotten	shine	shone	shone
forsake	forsook	forsaken	shoot	shot	shot
freeze	froze	frozen	show	showed	shown
get	got	got (gotten)	shrink	shrank	shrunk
give	gave	given	sing	sang	sung
go	went	gone	sink	sank	sunk
grow	grew	grown	sit	sat	sat
hide	hid	hidden	slay	slew	slain
hold	held	held	speak	spoke	spoken
keep	kept	kept	spring	sprang	sprung
know	knew	known	stand	stood	stood
lay	laid	laid	steal	stole	stolen
lead	led	led	stride	strode	stridden
leave	left	left	strike	struck	struck
lend	lent	lent	strive	strove	striven
lie	lay	lain	swear	swore	sworn
light	lighted, lit	lighted, lit	swim	swam	swum
			swing	swung	swung
lose	lost	lost	take	took	taken
make	made	made	teach	taught	taught
mean	meant	meant	tear	tore	torn
pay	paid	paid	tell	told	told
put	put	put	think	thought	thought
read	read	read	throw	threw	thrown
rend	rent	rent	wake	woke, waked	waked
rid	rid	rid	wear	wore	worn
ring	rang	rung			

DECLENSION OF PERSONAL PRONOUNS

First Person

	SINGULAR	PLURAL
Nom.	I	we
Poss.	my, mine	our, ours
Obj.	me	us

Second Person

	SINGULAR	PLURAL
Nom.	you	you
Poss.	your, yours	your, yours
Obj.	you	you

Third Person

SINGULAR

	Masculine	Feminine	Neuter
Nom.	he	she	it
Poss.	his	her, hers	its
Obj.	him	her	it

PLURAL

All Genders

Nom.	they
Poss.	their, theirs
Obj.	them

DECLENSION OF RELATIVE AND INTERROGATIVE PRONOUNS

Nom.	who	whoever	whosoever
Poss.	whose	whosever	whosesoever
Obj.	whom	whomever	whomsoever

COMPARISON OF ADJECTIVES AND ADVERBS

	Positive	Comparative	Superlative
BY ADDING -er, -est	old	older	oldest
	warm	warmer	warmest
	heavy	heavier	heaviest
	soon	sooner	soonest
	fast	faster	fastest
BY ADDING *more, most* less, least	beautiful	more beautiful	most beautiful
	famous	less famous	least famous
	rapidly	more rapidly	most rapidly
	carefully	less carefully	least carefully
BY EITHER METHOD	handsome	handsomer	handsomest
	handsome	more handsome	most handsome
	handsome	less handsome	least handsome

450 WORDS FREQUENTLY MISSPELLED

absence
absurd
accept
accessible
accidentally
accommodate
accomplish
accumulate
accustom
achievement
acknowledge
acquaintance
acquire
acquitted
across
address
advantageous
advice
advise
affect
aggravate
aisle
all right
alley
ally
almost
already
altar
alter
although
altogether
always
amateur
among
amount
analysis
analyze
angel
angle
annual
answer
apartment
apologize
apparatus
apparent

appearance
appetite
appreciate
appropriate
arctic
argument
arithmetic
around
arrangement
ascend
asked
athlete
attacked
attendance
audience
auxiliary
awkward

balance
balloon
barbarous
bargain
beautiful
becoming
beggar
beginning
believe
benefited
biscuit
boundaries
breathe
brilliant
Britain
buoyant
bureau
busily
business

calendar
candidate
can't
capital
capitol
captain
career

casualty
cavalry
ceiling
cemetery
certain
changeable
changing
characteristic
chauffeur
choose
chosen
climbed
clothes
coarse
column
coming
commission
committee
comparative
compelled
competent
competition
completely
compliment
concede
conceit
conceive
condescend
conferred
confident
conquer
conscience
conscientious
conscious
consistent
continuous
controlled
convenience
counsel
countries
course
courteous
criticism
criticize
cruelty

450 WORDS FREQUENTLY MISSPELLED

curious	entirely	handsome
curiosity	environment	harass
	equipped	height
dealt	especially	heroes
deceive	exaggerate	hindrance
decision	exceed	hoping
deferred	excellent	humorous
deficient	exercise	hundredths
definite	exhaust	hungry
democracy	existence	hurriedly
dependent	expense	hypocrisy
descendant	experience	
describe	explanation	identity
description	extraordinary	imaginary
desirable	extremely	immediately
despair		immensely
desperate	familiar	impromptu
dessert	fascinate	incidentally
device	February	independent
dictionary	field	indispensable
different	finally	infinity
dining	financier	influential
disappear	forehead	intelligence
disappoint	foreign	intercede
disastrous	formally	interesting
discipline	formerly	interfere
disease	forty	invitation
dissatisfied	fourteen	irrelevant
divide	fourth	irresistible
doctor	friend	
dormitories	fundamental	judgment
dropped	furniture	
dying		knowledge
	generally	
economic	genius	laboratory
ecstasy	government	laid
effect	governor	later
efficient	grammar	latter
eighth	grief	led
eligible	grievous	leisure
eliminate	guarantee	library
embarrass	guard	license
eminent	guidance	lightning
emphasize		literature
enemy	handkerchief	loneliness

450 WORDS FREQUENTLY MISSPELLED

lose	ordinarily	probably
lying	original	procedure
	outrageous	proceed
maintenance		professor
maneuver	paid	prominent
manual	pamphlet	pronunciation
marriage	parallel	propaganda
mathematics	parliament	prophesy
meant	particularly	prove
medicine	partner	psychology
merely	pastime	pursue
miniature	peaceable	
minute	perceive	quantity
mischievous	perform	quarter
misspelled	perhaps	quiet
momentous	permanent	quite
morale	permissible	quitting
mosquito	perseverance	
murmur	personal	realize
muscle	personnel	really
mysterious	perspiration	receive
	persuade	recognize
naturally	physician	recommend
necessary	picnicking	reference
neither	piece	referred
niece	planned	relieve
nineteen	pleasant	religious
ninety	poison	remembrance
ninth	politician	repetition
noticeable	porch	replies
	possess	representative
obedience	possible	restaurant
oblige	practically	rhythm
obstacle	prairie	ridiculous
occasionally	precede	
occurred	preference	sacrifice
occurrence	preferred	sacrilegious
o'clock	prejudice	safety
offered	preparation	sandwich
officer	presence	satisfied
omission	prevalent	scarce
omitted	primitive	scene
opinion	principal	schedule
opportunity	principle	scheme
optimistic	privilege	science

450 WORDS FREQUENTLY MISSPELLED

secretary	succeed	usually
seize	successful	
sense	superintendent	valleys
separate	supersede	valuable
severely	surprise	variety
shining	syllable	vegetable
shriek	symmetry	vengeance
siege		village
significant	technique	villain
similar	temperament	
sincerely	temperature	weather
sophomore	tendency	Wednesday
source	thorough	weird
speak	together	welfare
specimen	tragedy	whether
speech	tries	wholly
stationary	truly	whose
stationery	Tuesday	women
statistics	typical	writing
stopped	tyranny	written
straight		
stretch	undoubtedly	yield
studying	until	

Achievement Tests

NAME .... DATE .... SCORE ....

FINAL TEST—UNDERSTANDING THE SENTENCE

Decide whether each group of words appearing below is a complete sentence, two or more sentences run together, or an incomplete construction. In supplying your answers, use the following abbreviations:

    S—A complete sentence

    RT—Sentences run together

    F—Incomplete construction or fragment

.... 1. Though Charles Dean was known to most of the villagers as a proud, unbending aristocrat, he was regarded by his intimates as a kindly, charitable man with a genial wit.

.... 2. Hoping to find the missing receipt, he searched through the papers in his desk, but with no success.

.... 3. The waves, surging and pounding with relentless fury, sometimes tossing spray across the road on which we were walking.

.... 4. Plastics have come into general use as substitutes for metal, rubber, and glass, even as textiles they have found a wide range of applications.

.... 5. Making no effort to conceal his impatience, he slammed the telephone receiver back onto the hook.

.... 6. The farmer of that era worked from dawn to dusk, day after day, hence it was natural for his children to look toward the easier life of the town.

.... 7. My father, being the only Democrat in a family of militant Republicans, had learned to defend his convictions in a nimble, good-humored fashion.

.... 8. Many Englishmen having emigrated after the war to Australia, where sheep-ranching was a profitable enterprise.

.... 9. The first question on the test was surprisingly simple I had little trouble in answering it correctly.

.... 10. Then, too, there is the picnicker who, when he is ready to start homeward, forgets to clean up the papers and trash which litter the ground.

.... 11. When Uncle Jim comes home from work at the store, he settles himself in an easy chair and naps until dinner time.

.... 12. He had spent his early years on a Minnesota farm therefore he was keenly interested in the sports of hunting and fishing.

.... 13. The bookkeeper, a round, owl-faced man who looked up smilingly as I handed him the papers.

.... 14. The boy cranked and cranked the ancient vehicle, when the engine roared he hurried to the driver's seat and tugged at the levers on the steering wheel.

.... 15. Especially when, just after you have wrapped up the article, the customer changes his mind and decides to look further.

.... 16. The war over, Tom went back to his job as salesman with a wholesale drug firm.

.... 17. Icebergs were seldom seen in that latitude during the month of June, nevertheless the captain was taking no chances.

.... 18. A brilliant young violinist who, after performing in a concert tour of the East, was invited to appear as a soloist with the Cincinnati Symphony Orchestra.

.... 19. The state engineers, who had spent more than a year gathering data on the problem, recommended that a four-lane highway be constructed to accommodate the traffic between the two cities.

.... 20. Although I was very young, I remember the occasion vividly, my mother and I were alone on that particular evening.

.... 21. Some persons believe that the blacksnake is harmful, but this view is incorrect the blacksnake is actually of real usefulness in destroying rodents and other pests.

.... 22. Principally because television is a relatively new development which has tremendous possibilities for entertainment, education, and news reporting, to say nothing of its applications in business.

.... 23. Today's wrestlers try to please the crowd, in fact they are actors rather than athletes.

.... 24. Perhaps the most engaging of Stevenson's books is his *Travels with a Donkey*, written while he was still a young man.

.... 25. That afternoon, while he was at bat in the third inning, he swung at the ball and missed, wrenching his shoulder severely.

To obtain score, multiply number of errors by 4 and subtract total from 100.

FINAL TEST IN GRAMMAR

Draw a circle around any word incorrectly used and write the correct word in the margin on the left. If the sentence is correct as it stands, let the space remain blank. Errors are not to be corrected by rewriting the sentences or by fundamentally changing their meaning.

1. After lunch yesterday I laid down for a short nap.
2. Most any tourist agency can give you the information.
3. Why don't Edith change her hair-do?
4. May I take your order for the magazine?
5. The coach, as well as three members of the squad, were arguing with the referee.
6. Which would you say is the youngest of the two, his sister or he?
7. Here is one of the most important novels that has been published since the war.
8. Her primary concern at college were social activities.
9. Anyone could cook as well as she.
10. Each of the fraternities have a faculty adviser.
11. You are to young to remember these happenings.
12. He should of saved some of that money.
13. He has shook his fist at me several times.
14. The entire audience thought the best actor of the play to be him.
15. These packages are our's, aren't they?
16. There has been some disagreement between John and her.
17. Near the house there was three large pine trees.
18. Julia can play the piano as well as her.
19. You must not use his name as a reference without he gives his permission.
20. By six o'clock we were already for dinner.
21. For an old motor this runs exceptionally good.
22. They intended to have returned on the *Queen Mary*.
23. The methods now used in forecasting weather are quite different than those in vogue a generation ago.
24. The Smiths are especially proud of there flower garden.

.... 25. Ten dollars will be awarded to whomever sends in the best slogan.
.... 26. The jury mopped its brows as the trial dragged on and on.
.... 27. By the time of our arrival there was scarcely no food left on the table.
.... 28. Anyone traveling abroad should keep a list of their purchases.
.... 29. I wish he would try to speak more distinct.
.... 30. When will this new regulation take affect?
.... 31. The batter looked scornfully at the umpire.
.... 32. She looks very attractively in that blue suit.
.... 33. I believe that Elizabeth is younger than he.
.... 34. We have arranged a surprise party for her husband and she.
.... 35. Most of us seniors had ordered our caps and gowns.
.... 36. Mr. Marlow took Paul and I for a ride in the speedboat.
.... 37. That is the man whom he used to work for.
.... 38. Who do you think they have accused?
.... 39. He appeared kind of nervous.
.... 40. Whom are you taking in your car?
.... 41. Within a few minutes the storm had spent it's fury.
.... 42. He really looked like he had seen a ghost.
.... 43. The reason for my going home tomorrow is because my sister is getting married.
.... 44. I read in this magazine where many Americans are again studying art in Paris.
.... 45. Since 1939 the cost of food and other essential items have risen sharply.
.... 46. The flight was canceled due to bad weather.
.... 47. There taking a trip to Bermuda after Christmas.
.... 48. Who did you say was driving the car?
.... 49. Hire whoever is available at the employment agency.
.... 50. Earl, Walter, and myself were standing on the pier.

To obtain score, multiply number of errors by 2 and subtract total from 100.

FINAL TEST IN PUNCTUATION

Decide whether any changes should be made in the punctuation of the following sentences. To make changes, follow these directions. First, set down in the space at the left the word (or number) which immediately precedes the mistake. Then, if you wish to add *punctuation, insert the proper mark after the word.* To take out *unnecessary punctuation, insert the faulty mark after the word and draw a circle around the mark. If the sentence is correctly punctuated, leave the space at the left blank.*

EXAMPLE: *house* , = comma to be added
house ⊙ = comma to be taken out

1. Balboa, not Cortez was the discoverer of the Pacific.
2. There are few fences in that section of the country, and the cattle are allowed to roam at will.
3. We were scheduled to leave the Los Angeles airport at 10 30 A.M.
4. Out of the night came the throbbing whining drone of an outboard motor.
5. William Allen White was for many years editor and publisher of the Emporia Gazette.
6. The girl wearing the plaid coat is my cousin.
7. The word bantam is thought to be derived from the name of a village in Java.
8. Every student, who is enrolled in chemistry, must pay a laboratory fee.
9. John Hancock an eighteenth-century Boston aristocrat was the first signer of the Declaration of Independence.
10. I read in the *Atlantic* a short story called In the Park.
11. Three early American painters John Copley, Benjamin West, and Gilbert Stuart won a considerable reputation.
12. On her head was an enormous, straw hat.
13. Your suggestions I assure you will be welcomed by the committee.

_____ 14. On April 18, 1906 a severe earthquake rocked San Francisco, California.

_____ 15. Whether he intends to sell the property I have not heard.

_____ 16. W. H. Hudson's best-known work is a novel called Green Mansions.

_____ 17. Generally speaking women spend money more cautiously than men do.

_____ 18. The Whites live in an ornate stucco house built about thirty-five years ago.

_____ 19. Elaborate parades gay and colorful are a feature of the Mardi Gras.

_____ 20. He explored the pockets of his coat and brought forth a grimy piece of paper.

_____ 21. A contractor's estimate is based on the following considerations materials, labor costs, overhead, and reasonable profit.

_____ 22. "Is this the train to Boston" he asked breathlessly.

_____ 23. No I have not yet seen the evening paper.

_____ 24. This prefabricated cabin can be erected in a few days' time by any man who is handy with tools.

_____ 25. Oliver will you take this letter to the post office?

_____ 26. The child was feverish and uncomfortable consequently Mrs. West telephoned for the doctor.

_____ 27. Three Scandinavian countries Norway, Sweden, and Denmark were included in our tour.

_____ 28. My doctor who follows painting as a hobby displays his pictures in the reception room.

_____ 29. Many dogs become nervous when they hear the sound of thunder.

_____ 30. I was employed as a counselor at the Pinewood Camp, Orchard Hill, Maine last summer.

_____ 31. Many citizens of the community have urged, that the council take steps to acquire the land for use as a public park.

32. "Well I haven't yet finished my story," he continued.
33. With the radio turned on my roommate was playing a screechy accompaniment on his violin.
34. Although she had followed the recipe with the utmost care the cake was not a success.
35. The magician picked up a glass vase and held it aloft then he draped a velvet cloth over it.
36. March the fifteenth, which is the deadline for filing income tax returns is a busy day at the office.
37. That his latest novel is both readable and entertaining most readers will agree.
38. Respect for traditions is to say the least, a strong element in our national life.
39. The following persons have consented to let me use their names as references Mr. J. F. Walsh, principal of the high school; Mr. Thomas King, cashier at the Central Bank; and Dr. Hugo Smith, pastor of St. Luke's Church.
40. Since milk provides fat, protein, and lactose it ranks especially high in food value.
41. Did Falstaff say The better part of valor is discretion
42. He knocked on the door several times, and then walked away.
43. "It's time to leave" said Mother "if we are to be at the church by eleven.
44. On one side of the walk, was a low iron fence.
45. The initiation is a serious and impressive ritual it usually takes an hour or longer.
46. Decide how much you wish to contribute, Helen and then return the pledge card to me.
47. The necktie which he selected was a hand-painted creation of vivid design.
48. That he should have given a signal before turning left, he later admitted.

.... 49. The Finger Lakes they are in western New York are of glacial origin.

.... 50. Pictured in this photograph are Henry Ford, the automobile magnate Harvey Firestone, the Akron industrialist and John Burroughs, the well-known naturalist.

To obtain score, multiply number of errors by 2 and subtract total from 100.

NAME .... DATE .... SCORE ....

FINAL TEST IN SPELLING

In the space at the left, write each italicized word in full.

.... 1. The trial has been *defer—d* until April.
.... 2. In earlier times, *bel—f* in witchcraft was common.
.... 3. Dust storms were *prev—l—nt* in the Midwest that summer.
.... 4. They ordered spaghetti at an Italian *rest—rant*.
.... 5. His vanity and *conc—t* made him an unpopular figure.
.... 6. She has a neat, well-tailored *appear—nce*.
.... 7. The dent in the fender is hardly *notic—ble*.
.... 8. His remarks often had a *hum—r—s* twist.
.... 9. It was the twenty-fifth anniversary of their *marr—ge*.
.... 10. With neither side *conc—ding* a point, the parley ended in a stalemate.
.... 11. Some repairs will be *ne—sary* before the house can be occupied.
.... 12. You will find the bandages in the *med—cine* cabinet.
.... 13. I am *sincer—y* grateful for your help.
.... 14. The salesman leafed through the papers *hurr—dly* and then replaced them in his brief case.
.... 15. In the *orig—nal* sense of the word, a "gossip" was a godparent or a friend.
.... 16. According to legend, Helen of Troy was a woman of quite *irr—sist—ble* charm.
.... 17. Kindly give us an answer at your earliest *conven—nce*.
.... 18. Only one *p—ce* of candy remained in the box.
.... 19. Lincoln's early *envi—ment* was the Western frontier.
.... 20. Cologne was *practic—y* destroyed by aerial attack.
.... 21. The acrobats will *p—form* on that high trapeze.
.... 22. It was later realized that the Munich Pact, an attempt to appease the dictators, was a *gr—v—us* error.
.... 23. One philosopher has stated that the test of a man's character is the way in which he spends his *l—sure* hours.
.... 24. There is an old saying to the effect that *op—rtunity* knocks only once.
.... 25. He always *p—d* his bills promptly.

.... 26. Public executions were a common *occur—nce* in London during the eighteenth century.
.... 27. The lands bordering the Persian Gulf are believed to hold a vast *quan—ty* of oil reserves.
.... 28. Many *wom—n* of this country have been active in public life.
.... 29. The company *repl—d* encouragingly to his letter.
.... 30. No *expl—nation* has been found for the mystery.
.... 31. It was a *signifi—nt* discovery.
.... 32. The waiter led us to a table in the *din—ng* room.
.... 33. He was an *influen—al* citizen of Clayville.
.... 34. The monotony of the work filled him with *d—spair*.
.... 35. The Navy oarsmen won the race with *compar—tive* ease.
.... 36. Aptitude tests should be helpful to a student about to *ch—se* his career.
.... 37. A super market is similar in *princip—* to a cafeteria.
.... 38. This action is not *consist—nt* with our usual policy.
.... 39. Threshing results in the *sep—ration* of the grain from the stalk.
.... 40. The daily market reports are scanned by *b—s—ess* men.
.... 41. He accepted a *com—s—n* in the Army.
.... 42. A depression would seriously *—ffect* our economy.
.... 43. After *inherit—ng* the money, he bought a farm.
.... 44. Was there any reason for *omit—ng* his name?
.... 45. The Normandy invasion was a *moment—us* undertaking.
.... 46. He was always a confirmed *opt—mist*.
.... 47. It was a *disast—us* fire.
.... 48. His spirit of *pers—verance* is indeed remarkable.
.... 49. Is he a *priv—l—ged* character?
.... 50. He never shirked *unpl—s—nt* tasks.

    To obtain score, multiply number of errors by 2 and subtract total from 100.

INDEX

Numbers refer to pages. Italics indicate words discussed individually.

accept, 165
access, 165
adapt, 165
Adjectives, 111; as objective complements, 112; comparative and superlative degree of, 112; misuse of to modify verbs, 111; misuse of to modify adjectives and adverbs, 112; not comparable, 113
adopt, 165
Adverbs, 111; comparative and superlative degree of, 112
advice, 165
advise, 165
affect, 165
aggravate, 165
Agreement, pronoun with antecedent, 47; verb with subject, 33
allow, 94
all ready, 165
all together, 166
already, 165
altar, 166
alter, 166
although, 136, 138
altogether, 166
among, 139
and which, 135
and who, 135
angel, 166
angle, 166
Antecedent, reference of pronouns to, 48; vague use of with pronouns, 48
Apostrophe, 198; to indicate omission, 200; with numbers, signs, etc., 200
Apposition, case of words in, 61, 62; possessive of words in, 64
as, 136, 137
As, case of comparisons with, 63
aside from, 139
asked, 94
assert, 94
Auxiliary verbs, correct verb forms with, 93; necessary use of, 35

balance, 166
before, 137
behind, 139
beside, 139

besides, 139
between, 139
born, 166
borne, 166
Brackets, 189
burst, 94

can, 91
canvas, 166
canvass, 166
capital, 166
Capitals, use of, 196
capitol, 166
Case, objective, 62; possessive, 64; subjective, 61; with verb *to be*, 63
caused by, 124
choose, 94
chose, 94
cite, 171
claim, 94
Clauses, elliptical, 124
coarse, 166
Collective nouns, agreement of verbs with, 35; use of pronouns with, 50
Colon, 187
Comma, conventional uses of, 194; main uses of, 190; wrong uses of, 194
Comma fault, 18; correction of, 19
Comparative degree of adjectives and adverbs, 112
complected, 166
complement, 166
complexioned, 166
compliment, 166
Conjunctions, co-ordinate, 135; correlative, 135; subordinate, 135
Connectives, 135
conscience, 166
conscious, 166
consul, 167
contemptible, 167
contemptuous, 167
continual, 167
continuous, 167
Conventional punctuation, 195
could, 92
council, 167
counsel, 167

301

course, 166
credible, 167
creditable, 167
credulous, 167

Dangling modifiers, 123
Dash, 188, 189
Declension of pronouns, 283
desert, 167
dessert, 167
different from, 139
disinterested, 167
dived, 94
don't, 94
Double comparatives, 113
Double negatives, 115
Double superlatives, 113
dove, 94
dragged, 94
drug, 94
due to, 124, 139
dyeing, 167
dying, 167

each other, 167
effect, 165
Elliptical clauses and sentences, 18, 124; punctuation with, 186
eminent, 168
enthuse, 94
except, 165
excess, 165
Exclamation point, 186
expect, 168
extra, 168

famous, 170
farther, 168
fewer, 168
formally, 168
formerly, 168
forth, 168
fourth, 168
Fragmentary sentence, 16; how to correct, 17
further, 168
Fused sentence, 20

Gerund, misuse of tense of, 83; use of possessive case with, 50, 65
got, 94

healthful, 168
healthy, 168
human, 168
humane, 168
Hyphen, 200; to syllabicate, 200; with numbers, 201

Idiomatic use of prepositions, 139
if, 137
imminent, 168

imply, 168
in, 139
in back of, 139
Incomplete comparisons, 113
Incomplete sentence, 16; how to correct, **17**
Indefinite pronouns, agreement of verb with, 34
infer, 168
Infinitive, misuse of tense of, 83
ingenious, 169
ingenuous, 169
inside of, 139
instance, 169
instant, 169
Interrogative pronouns, declension of, 284
into, 139
Irregular verbs, list of, 282
It, as grammatical subject, 37; indefinite use of, 48
Italics, 196
its, 169

kind, 38, 114
kind of, 115

last, 169
later, 169
latest, 169
latter, 169
lay, 92, 93
lead, 94
learn, 169
leave, 94
led, 94
less, 168
let, 94
liable, 169
lie, 92
Like, as conjunction, **137**
likely, 169
locate, 171
loose, 169
lose, 169
luxuriant, 170
luxurious, 170

maintain, 94
may, 91
Mechanics, 196
might, 92
Misplaced modifiers, 124
Modification, separate, 114
Modifiers, dangling, 123; misplaced, 124; squinting, 125
Mood, subjunctive, 81
moral, 170
morale, 170
myself, wrong intensive and reflexive use of, 50

Negative, double, 115
nor, 136
notorious, 170

observance, 170
observation, 170
of, wrong use for *have*, 139
on account of, 139
one another, 167
outside of, 139
owing to, 124

Parallel constructions, 135
Parentheses, 189
Partial sentence, punctuation of, 18
Participial phrase, loose, 123
Participle, misuse of tense of, 83
pay, 93
Period, 185
Period fault, 16
persecute, 170
personal, 170
Personal pronouns, declension of, 283
personnel, 170
Plural, mistaken for possessive, 64
Possession, joint, 64; separate, 64
Possessives, errors in formation of, 198; of indefinite pronouns, 199; of personal pronouns, 65, 199; of proper names, 199
practicable, 170
practical, 170
Predicate defined, 15
Predicate noun, attraction of verb to, 35
Prepositions, compound, 135; idiomatic use of, 139; simple, 135; superfluous, 138; wrong omission of, 138
principal, 170
principle, 170
prophecy, 171
prophesy, 171
prosecute, 170
Punctuation, 185; conventional, 195

Question mark, 185
quiet, 171
quite, 171
Quotation marks, 188

raise, 93
Reference, vague with pronouns, 48
Relative pronoun, agreement of verb with, 36; antecedent of, 47; case of, 63; declension of, 284; squinting, 125; with vague antecedent, 49
remainder, 166
respectfully, 171
respectively, 171
rest, 166
rise, 92, 93
Run-on sentence, 20

say, 93
Semicolon, 186
Sentence defined, 15
Sentence fragment, 16; how to correct, **17**
Separate modification, 114
set, 92
settle, 171
shall, 91
should, 91
since, 136
sit, 92
site, 171
so, 137
so that, 137
sort, 38, 114
sort of, 115
Spelling, list of words, 285; rules for, 260
Squinting modifiers, 125
stationary, 171
stationery, 171
Strong verbs, list of, 282
Subject, compound, 33; defined, 15; how determined, 16
Subjunctive mood, 81
suit, 171
suite, 171
Superlative degree of adjectives and adverbs, 112
supposed, 94
suspect, 94
suspicion, 94
Synopses of verbs, 279

teach, 169
Tense, 82; historical present, 83; logical sequence of, 83
than, 137
Than, case of comparisons with, 63
that, misused for *so*, 115
that there, 115
their, 171
them, misused as adjective, **114**
there, 171
They, indefinite use of, 48
this here, 115
to, 171
too, 171

uninterested, 167
unless, 138
used, 94

Verbs, list of strong and irregular, 282; past tense and participles of strong, 93; synopses of, 279

weather, 172
when, 137
where, 138
whereas, 136, 138
whether, 137, 172
Which, loose reference of, 124

303

while, 136, 137
will, 91
within, 139
without, 138

Words frequently misspelled, list of, **285**
would, 91

You, indefinite use of, 49